MW01048205

Adventure Careers

Second Edition

By
Alex Hiam and Susan Angle

CAREER PRESS
3 Tice Road
P.O. Box 687
Franklin Lakes, NJ 07417
1-800-CAREER-1
201-848-0310 (outside U.S.)
FAX: 201-848-1727

ADVENTURE CAREERS, SECOND EDITION

ISBN 1-56414-175-6, $11.99

Cover design by Dean Johnson Design, Inc.

Printed in the U.S.A. by Book-mart Press

To order this title by mail, please include price as noted above, $2.50 handling per order, and $1.00 for each book ordered. Send to: Career Press, Inc., 3 Tice Road, P.O. Box 687, Franklin Lakes, NJ 07417.

Or call toll-free 1-800-CAREER-1 (Canada: 201-427-0229) to order using VISA or MasterCard, or for further information on books from Career Press.

Library of Congress Cataloging-in-Publication Data

Hiam, Alexander.
    Adventure careers / by Alex Hiam and Susan Angle -- 2nd ed.
        p. cm.
    ISBN 1-56414-175-6 (pbk.) : $11.99
    1. Vocational guidance. 2. Young adults--Employment.
  3. Vocational interests. 4. Self-realization. I. Angle, Susan,
  1962-   . II. Title.
  HF5381.H44 1995
  331.7'02--dc20   95-96
                                                                      CIP

Know thyself.
—The Oracle at Delphi

Something we were withholding made us weak
Until we found out it was ourselves
We were withholding from our land of living
And forth with found salvation in our surrender
—Robert Frost

Contents

Preface

The second edition came about because of the thousands of readers who embraced the notion of adventure careers and went forth to create their own adventures. They have inspired others, contributed immeasurably to society and found more fulfilling careers and lives than many of us ever do. Congratulations! This second edition is designed to update and extend the information and directories for the next generation of career explorers. To them, we can offer no better words than those of some of their predecessors.

Abigail wrote to tell us that:

> "Adventure Careers *has not only changed the course of my life, but given me great hope for the countless others who have surely devoured the book as I did. I have referred to it many times over, consulting the chapters on 'good works' and the political arena in particular. As a result, I am awaiting acceptance into the Eastern European program of the Peace Corps and hope to get my doctorate in history or government upon my return. In the meantime, I am volunteering at NYPIRG and Amnesty International. It was your book that jump-started my withering ambition and reminded me that the 'something I was withholding' was indeed myself. Your book was like the constant 'faculty adviser' that I so needed during these months of turmoil that are the rite of passage of turning 26 years old!"*

Susan and I would like to take the credit, Abigail, but in truth the inspiration for our book, and your wonderful adventures, came from the hundreds of people and organizations we write about. All of us need jump starts on occasion, and I think we all withhold more than we need to. By acting on this insight you have changed your own life, but we are happy this book was of some assistance.

Similarly, Buff wrote to say that reading *Adventure Careers* "has been an enlightening and encouraging experience," and:

> *"For the last several weeks I have been researching pro-grams for graduate study and designing my last two semesters in school to bring myself closer to a dream career. I am in the last year of night school at Georgetown University and had been getting nervous as to what I should do after graduation. During the day I work as a legal secretary and had come to think of myself as such. I used the worksheets [Chapter 2] to take stock of other areas of my life and used the resource lists [Chapters 3-12] to consider what the next step in my own 'adventure' should be."*

Wow, it works! This is just how we hoped the book would be used by readers to analyze their own situation, explore alternative paths and develop practical plans. To help the next generation of readers use the book this way, we have updated all the resource lists and have added some new ones as well.

This book generated more public attention than my other eight books (I guess I should collaborate with Susan more often!), and I often found myself taking questions at a bookstore event or on a radio or television interview. Susan and I learned from these many conversations with the public that there is *a great need for information, strategies and role models to help people jump-start their careers or explore career alternatives*. We learned also that the principles of adventure careering apply to everyone, regardless of age or economic situation. Whenever someone begins to take charge of their career in order to get more from it and give more to it, then they are embarking on their own adventure career path.

Our readers also told us that many employers do not understand adventure careers as well as they might. This is a serious concern, and we realized we had to figure out what to do about it. The adventurer offers many benefits to an employer—creativity, breadth of experience, initiative, self-confidence and hands-on expertise in many practical management, interpersonal and communication tasks. *But* the employer who has not experienced the adventure career path may fail to see these strengths in the average resume or interview. For that reason, we created the checklist that follows and have tested it with the help of adventurers around the country. It works.

The checklist on pages 11-14 describes 39 specific job skills that are often acquired during the kinds of career adventures accessed through this book. Use the checklist to analyze each of your adventures, whether a part-time volunteer job, a year in the Peace Corps, a stint as an entrepreneur or a semester abroad. The checklist will help you *define the skills you gained in ways that employers can understand*. For instance, if you became an Outward Bound trainer, the checklist will show you that you gained specific leadership skills, team skills, personnel management skills, reporting skills, collaboration skills, spoken communications skills, teaching skills, problem-solving skills, conflict resolution skills, planning skills, goal-setting skills and event-planning skills. While the typical company does not rate your ability to climb a cliff or survive in the wilderness as relevant to an office job, the same company is probably desperate to find people with all the skills listed above! After using the checklist to analyze each adventure, borrow liberally from its language to describe the job-related skills you gained as you write your resume or cover letter or as you present yourself verbally in an interview. We want you to be able to slip easily between wild career adventures and more conventional work, always gaining respect and earning power by leveraging everything you learn.

This second edition was made possible by two career adventurers, Christina Towe and Hannah Gordon, both recent graduates from Hampshire College. They researched hundreds of organizations and sources in order to update and extend the directories and also helped edit and update the text. Hannah, a music composition major in college, has done more than her share of childcare and waitressing jobs in order to fund her efforts to work in the music industry. She has recently directed a musical and run a music festival, and while working on this book she finally landed a full-time job in her field! Good luck, Hannah, and thanks for all your help. Christina, a talented painter and budding writer, works part-time in my management consulting office and did the bulk of the research on this second edition. She often laughs at me as I labor frantically to complete a book by its deadline, and it gave me great pleasure to see her sweating this deadline for a change. Thanks for all your help, Christie. Are you ready for the next book?

Adventure Careers

Buff concludes her letter to us as follows:

"It's not so much realizing what I want to do that I've gained, but the whole perspective I have now on my life and the feeling of possibilities that your book has given me. Somewhere I had learned that work was one thing, and what one enjoys in life was something separate. Your book helped me to dissolve those categories. I'm not sure exactly what I'll be doing in a year, but I am positive now it will be something extraordinary."

We are positive too! Susan, Hannah, Christie and I all wish you the best of luck as you pursue your own adventures. While we do not know what each of our readers will be doing in a year's time, we certainly hope that it will be something extraordinary, too.

Please let us know what you find on your adventures and how we might add to or improve this book when it comes time for yet another edition. You can reach us through my office: Alexander Hiam & Associates, 69 South Pleasant Street, Suite 204, Amherst, MA 01002. Thanks, and bon voyage.

Alex Hiam
January 1, 1995
Amherst, Mass.

How Did You Benefit From Your Adventure?

Until adventure careering becomes the norm (it will eventually!), it is up to the adventurer to explain his or her career path to employers. Here is a checklist that helps you decide—and communicate—what you gained from your experience. Check each benefit that applies:

Interpersonal Skills

❑ **Leadership.** I was responsible for leading a group of people in challenging circumstances.

❑ **Written communications.** I wrote or edited memos, reports, instruction manuals, press releases, newsletters, articles and/or other material on behalf of the organization I worked with.

❑ **Spoken communications.** I lead workshops or training sessions, gave verbal presentations to groups, made speeches and/or presented reports to program managers.

❑ **Collaboration.** I had to collaborate with a diverse group of associates, with people from multiple organizations, with people from different disciplines and backgrounds, in order to accomplish my (or my employer's/sponsor's) goals.

❑ **Cross-cultural skills.** I worked with people from different cultures, countries and/or religious and economic backgrounds and developed unique understanding and communication skills as a result.

❑ **Language skills.** I traveled in foreign countries and had to operate in areas in which the primary language was not my own.

❑ **Teaching.** I taught young people or adults and gained valuable experience in training as a result.

❑ **Networking/referrals.** I provided referrals and/or helped connect people or organizations. This required development of a specialized knowledge and an ability to listen and diagnose needs.

- ❑ **Counseling.** I helped people understand and solve their problems.

- ❑ **Personal presentation.** I gained confidence and polish in my communications skills.

Knowledge Skills

- ❑ **Unstructured problem-solving.** I was required to handle difficult, unstructured problems and to find solutions to them through analysis, consensus-building and other important problem-solving skills.

- ❑ **Conflict resolution.** I learned to mediate disputes, deal with conflict and help other people or organizations negotiate and achieve win-win solutions.

- ❑ **Knowledge.** I was exposed to new ways of thinking and new information that will help me be more creative, flexible and resourceful in any future job.

- ❑ **Quantitative skills.** I had to learn and/or apply mathematical or logical techniques in my work.

- ❑ **Creativity.** I had to find innovative, creative approaches to accomplish my goals.

- ❑ **Self-confidence.** I gained confidence in my thinking and problem-solving abilities through these experiences.

Practical Job Skills

- ❑ **Organization.** I organized the work flow of an office or other job site. I had to structure or improve the design of my own work or project.

- ❑ **Management.** I had management responsibilities that gave me experience in coordinating and tracking the work of others.

- ❑ **Planning.** I helped plan and implement activities for an organization or project.

- ❑ **Goal-setting.** I helped define goals for an organization or project.

❑ **Design/layout.** I developed artwork or designed brochures, posters or other communications.

❑ **Office equipment.** I operated office equipment such as photocopier, fax, PC, overhead projector or audio-visual equipment.

❑ **Typing/word processing.** I used a typewriter or computer to prepare written materials.

❑ **Computer skills.** I worked with spreadsheets, databases or other computer programs. I helped purchase, configure, install or operate computer equipment. I wrote application programs or utilities.

❑ **Accounting/financial management.** I was responsible for budgeting and controlling funds for my own or an organization's project.

❑ **Event and travel planning.** I gained experience in travel planning and/or the organization of public events (such as workshops, rallies, sports events, lectures, performances or trips.)

Management Skills

❑ **Leadership skills.** I lead others in the accomplishment of goals or completion of tasks.

❑ **Team skills.** I coordinated the efforts of a team (and/or worked in a team environment.)

❑ **Employee motivation.** I was responsible for motivating employees, associates or volunteers to work on a project.

❑ **Personnel management.** I was responsible for dealing with the interpersonal problems of others, such as disagreements, complaints and misunderstandings.

❑ **Control.** I was responsible for organizing, tracking and evaluating the work of others.

❑ **Interfacing.** I worked within an organizational structure that required me to interact with people above and below me and/or in other departments or areas.

Adventure Careers

❑ **Spokesperson.** I was responsible for representing an organization or project to external groups, such as the public, regulatory agencies or other organizations.

❑ **Hiring/selection.** I was responsible for an recruiting or selecting individuals to work for an organization or project or as part of a team or educational program.

❑ **Reporting.** I reported on the activities of my group or project to the organization within which it operated.

Marketing Skills

❑ **Communications.** I helped develop a communication strategy and prepare communications to publicize an organization, program or project.

❑ **Publicity.** I interacted with media and the public to publicize an event, story, candidate or organization.

❑ **Sales.** I made personal presentations to individuals or groups to publicize or market an organization, program or project.

❑ **Fundraising.** I raised funds for an organization, program or project through grant applications, donor solicitations, loan applications or other activities.

Introduction

Life is either a daring adventure or nothing.
—Helen Keller

Young adults are finding it harder to stand alone as
productive citizens.
—Peter Francese (Publisher, American Demographics)

This book is about your career and making it into a daring adventure. Many aspects of your adult life will make up your work in the world: your professional work, volunteer activity, political involvement, personal and spiritual work. Your schooling and training, your adventures and experiences, your values, goals and dreams all play a part in shaping your career. But, it is up to you to make your work, your career, a daring adventure—one that will last a lifetime. Only you can discover your own adventure career.

It is hard for people in their college years and 20s to take an optimistic, open-minded view of career development right now. Young adults are experiencing shrinking incomes and in-creasingly limited job opportunities. Census Bureau statistics show, for example, that the average incomes of 15-to-24-year-olds dropped by 11 percent last year, while the incomes of 25-to-34-year-olds dropped 1 percent. These groups were the only ones to experience drops in income during the recession. Those 65 and older actually experienced a 21-percent *increase* in income. Conventional wisdom pities the elderly on fixed incomes, but the reality is that Americans in their late teens to early 30s are now on *shrinking* incomes while many older Americans experience income growth.

According to the publisher of the journal *American Demographics*, "A record number of people in their 20s still live with their parents. The

15

home ownership rate is not rising, and there has been a sharp rise in the number of children living in poverty...In short, young adults are finding it harder to stand alone as productive citizens." (March 1992 issue.)

In times like these, well-paying jobs are hard to come by, and the struggle for economic independence seems an impossible challenge. It's harder than ever for young people just to make a living in America. So the tendency is to postpone personal experience and development. Symptomatic of this is the college-level shift from humanities majors to business and science. And everyone is rushing to interview for the few good-paying jobs available.

We are not sure what the solution to the failure of the American dream is, but we're certain that it will fall to those with the most at stake to find that solution. And therein lies both a difficult problem and a wonderful opportunity. Take advantage of the *opportunity*, rather than allow yourself to fall victim to the *problem*. Choice is possible.

Transforming breakdown into breakthrough

Amidst every breakdown is the fertile possibility of break-through. Through your work and your commitment, you can go beyond the breakdown—the idea that "this isn't working," to breakthrough—the commitment to make it work. You'll do this by taking on new work and entering into different experiences, whether you are teaching English in Costa Rica, studying art restoration in Italy, or working in your office in downtown Chicago. You'll know you've achieved breakthrough in your own life and work when you no longer have to ask "Why am I in school?" or "Is this job worth the paycheck?"

Here is an exercise that demonstrates what we mean by going beyond the breakdown—to breakthrough—finding a way to make it work. The goal is to connect all nine dots with four straight lines, without lifting your pen from the paper.

•   •   •

•   •   •

•   •   •

16

When the standard boundaries are broken, new answers and solutions are discovered. As seen here, new possibilities are also created with the discovery of two new points.

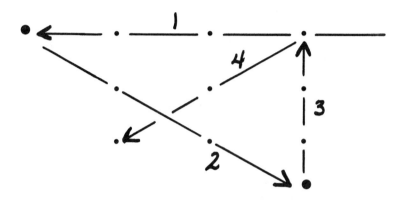

When you believe that only "what is" is possible, you take away the potential of discovery. If you get stuck in the idea that this is a time of economic (not to mention political, social and environmental) breakdown, you lose the power to create a different future.

Hitting the ground running

We have designed this book to help you leap through the window of possibility and hit the ground running. Use this book as a resource for your job of creation. Its focus is on non-traditional and extraordinary experiences. This means, on the one hand, pursuing experiences of value to you that are not offered in conventional school and career environments. On the other, it also means taking control of *all* your experiences and shaping them, even those within traditional arenas, into something extraordinary. The book invites you to enter into a personal journey that will help you expand your own vision, understanding and knowledge.

The book also defines a new view of your career—one that is applicable to anyone of any age, but is especially helpful for people at or near the beginnings of a career. Three attributes characterize this new career path:

Adventure Careers

1. It is planned and controlled by the *individual*, not employers, parents, unions or teachers.

2. It is personal, building on a diversity of experiences, not all of them traditional (and should therefore be judged by how much you *learn*, not how much you earn).

3. It is characterized by periodic lateral "hops" in addition to the traditional linear climb up a career ladder.

In addition to being a field guide for work, experience and exploration, the book will provide a platform for value clarification and personal expression. The exercises in Chapter 2 will help you clarify your values, work through goal setting, prioritize your goals and establish strategies to meet these goals.

Chapters are introduced by text addressing topics such as education, economics, entrepreneurship, travel and the environment. The personal accounts and directories are intended to inspire thoughtfulness and clear a pathway to action in one or more of these areas. They offer only a sampling of opportunities.

Remember that researching these opportunities, making choices and developing your personal plan is of great importance. A book cannot do this for you. It's your career, your adventure and your life. This is just a field guide to stick in your pocket before you set out. The organizations, programs and resources we list are worthy of your attention, but you must design your own adventure. Don't take our word for it. Instead, employ this as a resource to develop your own experience and discoveries.

The process of personal discovery and development ought to be made part of your education and career, and *vice versa*. This book is called *Adventure Careers* because it is important, more important than ever, for people to think about their careers as *theirs,* and as *adventures.* In this view, careers are crafted as an artifact of personal exploration and discovery, and of your efforts to come to terms with today's challenges and opportunities. This process may lead to a traditional 9-to-5 job in business management, or to the law or medical degree your parents always hoped you would earn. And it may not—more and more careers are now in nontraditional areas such as those described in this book.

Regardless of your destination, the path needs to be experiential, adventurous and very much your own. Don't allow concerns about career planning to get in the way of personal development and growth. Life can be a career, but no career should be allowed to become a life! Yet most people, when asked what they are doing with their life, answer by saying "I'm working for a Fortune 500 company" or "I'm looking for a job."

As you read the next chapter, think about your own career plans in the context of the new adventure career path. And then go on to the following chapter and spend a little time evaluating your goals and aspirations. Oh, and one other thing: Have fun!

Chapter 1

The Adventure Career Path

Adventure Careers

Bob started out in college majoring in business. But he liked to cook. So, against the advice of his parents and career counselor, he transferred to the Culinary Institute of America. As a fully trained "CIA chef," he worked in the kitchens of a major U.S. hotel chain under master chefs. His parents were pleased when he had finally landed on a solid career path, and urged him to stick with his job until he worked up to a senior position with his employer.

But Bob also liked to sail and waterski. In fact, he had always devoted much of his spare time to water sports. When he saw an ad for a lower-paying chef's job in the struggling restaurant of a new hotel in the Virgin Islands, he quit his job on impulse and moved to the Caribbean. He successfully ran the hotel's kitchen for two years, helping to develop the resort into a popular vacation destination. But he also acquired several small boats and rented them to vacationers. Then, again acting against the advice of his family, he quit his now-lucrative chef's job, teamed with another ex-hotel employee, and formed a small business offering water sports off the dock in front of the hotel. Both partners plowed their personal savings into an expanded fleet of boats, and now the business offers sailboarding, waterskiing and sailboat rentals, as well as waterskiing and sailing lessons. Bob and his partner are now married, and their business is a booming success.

Bob changed directions as many times before his 30th birthday as most people do by the time they reach 65, the traditional age of retirement. Each new direction threw his family into temporary panic, and exposed him to risks and a temporary reduction in income. But because Bob focused on developing expertise in areas of personal interest, each step helped build upon the previous ones and, together, they led him to a career and life far more rewarding and suitable for him than any the on-campus recruiters would have offered him had he stayed in his traditional college business major.

Carol majored in biochemistry in college, achieving high honors and strong recommendations from her professors to pursue a Ph.D. and research career. But she didn't feel enthusiastic about another lengthy round of education, so she took a year off to travel and work in Nepal. During this time, she developed a deep interest in public health issues, and came home eager to help women in Third World countries improve their lives.

This interest led her to volunteer work and internships with several nonprofits, to an intensive foreign language course, and to further travel in Third World countries. Three years later, she was ready to apply to graduate schools, but this time she knew what she wanted to study. She went on to do important work in public health, and her doctoral research led her back to Nepal and the public health issues she first encountered on her post-college trip to the region.

Adventure career paths

These are not conventional career paths. They are not the kinds of career paths parents, counselors and teachers recommend. They are characterized by multiple steps *off* the ladder—steps that look more like *falls* to some parents and advisers. Conventional wisdom says you pick a career ladder and climb it, gradually working your way to the top.

The career environment no longer offers long-term job security, or even *skill* security. Many workers laid off in the recent recession found that their job skills were no longer needed by U.S. industry. And companies no longer feel loyalty to their long-term employees, or expect it from them. Job and career shifts are increasingly common, and today's college graduates should expect to change directions a minimum of three times during their working lives. Those who change directions frequently used to be stigmatized and were unable to climb to the top of the ladder. Now they are the ones who have an advantage, developing a constellation of varied skills that add up to multifaceted capabilities and talents. Their varied skills can bring them closer to their own personal goals, rather than higher up a narrow, predetermined job ladder.

Even more important is the change in the individual's life cycle. People are living longer—their productive years now stretch far beyond the traditional retirement age. They are starting families later. They are changing careers, going back to school, and making many side-steps and turnarounds during the course of their lives and professional careers. The new life cycle is, as the name implies, cyclical, leading people into specialized work and specific roles, then, periodically, back to an active learning phase that opens up another specialized career path. In this new life cycle, people learn and change *throughout* their lives, not just in their early years. Every year is formative.

The career jungle gym

As a result of the new life cycle and the new career environment, the old vision of a career ladder is no longer appropriate. Now people move around on a three-dimensional structure offering many paths, both lateral and vertical. The career ladder has been replaced by the career jungle gym.

Or ought to be. The problem is that traditional values continue to constrain the new entrant into the job market, and society has not yet learned to support and encourage the young adult's efforts to develop a multidimensional career path. Few older adults have taken such a path, and so few mentors and role models exist for young adults. Many people still see efforts to explore the career jungle gym as *play*, not work. They offer advice like, "Stop fooling around and start developing a serious career." What they really mean in many cases is, "Get off the *new* career jungle gym and get on the *old* career ladder." And this is not helpful advice.

It's fun, but it's not play

One reason exploration of the new career jungle gym looks like play is that it is, or ought to be, directed by personal interests and convictions. Otherwise it is just a random process, and will never add up to any higher level of personal competence and fulfillment.

As you enter today's work force, you need to nurture personal interests and goals through a series of different experiences. The experiences may be education-oriented, they may be conventional jobs, they may be volunteer jobs and internships, and they may even be personal adventures such as travel or mountain climbing. When your interests provide a common thread to link these diverse experiences together, they'll support each other and add up to something greater than the sum of the parts. They will provide you with an adventure career and an adventurous life full of learning and excitement.

For many people in their late teens and 20s, social problems provide that common thread of interest and experience. A growing number recognize that they have inherited a great many pressing issues and problems and they are drawn to experiences and adventures that focus on solving these problems.

Others are motivated more by their personal interests in a sport, an art, or one of the many other fields of interest that tend to fall outside the traditional selection of career ladders. Many adventure careers can also be built on the foundation of these interests.

How to use this book

Adventure careers are built out of many, varied experiences. And often they start with a series of short-term experiences. This book offers access to many of the building blocks needed to start an adventure career. They include unique educational experiences, internships, unconventional jobs, travel and volunteer work.

Finding the right exploratory experiences can be difficult. Career counseling offices and conventional job-finding books do not cover these kinds of experiences, and they do not appear in the course catalogs of colleges and universities. Yet they are everywhere—for those who know where and how to look. Use this book to gain access to the wide selection of building blocks out of which you can build your own career jungle gym.

Also use this book to help you find and develop the personal interests and goals that will unify your various adventures and ensure that they add up to a satisfying career and life. There are exercises, observations and accounts from other career adventurers throughout the book.

In using this book, and in planning your own adventure career, try not to think of learning and working as two separate activities. Learning does not end with a diploma. In fact, the development of a reservoir of personal experience and wisdom is better done *outside* the classroom than in it. Think of school as the best place to build your explicit knowledge, and other experiences as best for experience-based knowledge. Life-long learning requires periodic use of both kinds of educational experiences.

No one is through learning when they leave school. They are just beginning to learn. Plan your career as you would your education, and plan your education as you would your career, by following your interests and seeking novel and valuable experiences and viewpoints.

An action orientation

Adventure careering is an *active* endeavor. You must take charge of your journey, rather than follow a narrow ladder provided by someone who went before you. This means you must rely first on yourself, and only secondarily on family and advisers, when it comes to discovering and planning your next experience. *You* are fully capable of finding something wonderful for you to do, and of working out the often complex logistics to make it happen. This book can help you tackle these tasks, but it is up to you to use it as a starting point, not an end point. Take on the initiative of creating and sustaining an adventure career.

Chapter 2

Planning Guide: A Brief Introduction to Your Life

Life is a game.

*In order to have a game
something has to be more important
than something else.*

*If what already is,
is more important than what isn't,
the game is over.*

*So, life is a game in which what isn't
is more important than what is.*

*Let the good times roll.
—Werner Erhard, 1973*

By now you must be tired, as well as bored, of playing games that are not of your design. You know the ones: the good grades game, the success game, the get rich game, or the I'm different game. Even if you are spending your time breaking all the rules of someone else's game, it means you've never created your own. Now it's time to create your own game. One with your rules, training schedule, objectives and prizes. It's time for your game to begin. Let the good times roll.

The development of your own game is not something that happens automatically when you turn 21, graduate from college or print your first business card. There is work, consideration, study and commitment involved. This is the entry-level work of your own adventure career. Some people delay this work until well into their careers, and everyone has to come back to it occasionally.

Older readers should not be put off by our focus on people in their teens and 20s—the following planning exercises work for people of all ages.

Note to the "too cool for this stuff" crowd

While some of you would rather be caught dead than wear a name tag in a group, participate in a classroom exercise or work through the type of "self-help" exercises in this chapter, we are, with all due respect, asking you to get over it and give this stuff a try. The best part is, you don't have to do it in public, or confess to anyone that you worked through a goal-setting exercise. And, as Robert Frost says in the introductory poem to this book you may find great salvation in your surrender. Just think how cool you will seem if these exercises move you toward being more clear or decided about the design of your future career and your path to reach your goals.

Before you begin: A look at problems

In general, we are taught that problems are bad. "Things shouldn't be this way." "If only there weren't this difficulty, life would be good." We learn very early that when confronted by problems, the *reasonable* thing to do is to head quickly toward the nearest exit. Escape and avoidance are the primary goals. But if the Wright Brothers had been reasonable and bailed out when confronted by the complexity of aviation, we may never have gotten off the ground.

So, welcome to the world of unreasonableness. The unreasonable request is for you to *love* your problems. By learning to love

29

your problems you can take control of them. You can seek a positive solution and start working toward it. You can choose action that is empowering to you and to those around you.

Life is about problems. The challenge of solving a problem, from the situation of the economy to the situation with your boyfriend or girlfriend is a valuable experience. Working to solve problems is a process of self-growth and character development, according to M. Scott Peck, M.D., author of *The Road Less Traveled:*

> *It is in this whole process of meeting and solving problems that life has its meaning. Problems are the cutting edge that distinguishes between success and failure. Problems call forth our courage and our wisdom. It is only because of problems that we grow mentally and spiritually. When we desire to encourage the growth of the human spirit, we challenge and encourage the human capacity to solve problems.*

This way of looking at problems will be invaluable to you as you answer and reanswer the questions posed at the outset of this chapter. What you want to do, and how you want to do it are worthy "problems" to solve. Work through the value clarification and goal-setting sections that follow with this in mind.

Reading through this chapter, clarifying your values, working through the goal-setting exercise, taking another look at problems and problem-solving, you may find your answers already changing. This is your life, not an exam, so feel free to edit or expand the worksheets at the end of this chapter to fit your needs. But remember, you can only edit the future, so don't wait too long to think about it. Your answers are about possibility, about breakthrough and about establishing a momentum in your life. Take some time, shoot for the stars, enjoy yourself, and write down some answers.

Worksheet 1: The three big questions

At the outset of your exploration we encourage you to ask and to answer the seemingly impossible questions of life: Who am I? What do I want to do? How do I do it?

These questions are often relegated to the "definitely no answer," "without a doubt unsolvable," or the "no way am I talking about that now" category. But the simple truth is that the answer to the question "Who am I?" is just what you say. The answers to "What do I want to do?" and "How do I do it?" are based, then, on who you say you are. For example:

1. Who am I?
   I am a person who believes in the possibility of a clean, safe environment.

2. What do I want to do?
   I want to spend my time working toward the reality of a clean, safe environment.

3. How do I do it?
   I work as an intern with an ecology group to gain experience and understanding about the environment (and about who I am) and begin a job search for a paid position in this field.

This example is presented in its simplest form. This is not to minimize the complexity of the process you must go through to answer these questions, but, instead, to suggest that within the complexity there are simple and complete answers waiting to emerge. The most important element of this exercise is to get you started answering these questions, and to get you beyond the "impossibility" of them. (Remember, you can always refine or modify your answers as you mature.)

The rest of the worksheets in this chapter will help you clarify, confirm and expand your answers. When you've completed all the exercises, review the three biggies again to see if your answers have changed or have just been more firmly established. Be flexible with yourself, experiment and enjoy.

Worksheet 2: Value clarification

A good project prior to setting your goals is to take some time to look at and articulate your values. Values provide the unseen foundation for all actions, from everyday habits to once-in-a-lifetime decisions. They function as rules of a game.

Step one: List your values

Make a list of values, ideals and principles that you consider important. Not only in the context of your personal experience, but to the world. What ideas carry meaning in relationship to your life? When you stop looking at values through the porthole of your own life, you may be surprised how many are important to you and are relevant to the manner in which you work. Here are a few to get you started:

Honesty	Achievement
Compassion	Loyalty
Kindness	Family
Steadfastness	Financial Success
Love	Consistency
Charity	

Step two: Select your most important values

After you have constructed your list, pick four to six values that seem most important to you. List them and write out a definition of what these values mean. For example, perhaps one of your core values is *kindness*. And perhaps kindness means to you the willingness to act on your concerns about the health and welfare of others. (Most meanings of values are action-oriented.)

Perhaps, to continue the example, you have done some volunteer work in the past that expresses the meaning of kindness, but you had not recognized that it was a central part of your value system. Now, having articulated it, you are able to recognize that experiences based on this value are meaningful and rewarding for you. As you plan your next moves and build your next adventures, you will be able to focus on those that permit you to implement this value.

Step three: Define your values personally

Now recast the definition of values in a personal tone. Which of these values influence your actions most profoundly? Which values affect the way you make decisions?

Step four: Create action plans

Now it is time to create possibility. How are you committed to living out these values in your life? How far are you willing to extend their influence in your actions? Explore your commitment by being very specific. Remember this is not a test. If charity is your number-one value, and helping the poor is the specific commitment you want to make, you don't have to beat yourself up for not having fed all the homeless people in New York City. You are charting your courageous course. Make your map and take it step-by-step.

Pick only two or three values and indicate how you are committed to expressing each in your life.

Making a commitment is a structure meant to support you, to support progress and breakthrough. This is not about setting you up for failure. If you don't keep your commitment, then acknowledge it and *remake* your commitment. Do it by working through these exercises as many times as you need.

The clearer you are about your values from the outset, the more effectively you will first set and then reach your goals. Values, your commitment to them and your adherence to them in action, will establish a strong foundation of personal integrity for you to work from. You will be able to have a hierarchy, or a sense of urgency related to action that will influence your life for the better.

Worksheets 3 & 4: Identify, prioritize goals

Here is an exercise to clarify your short-term and long-term goals. What kind of work do you want to do now, and what are your long-range professional goals? How do you want to spend the next year? What do you want to accomplish in the next five years? The next 20 years? How do your actions *this* year influence your five-year plan? This exercise helps you answer these questions by building a plan to guide you.

When you've completed listing your goals for all the topics, read through them and analyze them. Take a look at your short-term goals (six months to a year) and compare them to your long-term goals (five to 20 years). Do they relate to each other? Are they consistent? Do your short-term goals support your five-year goals? If not, you may want to rethink some of the goals. If you want to move to New York City and work in the hottest ad agency in town, don't forget to take a typing class or learn to use a PC while you're in college. Or, if you want to have your own bike tour business someday, start to learn about bike mechanics and repair right now.

Next, prioritize your goals on Worksheet 4. Pick the one goal from the worksheet that seems most important to you *now*. Then pick the second most important goal, and so on. Stop after you pick five or 10 goals. This is to help you focus on a few things, to give some of them great importance and a sense of urgency. Urgency is a great and inspiring fuel to fire your motivation.

(You will find other helpful exercises in *The Inventurers: Excursions in Life and Career Renewal*, by Janet Hagberg and Richard Leider, Addison-Wesley Publishing, Inc., 1988. Specifically, the life cycle review and the excursion map are valuable exercises for career planners at any stage.)

Worksheet 1
The Three Big Questions

1. Who am I?

2. What do I want to do?

3. How do I do it?

Worksheet 2
Value Clarification

Step 1: Make a list of the values, ideals and principles that you consider most important in your life. List as many as you can.

Step 2: Pick four to six of the most important values from your list above, and include them here with a description of what these values mean to you.

1.   Value:
        Meaning:

2.   Value:
        Meaning:

3.   Value:
        Meaning:

4.   Value:
        Meaning:

5.   Value:
        Meaning:

6.   Value:
        Meaning:

Step 3: Now expand on the meaning of these values, by writing what these values mean to you *personally*.

1. Value:
    Its meaning in my life:

2. Value:
    Its meaning in my life:

3. Value:
    Its meaning in my life:

4. Value:
    Its meaning in my life:

5. Value:
    Its meaning in my life:

6. Value:
    Its meaning in my life:

Step 4: Choose two or three values and explain how you want to express each in your life.

1. Value:
    I am committed to expressing it in my life by:

2. Value:
    I am committed to expressing it in my life by:

3. Value:
    I am committed to expressing it in my life by:

Worksheet 3
Goal Setting: Creating Your Future

<u>EDUCATION</u>

Goals for next six months:

Goals for next year:

Goals for next two years:

Goals for next five years:

Goals for next 20 years:

Worksheet 3
Goal Setting: Creating Your Future

<u>CAREER/PROFESSION</u>

Goals for next six months:

Goals for next year:

Goals for next two years:

Goals for next five years:

Goals for next 20 years:

Worksheet 3
Goal Setting: Creating Your Future

FINANCIAL

Goals for next six months:

Goals for next year:

Goals for next two years:

Goals for next five years:

Goals for next 20 years:

Worksheet 3
Goal Setting: Creating Your Future

TRAVEL

Goals for next six months:

Goals for next year:

Goals for next two years:

Goals for next five years:

Goals for next 20 years:

Worksheet 3
Goal Setting: Creating Your Future

<u>LEISURE</u>

Goals for next six months:

Goals for next year:

Goals for next two years:

Goals for next five years:

Goals for next 20 years:

Worksheet 3
Goal Setting: Creating Your Future

HEALTH/WELL-BEING

Goals for next six months:

Goals for next year:

Goals for next two years:

Goals for next five years:

Goals for next 20 years:

Worksheet 3
Goal Setting: Creating Your Future

<u>FAMILY</u>

Goals for next six months:

Goals for next year:

Goals for next two years:

Goals for next five years:

Goals for next 20 years:

Worksheet 3
Goal Setting: Creating Your Future

CONTRIBUTION TO COMMUNITY

Goals for next six months:

Goals for next year:

Goals for next two years:

Goals for next five years:

Goals for next 20 years:

Worksheet 3
Goal Setting: Creating Your Future

PERSONAL ACCOMPLISHMENTS

Goals for next six months:

Goals for next year:

Goals for next two years:

Goals for next five years:

Goals for next 20 years:

Worksheet 4
Prioritizing Goals

Now select your 10 most important goals and prioritize them here. You may select from all categories, and from short-term to long-term goals.

Prioritized Goals:
1.

2.

3.

4.

5.

6.

7.

8.

9.

10.

With a clear vision of the future, answer the three questions again.

1. Who am I?

2. What do I want to do?

3. How do I do it?

Chapter 3

Adventure Education

Adventure Careers

*The most important motive for work in school and
in life is the pleasure in work, pleasure in its result, and the knowledge of the value of the result to
the community.*
—Albert Einstein (in an address in Albany, N.Y.,
    Oct. 5, 1936)

Why did you go to college? Is it because it's what you should do
after high school and before entering the "real world?" Is it because
you heard it was a great party? Is it so you could get a higher position on the corporate ladder, or a higher-paying job? Or is it because you just didn't want to work yet?

It is helpful to consider your motivations. Often they are surprisingly vague. Most of us find that our reasons for pursuing college or graduate education have little to do with the values and
goals we consider important—those that surfaced in the exercises
in the preceding chapter, for example.

One thing is certain: When asked why they enrolled in an academic program, most people would not answer with Einstein's
words—"for the pleasure in the work, pleasure in its result, and the
knowledge of the value of the result to the community." Similarly,

your first answer will probably not be to prepare for, cultivate and defend the condition of happiness, as a psychologist might put it.

But below the surface we all feel more complex motivations springing from the desire to learn, to become skilled and competent in preparation for a career, and to practice the art of making our lives work: to build a structure that supports health, happiness, love and self-expression. These half-hidden motivations can be tapped to make educational experiences a daring adventure, and to help make them contribute to the creation of an adventure career.

There is an old saying that education is what is left over after you've forgotten everything you learned in school. If the sum total of what you get from college or grad school is what you recall of your lectures, labs, readings and exam crams, your education will not be of any value. If, instead, you are left with a structure that supports you in being effective in your work and in leading a rich and fulfilling life, the result of your college experience will be beyond value.

This chapter is to aid you in your formation of this structure. Provided are exercises that allow you to create your own college (or other) curriculum, which will offer the frame upon which to build an educational experience with lasting value.

Information on education alternatives, such as study abroad, unique transfer programs or colleges with alternative course work is provided in the directory of this chapter. These experiences are a powerful means for personal and academic breakthrough and are available not only in college and graduate school, but at any time during your career and life. On the new adventure career path, education is a lifelong project.

Worksheet 1: Identify your motivations

The first step in creating an adventure education is to consider your *real* motivations. Ask yourself why you are in school, why you went or why you plan to go. If you are now in college, this is a powerful exercise with direct application. If you have not yet gone, identifying your motives can confirm your decision to attend—or not attend—and will help direct your actions as you prepare. If you have finished college, this exercise and others in this chapter are tools for pinpointing how that past experience is relevant to your life now, and what additional educational experiences might be of value to you in the future.

In the same speech quoted at the beginning of this chapter, Einstein observed that:

> *Behind every achievement exists the motivation which is at the foundation of it...Here there are the greatest differences...The same work may owe its origin to fear and compulsion, ambitious desire for authority and distinction, or the loving interest in the object and desire for truth and understanding, and thus to that divine curiosity which every child possesses, but which so often is weakened early.*

To further explore the motivations behind your educational experiences, ask yourself whether you pursued them as a result of fear and compulsion, or from a desire for truth and understanding. Take some time to identify your motives for higher education and write them down in the space provided on Worksheet 1. While considering your motives, think in terms of your whole life and what you want to accomplish. It may be helpful to refer to your answers from the goal-setting exercise in the previous chapter.

Your motivations will change with time, and maybe even as you work through this chapter, but writing them down now is a way of laying the first brick of your foundation.

You can use this chapter to expand on the standard education format, to create "alternatives," and to create a curriculum that will support your work in life. The value retained after you have forgotten everything you learned depends upon how broad your vision is and how you implement your vision. College years are an important part of this project, but graduate schools, weekend workshops, educational travel and many other experiences also contribute to it.

When you enter college, you enter into a modern rite of passage that catapults you from the life you lived with your parents for the last 18 or so years, into your life as an independent adult. In a culture with few such rites of passage, college can be a very important and potent period of growth and personal development. Many people go back to school or continue their education. Sometimes these nontraditional students are back in school simply to take charge of their educations and shape them into something more meaningful and worthwhile than what was left over after college.

Taking charge of your education is a worthwhile endeavor, and is possible no matter where you are in the educational system and in your own learning process. If you are still in college, start the project earlier than most of those who went before you. But be forewarned that this endeavor is not always supported by the education system, which rewards the single-minded and fails to support the open-minded explorer.

The standard college curriculum is designed to offer a sum of critical knowledge, facts and theory, but not really to aid in personal discovery. Colleges and universities are not designed to nurture the student that is "hoping to find out what career they want to have, or are simply looking for an adventure with themselves," says Allan Bloom, author of *The Closing of the American Mind* (New York: Simon & Schuster, Inc., 1987, p. 399). He explains that, "This undecided student is an embarrassment to most universities, because he seems to be saying, 'I am a whole human being. Help me to form myself in my wholeness and let me develop my real potential,' and he is the one to whom they have nothing to say."

Worksheet 2: Creating your own curriculum

This exercise will take you beyond what is probable and help you create what is *possible* from your college or other educational experience. For simplicity, we will write with the standard college experience in mind, but the exercise can easily be adapted to any other kind of educational experience.

The power of this exercise is in being specific, developing a vision and being committed to creating it. Work through the complete exercise at the beginning of each semester or term. Focus on the term that you are about to begin and be very specific. Refer to this exercise throughout your education to keep on track. Also sketch out your plan for all the terms that follow. As you move through each term, be specific. Challenge yourself. Be more committed and allow your vision to develop.

First write down what is *probable* for you during the term, what is predictable, what is likely. What kinds of experiences, learning and accomplishments are you fairly certain to obtain? With that behind you, create what is *possible*. All you need to do is write it down and it has become your possible experience. Create, enjoy, even dream. Now make it real. Again, this is not to set you up for failure or disappointment. It is to support you in challenging yourself, breaking through what you assume to be your limitations.

Then, articulate your vision based on the options you have created. Where do you think these specific educational experiences will lead you and how will they tie into your short-term and long-term goals?

If you are in the midst of college or graduate school, you can pick this up at any time. Don't wait until the end of the term. If you have already graduated, you may also go back and do this exercise in hindsight to give you a clear reflection. And finally, you may also find the exercises helpful at the beginning and end of shorter nontraditional educational experiences such as those that appear in the directory to this chapter.

We have included one worksheet, but suggest you make photocopies so you can use them throughout your educational experiences.

Creating possibility in the "real world"

Paul White graduated from the University of Massachusetts at Amherst in the spring of 1990. His greatest dream was to work with a major sports organization. Within weeks he was hired as an intern with the National Basketball Association, and by the end of the summer he had a challenging full-time job at their New York headquarters. Luck? Superior grades? Good interviewing skills? In part, but most important, two years earlier Paul had created his own college curriculum. He took the steps while in college to make his dream come true upon graduation. He turned possibility into reality.

In 1988, Paul realized that his course work would probably qualify him for work in a small business, but that he lacked the relevant work experience and professional contacts to work for a major sports organization. He was majoring in sports management (an unusual program, and an excellent choice for his career goal). But his jobs were the typical eclectic collection of the self-supporting student, ranging from road builder to bartender. He decided he needed actual experience in business, especially in marketing and public relations. He filled these gaps by doing an internship in public relations with a nearby company. He also took a marketing course that paired students with businesses to write a marketing plan, gaining relevant experience and college credit. He also found that one of his professors placed students in internships, and this contact led eventually to his internship with the NBA.

What if he had waited until the spring semester of his senior year to ask if he was doing what was needed to support his career goals? He would have found himself interviewing for sales jobs with the pharmaceutical companies that recruit on campus. But there would have been little time or opportunity to develop the specialized experience and contacts needed to land his dream job.

Paul took a hard look at his resume. How do you evaluate your resume as a college student? There are two alternatives: The first is to draw it up as it would read if you were to graduate (or apply for a job) today, and ask yourself—as well as the career placement counselor, your professors and anyone you know in the working world—what it lacks in relationship to reaching your goals. Secondly, imagine you are a cold-hearted employer. Are you a shoe-in on the strength of your current resume? If not, it is time to take the action it takes to *become* a shoe-in, to create your dream.

Writing next year's resume

We will start with the educational side, since it's easier to add for-credit experience than for-pay experience if you are currently a student. Should you take different courses? Would a year abroad help? Would specialized study be an asset? Look through the directory at the end of this chapter for inspiration. Once you have maximized the potential of conventional and alternative education, then consider adding work experience through volunteer programs, civil service, summer jobs or other options listed throughout this book. (Note that even people with full-time jobs can easily add qualifications through night courses, educational travel during vacations, and so forth.)

Of course it's difficult to anticipate what a cold-hearted employer will actually think of your resume. So why not ask? There are plenty of cold-hearted employers around. Take your experiment a step further, and send your current resume to some of the employers you would like to work for in future years. In your cover letter, explain that you are trying to make wise decisions about your education to prepare for a job with them in two years (or whatever). Ask them to let you know what they think your weak points are, and whether any of the options you are considering will make a difference. Select the appropriate person in a specific company, addressing the letter and your phone inquires to him or her personally. Call the next week for feedback, always attempting to set up an in-person meeting. (Be prepared to call back as many as five times before giving up on an individual.)

Creating your alternative

Through the processes of creating your own curriculum and evaluating your resume, you may find that you need to pursue an alternative experience: something out of the mainstream college curriculum. The following section will address alternatives directly related to your scholastic pursuits in the United States and overseas. Please note that the specifics of how to implement many of these alternatives are addressed in Chapter 12. You may need to arrange international travel, obtain a special rail pass, find a part-time job or an inexpensive place to stay, and so forth. Start thinking about logistical concerns early—six months to a year in advance if you plan a lengthy stay in a foreign country, are applying to a new college or university, or have to raise the funding for an educational trip. Please consult Chapter 12, as well as the personal accounts and the directory that follow.

Worksheet 1
Identify Your Motivations

1. (Query / Response). I went to school because I . . .
[examples: felt I ought to get a degree; didn't want to disappoint my family; expected I would earn more money; need to do this in order to qualify for the career I want.]

2. (Visual Imagery). My educational experience is like a . . .
[examples: horse race; cattle drive; book without an ending; rising sun; ant farm; chrysalis; fireworks display; long corridor.]

3. What are the positive aspects of my motivations?

4. *What are the negative aspects?*

5. *How would I like to change them?*

6. *Is my education consistent with the reason I went to school (from 1)? Does it live up to its image (from 2)?*

Worksheet 2
Self-created Curriculum

Term _____

Probability:

Possibility:

Commitment to Creating Possibility:

Vision:

Personal Accounts

Barbara: A story of breakthrough

Barbara Bryant, at 25, is a regional manager for the retail chain Westminster Lace, a position of responsibility and clout that she would never have imagined as a college student. Here she describes her six-month program at Oxford University in England and explains how it led to a new approach to school and, eventually, to an interesting career.

Immediately after her college graduation in 1987 she went to work for Westminster Lace, a new retail venture selling British antiques, lace and clothing.

Wearing a lace dress suitable for an elegant English tea party, Barb takes time at her Stamford, Conn., store to talk about the trip to England that so profoundly affected her life.

I grew up on the North Shore of Chicago. It is a suburban fairyland known for its beautiful lake front, affluence and conservatism. I attended the local high school, which boasts a national top-10 rating each year and 80-percent college matriculation. Quality education, but with a catch. If you're not on the fast track to Columbia, if you don't score well on standardized tests, the system shuffles you into level-two (nice way of saying remedial) courses and spends a whole lot of time telling you how to cope with your "academic limitations" instead of how to develop your strengths and personal assets.

This is what happened to me. I was frustrated by school, felt I could only fail and thought this was all my problem, to either hide or cope with on my own. I was also frustrated by the people around me. I found them limited by their easy acceptance of the status quo. There was no room for creativity and no support for someone with individual needs.

I was told that my only shot at higher education was to attend an all girls college that was not very academically demanding. So I went. Very conservative, with little, if any, academic substance. I did poorly, spending more time socializing and drinking than doing school work. I dropped out in the first year and returned to the Midwest. I was really discouraged. But I heard about a special program at a nearby college, Barat College, for students who were struggling with academics. I was admitted with very low grades into this special program and it provided a great structure that allowed me to begin to trust myself, just a little.

During my junior year at Barat, the American representative for Keeble College, one of the 25 colleges that comprise Oxford University, was working on our campus. I was interested in the exchange programs, interested in an adventure and, ready for a challenge. Requirements for admission to Oxford are often very high, but with the pull of the representative I was accepted into the Center for Medieval and Renaissance Studies with a lower-than-standard grade point average.

The system I came into contact with in England, so different than that in America, changed the way I felt about myself and my potential. The system was set up on the lecture/tutorial format in which formal lectures were given to the class twice a week and a tutorial was held once a week between the student and the instructor. The course work for my Shakespeare class involved reading the text of whatever play was being performed at the local Shakespeare playhouse and, after seeing the performance, writing an analytical review. Once a week I would walk to a small house on the bank of the Thames to sit and discuss the play and drink tea with my tutor, the playhouse's director. My tutor was so supportive. She wanted to see women become successful in the arts. Her attitude toward me was very motivating.

I found myself not only learning, but *loving* to learn. Taking exams conducted on the honor system was a rewarding challenge and I had a chance to demonstrate everything I had learned. They wanted the student to decide what was important, to take responsibility.

Adventure Careers

At the end of the semester, in the British system, you take your only written exam. It's called sitting for exams. Done on the honor system, you receive the questions a few days prior to the exam date. It was amazing for me to see how much my behavior had changed in those few months. Before, I had always hated taking tests, felt so much pressure and a certainty I would not do well. Funny, if that same situation had happened at home, I would have gone straight to the library and copied my answer to the exam out of a book. But I had learned so much in this class on British architecture that answering the question "How did the style of the Italian Renaissance influence British architecture?" was an exciting challenge.

The environment was so supportive for study that everyone did well. It was such a different view than had been common at home. Here at Oxford, students considered education a privilege, not a duty. They felt it a great honor to be among this esteemed group and, in turn, honored their positions. As a transfer student, you also were exposed to a collection of superior American students that had come to England from schools such as Columbia or Brown. And the vast majority shared a mentality of purpose. The purpose was to learn and to enhance your life with that learning. Before your eyes you would see people changing, growing and maturing.

The student social life was also different. In England, if someone said, "It's so nice to see you. We should get together next week for dinner," you could be sure that you would be called and an evening of food and conversation would follow. But, at home that statement is so empty that you may never hear from that person again. Things seemed to have a time and a place at Oxford. And in their appropriate time and place, these things were experienced to their fullest. The libraries were for study, not for checking people out. Dinner was a social and friendly time. And parties were polite and casual, but not unruly like the typical frat party you endure at home.

Culture and tradition were a wonderful part of everyday life. It is true that some of the tradition and quirks of this culture took a bit of getting used to. I couldn't believe how cold every room was. For the first two weeks, I would grumble to myself: "Why don't they just turn up the damn heat? And what do you mean the buses aren't running because of the half-inch of snow that fell this morning?" But, you get over it and get used to it, and get in the habit of wearing a lot of layers. But it's a culture with a context. With a history. And the students know and understand that history. In America, the average student couldn't count back four presidents. But at Oxford people knew history and current news and politics, and they loved to talk and exchange ideas.

After Oxford, I returned to school in the States and completed my remaining three semesters of course work in only two semesters. I felt completely different about school. After graduating, I was hired as a store manager for a new independent retail store specializing in the sale of British lace and antiques. In four years, the retail venture has been extra-ordinarily successful, expanding from its first store in Seattle to 29 locations throughout the states.

I blossomed at Oxford. I thrived on the school and the cul-ture. I saw that I had a brain and knew how to think and could participate. I realized that life is what you make of it and I became determined to make the best of it.

Laurie: From adventure education to an adventure career

While at the University of California-Santa Cruz, Laurie Cole enrolled in the alternative Sea Education Association (SEA) semester at sea program. SEA offers a rare opportunity for university students to learn and practice the true craft of open-sea sailing and to experience a three-month sea voyage on one of the association's 110-foot sailing ships.

After receiving her degree from UC-SC, Laurie spent many years traveling and adventuring. Working for the French resort outfit Club Med, Laurie lived in Haiti, the Bahamas and St. Lucia. Now Laurie has returned to Santa Cruz, where she teaches sailing, rowing and windsurfing at her alma mater.

You need a lot of initiative and motivation to do something out of the mainstream, but there is room for it. Students know that there are options and alternatives for them while they are in college, that there are other ways to get educated than in the classroom. But the university is getting more crowded and competitive all the time. It is so easy to get wrapped up in the routine and the idea that getting through all the required classes is the only goal. This ignores the practical parts of education and of life.

When it comes to getting out in the world and getting a job, many people don't have the proper perspective. My experience at sea changed my whole view of education, of work and of my life. Kids growing up get so involved in how they will be a success. They forget that in the whole grand scheme of things, life is very basic and simple.

After graduation I had no interest in getting a mainstream job. It was not even a consideration. I wanted to experience life. Looking back, I think of that time as very special. I was so flexible and so driven by wanting to explore the world. I chose to work for Club Med because it combined my interest in travel and language with the reality that I had to work.

I interviewed with Club Med in Chicago during one of their bi-annual interviews and the next week I was on a plane to Haiti to teach windsurfing. During the interview they told me that they would be in touch within the next few months. The following week the recruiting office at Club Med phoned to offered me a position teaching. The first thing I did was go to the travel agency to get a brochure on Haiti—to check out this unknown place—then I called them back and said yes.

That's how it works with Club Med. They expect you to drop everything, but they also offer you a ticket to beautiful places all over the world. They pay your round-trip transportation, you live free of charge at the Club Med complex and get a small salary. While working at Club Med, my language skills improved dramatically. I made friends that I still have today and I got to travel all over the Caribbean by boat. My experience with SEA made me a very skilled boat hand. So, between Club Med assignments I would hop on boats and go all over. I did three six-month sessions with Club Med. I worked first in Haiti, then the Bahamas and then Saint Lucia.

When you're employed by Club Med you can expect to work very hard. I worked my first two-and-a-half months without a day off. And you're on all the time, catering to the guests. While the work is very hard and you have to make some compromises, attitude is everything.

I started getting one day off a week and it was my goal to see the real Haiti and the people. So on my days off I would plan my own adventures up into the hills or to the small towns. We would ride out on horseback to places where the locals had never seen blond hair before. I have long blond hair and people would stop me and want to touch it, and touch my fair skin.

I remember quite vividly getting off the plane in Haiti. There was nothing as shocking for me as taking the bus from Port-au-Prince to the Club Med resort and seeing the way the people were living, seeing the poverty, the people walking around partially clothed. It was really shocking. These and other experiences during that time changed my perspective.

The experience confirmed what I already thought: that there was plenty of time to get a mainstream job; that the way most Americans lived was not the only way or the "ideal thing." Being exposed to vacationers continually validated my choice to take this time off and pursue an alternative. People would come from all over Europe, from New York, from Canada and it would take them half of their vacation to unwind from the pressure and the tension of their lives. They would all complain and say that they wished they had done what I was doing. It was clear to me that I didn't want a life in which I hated what I was doing. I did not want a life I would need a vacation from, to complain and struggle to regain my composure. People would constantly come up to me and say, "If I had only done what you are doing when I was young, my life would be different."

I know that it was a very special time for me. I have changed since that time. I want more consistency. I want a clean place to sleep. When I used to travel I could sleep anywhere, knowing it was part of the adventure. But what I still have is the determination to make the things that are important to me a standard part of my life, not something I have to go on vacation to find. So now I teach what I love to do, water sports. I live by the ocean in Santa Cruz, which allows me exposure to the marine environment. When I look back on my travels and adventures I think: Thank God I did what I did, when I did.

Adventure Education Directory

Throughout other directories in this book, education programs or experiences that you could arrange to undertake for credit are listed. If a topic covered in other chapters seems interesting, you may want to make one of those opportunities part of your education. Also note that Chapter 12 includes directory material that will help in arranging the basic planning and funding of adventure education.

The Council on International Educational Exchange (CIEE)
205 E. 42nd St.
New York, NY 10017
212-661-1414

CIEE offers international education programs in Australia, Germany, the Netherlands, Brazil, Argentina, China, Chile, Costa Rica, Czechoslovakia, the Dominican Republic, France, Hungary, Indonesia, Japan, Poland, Spain, Thailand, Russia and Vietnam. In all, there are 34 programs in 19 countries. From 1,300 to 1,400 people participate in its programs in a year.

CIEE serves as the administrator for international education programs arranged between sponsoring institutions (college or university where the student is enrolled in the U.S.) and host (institution abroad). For example, CIEE coordinates a program at the University of Alicante in Spain that is sponsored by 67 American universities. In general, students apply to specific programs through one of the sponsoring institutions. If a student is not enrolled in a sponsoring university, temporary transfers to other universities can be arranged. Credits can then be transferred.

Academic schedules, tuition, language requirements, travel plans and other details vary. Seventeen of the programs have foreign-language prerequisites, ranging from one semester to three years. One-semester fees fall between $5,200 and $7,550, including tuition, room, full board, insurance and school excursions. In most cases, accommodations are arranged as part of the program. If not, students are given support from CIEE to find their own lodging.

Note: It is through CIEE that all students going abroad can get the International Student Identity Card (ISIC)—even if they are not enrolled in a CIEE exchange program. The ISIC is the only official ID to confirm student status overseas. This card entitles students to privileges, discounts and travel benefits. A holder of a valid ISIC automatically receives accident and sickness insurance while out of the country. To be eligible for a card, a student must have been enrolled for a term during the academic year for which the card is valid. The 1995 price for an ISIC is $16. Contact CIEE at its New York address, or contact the nearest regional office of Council Travel:

12 Park Place South
Atlanta, GA 30303
404-577-1678

205 E. 42nd St.
New York, NY 10017
212-661-1450

2000 Guadalupe St.
Austin, TX 78705
512-472-4931

1210 Potomac St. NW
Washington, DC 20007
202-337-6464

1153 North Dearborn St.
Chicago, IL 60610
312-951-0585

1501 University Ave. SE
Room 300
Minneapolis, MN 55414
612-379-2323

919 Irving St., Suite 102
San Francisco, CA 94122
415-566-6222

729 Boylston St., Suite 201
Boston, MA 02116
617-266-1926

1314 NE 43rd St., Suite 210
Seattle, WA 98105
206-632-2448

A listing of regional Council Travel offices also appears in Chapter 12. More on Council Travel: Even if you aren't a student, you should call your nearest Council Travel office to check about reduced airfare, even for travel in the United States and especially for overseas. They have numerous resources that can prevent hassles and headaches. Milk the staff for all the advice they can give you since they are all experienced discount travelers.

American Institute For Foreign Study (AIFS)
College Division
102 Greenwich Ave.
Greenwich, CT 06830
800-727-AIFS, 203-869-9090

AIFS organizes full-year, semester and quarter academic programs in Australia, Austria, Britain, China, France, Ireland, Italy, Spain and the former

Adventure Careers

Soviet Union. The Institute also organizes 3- to 12-week summer programs in Europe, China and the former Soviet Union.

A student chooses a specific AIFS program from the Institute's catalog and applies to the foreign, or "host," university through AIFS. But it is the host university that issues the academic transcript at the completion of the program, and through the host university that credits must be transferred. To transfer credits from study abroad to degree programs in the United States, students need to make special plans with their universities. While, in almost all cases, the transfer of credit is easily arranged, those interested should check this in advance.

Students must be over 17, have a GPA of at least 2.5 on a 4-point scale, have good health and demonstrate emotional and social maturity. To apply, submit a completed AIFS application form, five passport-size photos, a $35 application fee, an autobiographical essay, student copy of transcript and two academic references. While costs vary, some scholarships are available. AIFS offers one minority scholarship for a free ride and 10 runner-up scholarships of $1,000. There are also 50 merit based scholarships of $1,000; students must have a 3.0 cumulative GPA and at least 24 credits.

The costs vary. Tuition, travel, and room and board are included in the program fee. Sometimes students will stay with a host family in a home-stay arrangement, but on the whole participants are housed in the student residence halls at the college they attend. No prior language skills are required, but some of the programs do require that language classes be taken as part of the overseas curriculum.

In addition to its semester offerings, AIFS has a summer program. Unlike the semester, the summer program does not require a formal application, students just need to have at least a 2.0 cumulative GPA. There are 10 $500 merit-based scholarships available for the summer, as well; students need a 3.0 cumulative GPA and completion of 24 credits. A deposit is required. The price changes yearly, but at the time of this writing, it is $400, which includes an application fee, basic insurance and a deposit on your airfare. While AIFS can quote you a price with or without airfare, they claim to get great prices with the airlines, but if you're a good bargain flight shopper, look around.

Friends World Program
Southampton College, Long Island University
Southampton, NY 11968
516-287-8466, Fax: 516-287-8463

"The purpose of the Friends World Program is to encourage men and women from every nation to treat the entire world as a university, to take the most urgent human problems as the basis of their curriculum, to seek together designs for a more human future and to consider all of humanity as their ultimate loyalty." This university has designed a course of study and established program centers around the world. The Friends World Program is a four-year, fully accredited program with centers in the U.S., China, Costa Rica, England, India, Israel, Japan and Kenya.

Students who enroll in the program as freshmen spend an average of two years abroad doing study and field work. The students themselves, along with faculty and field advisers, design curriculum to meet their personal and academic goals. The goal of the degree program is to combine individual interests with scholarship, social concerns and global awareness. Instead of being graded, students are evaluated by the faculty and receive 15 credits per academic semester.

Admission is based on a personal interview, application and essay, teacher and school recommendations, student experience and an official transcript. The average cost per year is $20,000. But before you gasp, that includes tuition, room and board, personal expenses, books *and* international travel expenses (and field travel when you get there). In addition, 75 percent to 80 percent of the students receive financial aid.

Alumni Lifelong Education
10 Kellog Center
East Lansing, MI 48824
517-355-4562

Evening noncredit programs for adults and eight travel-study programs in the U.S. and overseas.

School for International Training
The Experiment in International Living
Kipling Road, P.O. Box 676
Brattleboro, VT 05302
802-257-7751; Fax: 802-258-3500

The School for International Training offers study abroad programs for any student. Undergraduate study abroad programs are offered in more than 30 countries. These semester or summer study programs are for college students wanting to focus on language study, interdisciplinary seminars or independent study projects. Students are trained to analyze complex issues such as poverty, hunger, environmental degradation, overpopulation, war, racism and sexism. Fees range from $8,200 to $10,900 for tuition, travel, room and board. Credits are transferable.

In addition, there's a junior-senior year program in International Studies, called The World Issue Program (WIP). It is a combination of classroom training at the school and experiential learning that includes a seven- to 11-month internship anywhere in the world. According to the school, "students develop a unique combination of awareness, knowledge, skills and experience, which results in unusually strong resumes and contacts for beginning careers in a wide variety of fields—both in foreign countries and in the United States."

The school also offers a master's program in intercultural management, which can be completed between 16 months and three years. A master of arts in teaching is offered for people wanting to combine professional language teaching with innovative teaching methods and/or field work.

Adventure Careers

Summer Academy
School of Continuing Education
The University
Canterbury, Kent CT2 7NX, England
44-227-470402

Open to all 16 and over; a great variety of study holidays available at many British universities. Reasonable prices include room and board.

Summer Program in Italy
Italian Studies
Rosemont College
Rosemont, PA 19010
215-527-0200

Syracuse University
Division of International Programs Abroad
Summer Programs Office
119 Euclid Ave.
Syracuse, NY 13244
315-443-9420

Universita di Lingua e Cultura per Strainieri
Piazzetta Grassi, 2
53100 Siena, Italy

(U.S. Contact), Siena Program
Dept. of French and Italian
Herter Hall
University of Massachusetts
Amherst, MA 01002
413-545-2314

The Universita di Lingua offers well-established courses in Italian language and culture. The school is housed in an old palace in the historical center of Siena and has been operating for more than 70 years. Students can apply directly to the school on a quarter-by-quarter basis by contacting the Siena address above. Or they can attend a one-semester (spring) program organized through the University of Massachusetts-Amherst.

The fee for students registered at the university is $4,500; for out-of-state UMASS students, it is $5,500; and for all others the cost to go through UMASS is $6,500. This covers tuition, housing and group activities. Students cover the cost of board, books and travel.

Direct application to the Italian Universita may be better for those who want to arrange their own plans, and are not concerned with attaining college credit—especially for a person who plans to be in Italy already. Americans who apply directly to the Universita must have high school diplomas or other certification that would allow for admission to an American university. A prerequisite to any cultural studies is Italian language proficiency achieved by studying and receiving the Institutes "first degree diploma." Culture courses are divided into three major areas: Italian language and literature; archeology and history; Italian history and institutions. Students attending must arrange their own travel. The school will assist students in setting up accommodations. During the summer, housing in the Student Halls of Residence is often available, but again the student is solely responsible.

General Note: Many Italian institutions offer courses for non-Italian students. Some are designed in the manner of the Scuola di Lingua e Cultura, others focus on art or music, etc. For a listing of these institutions contact: The Italian Cultural Institute, 686 Park Ave., New York, NY 10021.

Antioch College
Office of Admissions
795 Livermore St.
Yellow Springs, OH 45387-1697
800-543-9436

Independent, intellectual, creative, humanitarian, imaginative, inventive, idealistic, nonconformist, sensitive, open-minded, a seeker of peace. If you've ever been labeled any of these, this program is for you. It's built on close student-faculty relationships, and a program that sends students into the real work world for much of their academic work. Antioch has a "tradition of academic excellence, social commitment and educational innovation" that supports just these types of people in their academic and community pursuits.

The calendar year is divided into four quarters, with students alternating on-campus study with off-campus co-op work experiences. Each student has two advisers; one academic, the other co-op. The faculty maintains an ongoing list of positions ranging from Associated Press reporters to hospital scrub nurses. Most of these are either paid positions or have a stipend for living costs. Students, along with their advisers, set up their own programs.

Sea Education Association
P.O. Box 6
Woods Hole, MA 02543
800-552-3633

The Sea Education Association (SEA) offers education through hands-on experience, combining classroom academics, laboratory research and open-sea sailing. SEA places high priority on the development of maritime skills but also personal integrity, self-reliance, and working with and supporting others.

SEA programs are one semester, divided into two six-week components. Students stay at the SEA campus in Woods Hole for the shore component, where they learn basic sailing skills, the fundamentals of navigation and other principles that will be applied during the sea component.

Adventure Careers

Then, students, along with the SEA crew and scientists, take to the water for sailing and study. Depending on the season and ship schedules, cruise tracks vary, with all cruises sailing approximately 2,500 nautical miles. Each cruise stops at several ports of call. Groups are sent out on land excursions to investigate the historic and current significance of these areas to the "maritime scholar."

SEA offers several different academic programs, including a SEA Semester which concentrates on deep-water oceanographic studies. Operating at full capacity, SEA has space for 48 students each semester. During its 20 years in operation, SEA has sent more than 2,000 students to study at sea.

SEA is a well-recognized academic institution, and college credit is easily transferred to most colleges. Nine colleges, including Boston University and Colgate, are SEA affiliates. For students from nonaffiliate colleges, SEA arranges for temporary enrollment to Boston University, through which credits are transferred. A full semester of credit is received.

The program cost is $9,450, which includes tuition, lab, fees and room and board on- and offshore. They have just begun a new tuition option for the March 20-June 16 session of $7,100. Supposedly it's the exact same program and credit, so check it out. SEA also offers need-based financial aid, so don't be deterred by the price tag.

Middlebury Language School
Sunderland Language Center
Middlebury College
Middlebury, VT 05753-6131
802-388-3711

If you want to learn to speak like a native in just one summer, Middlebury is the place to go. This is an option for someone who can't afford to go overseas to learn a language (or who might be afraid of flying.) Middlebury offers an intensive total immersion program. Each of the students makes a pledge to speak nothing but the language they are trying to learn. Most students say they learned more in one summer at Middlebury than in two years overseas.

The duration and costs vary. For Arabic, Chinese, Japanese and Russian, the program is nine weeks long and costs $5,435. For the European set (French, German, Spanish, Italian) the length is seven weeks and cost is $4,125. Financial aid is available, mostly in the form of grants. Some work study is also available. You must be at least a high school graduate to apply.

While it's not as glamorous as learning a language in a foreign country, the course at Middlebury will set you well on your way to being able to speak once you get there. The professors make every effort to teach about culture as well as grammar.

Additional listings

All the additional listings are programs that are open to Americans. While some schools, such as the London School of Economics, have transfer relationships with American universities, a student can apply directly to all the foreign universities listed below. Some of the colleges, like Oxford or Cambridge, have special classes and programs designed for foreign students; others introduce American students directly into their standard course work. Specific arrangements, requirements, fees and calendars vary, so remember to check out all the details. For more ideas and additional listings of foreign programs, contact the office of foreign study at your own college. If you are not in college now and want more information, contact any nearby college for help, or call American Institute for Foreign Study or Council on International Educational Exchange (numbers listed earlier in this section).

Alliance Francaise de Paris
101 Boulevard Raspail
75270, Paris, France CEDEX 06

The American College in London/
The American College for the Applied Arts
U.S. Admissions Staff
3330 Peachier Rd.
Atlanta, GA 30326-1016

Study-abroad opportunities for college seniors from over 45 U.S. colleges and universities in business administration, commercial arts, interior design, fashion merchandising or fashion design. Placement assistance and housing provided.

British Summer Courses
15 Bootham Terrace
York, England YO3 7DH
09 04-32 08 1

Contact for general information summer programs in England.

Cambridge
The Director/Board of Extra-Mural Studies
Madingley Hall
Madingley, Cambridge, England CB3 8AQ
09-54-21-06-36

Casa
Box 40148
Albuquerque, NM 87196
505-242-3194

Spanish language study in Guatemala, with individual instructions and family living.

Adventure Careers

City University
Northampton Square
London, England ECIV OHB
71-253-4399

Offers general programs for exchange students. Contact the University's political science department for information on classes on economics.

Cranfield School of Management
Cranfield, Bedford
MK43 OAC England
0234-752725

Ecole L'Etoile
4, Place Saint-Germain-des-Pres
75006, Paris
45-48-00-05
Fax: 45-48-62-05

Elderhostel
75 Federal St.
Boston, MA 02110
617-426-8056

Educational opportunities around the world for over-sixties only. Accommodations are modest—college dorms and biology field stations—but these sessions are cheap, educational and adventurous. Write or call for more details.

Escuela Azteca
APDO Postal, 76-005
Mexico, DF, CP 04201

Spanish language and cultural education that includes study tours of the pyramids. Students live with a Mexican family.

Home Language Lesson
Reservations Office: Dept. E
2 Cecil Square, Margate
Kent, England CT9 IBD
0843-227700

Courses in 10 languages, teaching on location in 50 different countries. Students live and study in teacher's homes.

Institut de Langue Francaise
15 Rue Arsene Houssaye
75008 Paris
42-27-14-77

The London School of Economics and Political Science
Houghton St.
London, England WC2A 2AE
71-405-7686

   Programs open to Americans. Also can provide information on which American universities organize transfer programs to LSE.

The Netherlands International Institute for Managers
Endepolsdomein 150, P.O. Box 1203
6201 Be Maastricht
43-618318

   Courses in general management, industrial project cycle management and sector technology and management.

Oxford University
Deputy Director/Department of External Studies
Rewley House, 1 Willington Square
Oxford, England OX1 2JA
08-65-27-03-60

   Contact for information on summer programs.

The Richmond MBA
MBA Office, Dept. EC
16 Young St.
London, England W8 6EH
71-938-1804
Fax: 71-938-3037

   Program in international management, in England.

University of London
The Center for Asia & Africa
External Services Division
Russell Square, London, England WCIH OXG
71-637-2388 ext: 2579

   Studies in Asian and African language, economic development and culture.

Version Francaise
23 rue di Rivoli, 6000
Nice, France
93-88-29-90

   Intensive French language courses for foreigners.

For further research

British Information Service, New York
845 Third Ave.
New York, NY 10022
212-752-5747

Information on colleges in the U.K. offering courses to U.S. students.

Canadian Council: Information Center
1251 Ave. of the Americas, 16th Fl.
New York, NY 10020
212-596-1600

Information on colleges in Canada offering courses to Americans.

Cooperative Education Association
655 15th St. NW
Washington, DC 20005

Provides information on schools offering co-op programs.

French Cultural Institute
972 5th Ave.
New York, NY 10021
212-439-1400

Information on colleges in France offering courses to Americans.

Italian Cultural Institute
686 Park Ave.
New York, NY 10021
212-879-4242

Information on colleges in Italy offering courses to Americans.

National Home Study Council
1601 18th St. NW
Washington, DC 20009

Provides information on home-study courses.

Reading and references

Academic Year Abroad
Institute of International Education (IIE)
809 United Nations Plaza
New York, NY 10017
212-883-8200; Fax: 212-984-5452

Academic Year Abroad is a comprehensive guide to programs for international study open to Americans. This publication includes almost 2,000 programs. IIE serves as a clearing house of information about international education. It publishes books, brochures and fact sheets for people looking for information on study-abroad programs, scholarships, grants and career opportunities in international education.

Transitions Abroad
TAAS Guides
P.O. Box 334
Amherst, MA 01004
800-293-0373

Call these people right away! If you are planning to go overseas, they have amazing resources. They offer a bimonthly Resource Guide and Fact Sheet that covers topics including student programs, study abroad for adults, responsible travel and a volunteer opportunity directory. They have a long list of resources on finding work overseas. Look for Guides on Solo Women Travelers, Fine Arts Study Worldwide and a range of other topics. Each year they publish an Alternative Travel Directory. This is one place you should definitely call to get the scoop.

Accredited Institutions of Postsecondary Education: Programs Candidate
Oryx Press
4041 North Central Ave., Suite 700
Phoenix, AZ 85012-3399
800-279-6799

An annual directory for planning graduate studies abroad. $39.95.

International Handbook of Universities and Other Institutions of Higher Education, F. Eberhard, Editor
Stockton Press for the International Association of Universities
15 E. 26th St.
New York, NY 10010

This biennial directory gives detailed information about the programs of colleges and universities in 115 countries. With a price tag of $180, those interested may want to check out a copy from the library.

Adventure Careers

The Whole World Handbook: Work-Study-Travel Abroad
Council on International Educational Exchange, Publications Dept.
205 E. 42nd St.
New York, NY 10017

A great guide for anyone who wants to spend time abroad. Full of good information and tips. Tells you what you need to know in developing your plan and how to get there.

A Guide to Educational Programs in the Third World
Council on International Educational Exchange, Publications Dept.
205 E. 42nd St.
New York, NY 10017

This is one of CIEE's many free publications with information on programs throughout the world. Contact them for a copy and a listing of other publications.

Advisory List of International Educational Travel and Exchange Program, Herwig and Dennis Pap, Editors
Council on Standards for International Educational Travel
3 Loudon St. SE, Suite 3
Leesburg, VA 22075

Lists high-school level programs.

Also see Chapter 12 for the directory of funding sources for alternative education and travel experiences. Look to Chapter 8 for a directory of short-term educational experiences, both for credit and not-for-credit.

Chapter 4

"Good Works:" Volunteer and Community Service Adventures

Adventure Careers

This is the true joy in life, the being used for a purpose recognized by yourself as a mighty one; the being a force of nature instead of a feverish, selfish little clod of ailments and grievances complaining that the world will not devote itself to making you happy.

I am of the opinion that my life belongs to the whole community, and as long as I like it is my privilege to do for it whatever I can.

I want to be thoroughly used up when I die, for the harder I work the more I live. I rejoice in life for its own sake. Life is no "brief candle" to me. It is a sort of splendid torch which I have got hold of for the moment and I want to make it burn as brightly as possible before handing it on to future generations.
—George Bernard Shaw

A young man and an old man were walking down the street one day. They were discussing the problem of homelessness, having just been stopped by a homeless women and her three children, asking passersby for spare change. "What can I give when I don't have any of this to hand out?" the young man asked, holding a wrinkled dollar bill in his hand.

"You have yourself to give," answered the older man after a pause. "That is what you have before and after you have money. You always have yourself to give."

This chapter is about the work of giving, and the directory material highlights some of the many volunteer, internship and job opportunities through which you can give of yourself. This kind of work enriches the lives of recipient and giver alike. It adds another dimension to an adventure career, and can be incorporated into a career in three ways. First and most obvious, it can be the main focus of the career. There are many full-time jobs available with social service agencies, nonprofits and other such groups (you will find many of these organizations in the directory of this chapter).

Secondly, socially beneficial work can be pursued on the side, as a part-time or occasional job or volunteer activity. When pursued in this manner, it enriches your primary career and helps build complementary skills and experiences. Third, it can form one of the short-term experiences that are the basic building blocks of adventure careers. An internship or summer job can provide fascinating and valuable experience that is applicable whether you continue in the same field or in a different one. For example, administrative and communication skills, interpersonal skills, and many other valuable work skills can be obtained in a "good works" job or internship and, later, applied in another job.

A glance at the organizations in the directory will spotlight the value of giving. Many of the people who work in these organizations have a different take on the standard social contract, expanding it to acknowledge and reward contributions made to the community as well as rewards for individual success. Their lives and their work seem to be at odds with mainstream culture, where money often equals value, and status is based on salary. Their experiences demonstrate that the value of one's work can also be measured by the richness of experience and the size of one's contribution to the well-being of the community.

Adventure Careers

This chapter will present volunteer and internship programs, as well as "good works" career opportunities. Whether working as a temporary volunteer for the Red Cross or an intern at UNICEF, whether building a career as a social worker at the community mental health clinic or volunteering with a refugee resettlement project, you can have priceless experiences that benefit society and, as a happy consequence, offer personal satisfaction and yet another way to build the multi-faceted knowledge and skills base of an adventure career.

You may have noted by now that the text of each chapter provides a vehicle for exploring another facet of the adventure career. In the previous chapter we explored the concept that adventure careers imply life-long learning. In this chapter the concept that work is more rewarding when it benefits society is introduced, suggesting another way to look at the adventure career path.

But how do you reconcile the giving required of altruistic experiences with the financial (and often social) pressure to earn a decent salary? The dictionary defines altruism as "unselfish regard for or devotion to the welfare of others." Yet in common usage the expression "to make a good living" means a comfortable or well-to-do living, not a socially beneficial one! (Perhaps it could more accurately be called "to *take* a good living.")

Volunteerism and the natural desire to earn a higher salary and live more securely and comfortably do not need to conflict, since they are on different levels in your bundle of priorities. Making money can be a goal, a stop on the road of some higher purpose. What that higher purpose is we cannot tell our readers, of course, but they may already have a clear vision of it through the value-clarification exercises in Chapter 2 of this book.

This conceptual approach is helpful in thinking about whether and how to pursue experiences such as those described in the rest of this chapter. It is often helpful to think about them in the context of your basic values and sense of purpose, and to pursue those that are close enough to this road that they make natural stopping places. Similarly, it is helpful to differentiate among the many ways of making money. In this perspective, volunteering or working at low salary is not a sacrifice or something done out of guilt, it is one of the many way-points that help you travel toward a desired purpose.

Volunteering as a job search strategy

By the way, volunteering is also a great thing to do when you are out of work and looking for a new job. Even if you are looking in some other field, you may find that volunteering helps you keep your sanity and build your job skills. And you can also use a volunteer job in place of an entry-level job if you are new to the job market and cannot find a paid position. The chance to get in and get working can be priceless when there are very few—and sometimes no—jobs for entry-level applicants.

At the end of this chapter are two personal accounts from Peace Corps volunteers. This is one of the better-known and best-organized of the available volunteer experiences that often leads to a "good works" career, but by no means the only one, so be sure to look at the directory as well. However, the personal accounts here do convey something of the feel of many "goods works" experiences, as you will see.

"Good work" careers

"Nourishing the taproots of an ever deeper democratic society can be considered one of life's great joys. Fulfilling one's talents and dreams in such a quest is the antithesis of jobs that, however well paid, make you feel that you are just putting your time in, that life begins after the nine-to-five drudgery is over."
—Ralph Nader (from his introduction to *Good Works* by
    Jessica Cowan, Barricade Books, N.Y., 1991.)

Work in social change can provide rewarding careers—not just short-term internships or volunteer opportunities. You can find work in this area. A great many options for "good works" careers exist, ranging from work in agriculture and the arts through citizen organizations, civil right groups, communications and consumer rights, on to work with the disabled, economic development, education, health care, human rights and more.

However, you may have to dig for information and do a lot of research to find such career opportunities. Most career counselors and job placement services seem to be uninformed about this sector of the work force. In fact, the reason this discussion follows the volunteer section is that it is often easiest to start a career in social service by working as a volunteer or intern. The experience and contacts will open many doors, and often lead to career options that were not visible before.

It's never too early to start building a network of contacts who might put you in touch with any job openings. Asking lots of questions can speed the development of a network—in essence this constitutes plugging into other peoples' networks. And there is also a wonderful shortcut available to people who seek careers in social change. Many organizations have begun to collect detailed information about other organizations that operate in their area.

These organizations have made themselves conduits in the information network, and are happy to offer referrals and access to their databases to any who seek careers in social change.

There is now one good reference on the topic, updated through periodic releases of new editions. It is called *Good Works: A Guide to Careers in Social Change*; the latest edition is edited by Jessica Cowan (published by Barricade Books, 61 Fourth Ave., New York, NY 10003, ISBN 0-9623032-8-3.) For phone orders: 212-627-7000. The price is $24 for 704 pages of information.

Because *Good Works* provides such a thorough directory of employers, we have not attempted to include an authoritative listing in our directory. However, in Directory 3, we do include a sampling of organizations that hire people for full-time, career-oriented positions, entry-level and higher. These organizations are generally well-established, with substantial budgets and professional management. Our list covers a broad range of interests and focuses, and provides a good starting point.

If you seek a career in social change, whatever your specific interests, be sure to refer to all these lists. Contact organizations that share your interest for job openings or referrals, and by all means network through those organizations that make it their business to help people like you find work! Also seriously consider purchasing a copy of *Good Works: A Guide to Careers in Social Change*. It is an extensive database, and when it comes to job searches, more is generally better.

Personal Accounts

The Peace Corps is perhaps the best-known of all volunteer programs, and in a sense it illustrates the fuzzy boundaries between voluntary work and full-fledged careers. Peace Corps volunteers have full-time, multi-year experiences, and are fully supported by the Peace Corps during these experiences. To many, this *is* a career—and a far more rewarding one than any of the more conventional options. Many people go on from Peace Corps experiences to rewarding careers in international aid, Third World economic development, teaching, public health or other fields that build directly on their Peace Corps training and experiences.

Erin: "Success was having meat on the table, learning a new word."

Excerpts from the journal kept by Erin McNulty, written while she served as a Peace Corps volunteer in Zaire from 1988 to 1991.

I was mistaken in thinking I would join the Peace Corps and somewhere, sometime find my "cause." I had thought that the cause was a Thing, an organization of like-minded people and resources. I thought I would have a life where I would fight for my cause from 9 to 5, and then rest. In the Peace Corps I did find my cause, but I also found reality. My work for justice and liberation is not a neat and tidy, 9-to-5 job. It is the commitment of my daily life to this work. It's all about me, about my personal choices, reactions and responses. We each are God in our ability to create, and our potential is beyond our own comprehension. We must test our beliefs and convictions to learn their worth, and sometime to discover the lack of worth of things we had held so dear.

February 1989

The day, as determined by my attitude, had not gone well. I was at my village four days, had the language skills of a 5-year-old, and foolishly, had plans about what I wanted to do, and how. The ideas, however, did not include the man who was walking ahead of me, but he had somehow become my guide, interpreter and partner in work.

I was hoping to go to the nearby town, in order to introduce myself and my work to local authorities. Well, this new friend would just not hear of it when I told him I planned to go on my own. He said something to the effect that it would be shameful to the community if others saw me alone—being new and all. So, as I grumbled under my breath, we set off together.

I'll never be the same because of the things that happened that day. During introductions made, he never mentioned that I had been vehement to go alone (accompanied only by my huge ego). Instead, he told people we were out walking to meet and talk to the general population. I felt I had been rude, and asked him, in broken phrases, why he said what he said to people when he knew I hadn't wanted him along?

He stopped on the footpath and asked me if I knew where we were. I had no idea. He responded wisely that he was in front and I behind because sometimes one person must lead so others don't stumble or get lost. He added it was his turn to lead, since he had the knowledge. But another time, with my own knowledge, it would be my turn to lead.

April 1989

I laugh at my smallness and how big fear really can be. I've definitely shed some fears and, of course, adopted some other ones. I've found myself cursed with a sense of responsibility that outweighs its need.

Learning to let go, when to open my mouth and when to listen. Choices are very important living in a strange culture and speaking a new language. Sometimes your choices and decisions are all you have control over. Here you depend so much on everyone else to watch out for you. Success was redefined because the "American Way" did not mean anything. Success was getting an idea across, having meat on the table, learning a new word and finally understanding the appropriate cultural responses to a situation.

Happiness now meant connecting with people under any circumstance. My reward was watching others discover their own abilities and strengths, not always my own. Success to me was helping others reach their own conclusions and doing what was best for them. No price can be put on the reward and recognition given by the smile of personal empowerment.

August 1989

One rare moment with a group of young men and women: We were talking about life. One boy asked me, "Where is it we all come from? We all seem pretty similar except for our colors. Why?" he asked. He said the whites he had come in contact with knew far more than anyone else. So he asked me to please explain to him what happens and where we go after we die. I learned right then that we are all the same—people asking the same questions.

Lisa: "Among the unusual delicacies at the market are caterpillars, live or roasted."

Lisa Boyd has been working as a Peace Corps volunteer in the Central African Republic (CAR) since 1990. She contributed this letter to her high school class notes (class of '82) and it is reproduced here courtesy of "The Andover Bulletin," Phillips Academy, Andover, Mass.

I was sworn into the Peace Corps on 3 July 1990 at the American Ambassador's house in Banqui, Central African Republic (CAR, formerly Cameroon). My months as a trainee included studying French and Songo, the main language in CAR; learning to instruct teachers in the School Health Education Program about ways of protecting children against diarrheal diseases and malaria; and learning to eat antelope and beef heart (but not monkey, bat or tripe) with my host family. No longer being a trainee felt good, almost as good as the moment when Ambassador Simpson called us "the best of America."

Since then I have worked in primary schools as a school health educator in Berberati, a city of 50,000 people near the rain forest—an area with many coffee plantations and rich with diamond mines. I also visit schools in other towns to present workshops and evaluate teacher delivery of health lessons ranging from information about measles to instructions about using a latrine to the needs of the newborn.

The pace of work here is very slow. I awake around 5:30 a.m. and crawl out of my mosquito net to take a shower before my breakfast of coffee, a banana and peanut butter on something resembling French bread. I arrive at my office, review training notes, read reports or visit schools. Mid-morning I shop at the open-air market. Among the unusual delicacies at the market are caterpillars, live or roasted. Some of the best offerings are fresh ground peanut butter, fruits and "white person" vegetables such as carrots, cucumbers and cabbage. I return to work until 2:30 in the afternoon. I will then leave work to spend the rest of my afternoon visiting friends, cleaning and cooking. By 9 p.m. I'm in my mosquito net, sure to have a kerosene lamp lit for those midnight trips to the "bathroom."

In mid-October 1990, Berberati hosted a national celebration by women's groups, agriculture groups, church groups and school groups from all over the country. Here I had my first glimpse of grass skirts, leather loin cloths, feather head-dresses, beaded necklaces, pounding drums and complicated rhythmic movements. A Central African women tried to teach me some dance steps. How my hips ached afterwards!

Shortly after the celebration, a teacher's strike closed the Regional Pedagogical Center and gave me more time to visit the health centers and the hospital. I viewed these facilities through two filters. Through my CAR filter, I saw a hospital with a pharmacy, a place for surgery and an incredibly capable midwife. The grounds were well-kept and the buildings looked solid. Through my American filter I saw an appalling place. Until a week ago there had been no outhouses. Water was hauled to the under-staffed hospital, which was short of beds and medicine. People seeking admission were often turned away. Although the hospitals and health centers are supported by UNICEF and USAID, they continue to be understaffed and overburdened.

I have now visited all nine schools, met 53 of the 70 teachers (all men), and have taught, in French, would-be teachers in primary schools. I feel very good about this work. But because the Central Africans are very stoic, I cannot gauge my students' responses very well. Also, evaluating the impact of the health programs is difficult since I do not work directly with the delivery of service: vaccination or oral rehydration therapy. More children are being vaccinated; my neighborhood children proudly display their vaccination scars. On the other hand, within a six-month period my neighbor's baby died one day after its birth, a 12-year-old host family "sister" to a fellow Peace Corps volunteer died of chronic malaria.

Working here can be discouraging—the slow rate of progress, local people who do not understand the Peace Corps mission and appear to resent our presence (and sometimes can harass women colleagues), foreign development agencies that attempt to solve all the problems for Central Africans rather that help them to develop their own lasting solutions. Yet working here can be exhilarating and many host country nationals are respectful and friendly.

There is a saying among those of us who train teachers: "If I see one teacher lead an exciting, challenging health lesson, it will have been worth it." I have. And it is.

"Good Works" Directory

This directory is divided into four parts: 1) volunteer and internship programs, 2) social change organizations offering career opportunities, 3) organizations offering job referrals, and 4) reading and references. We have presented some of the larger organizations and more well-known programs in detail. Other entries are brief, with a sketch of the programs and contact information.

Details regarding the volunteer/internship experiences vary greatly from organization to organization. Some positions are paid, some not. Sometimes travel costs are covered, and stipends are offered. In other cases the workers pay their own way. Be sure to check out all details before committing to a program. The reading and references list offers additional resources for your own continued investigation.

Although we haven't listed any in particular, keep in mind that good places to begin volunteering are at your local homeless shelter or abused women's shelter. Just because you can't leave your home tomorrow doesn't mean you can't start your own "good work" adventure. Shelters can often use a range of skills: office work, child care, legal advice, extra hands, etc.

1. Volunteer and internship programs

American Foundation for AIDS Research (AmFAR)
Intern Coordinator
1828 L St. NW, Suite 802
Washington, DC 20036
202-331-8600

AmFAR was founded to provide funding and encouragement for AIDS research. The Washington branch funds public policy research, and monitors federal AIDS efforts. This internship involves a great deal of research and writing, but it gets you in the thick of AIDS policy and research efforts. AmFAR only takes four interns a year: two may receive a $2,500 stipend, while the other two will volunteer for at least 20 hours a week.

Council on International Educational Exchange (CIEE)
International Voluntary Service
205 E. 42nd St.
New York, NY 10017
212-661-1414

The Council on International Educational Exchange (CIEE) coordinates the summer placements of Americans in workcamps in the United States, Europe, Canada and Africa. CIEE works in alliance with service organizations in the area of each workcamp to determine projects, coordinate operations, and recruit volunteers and leaders. The purpose of these camps is "to promote international understanding and a spirit of cooperation through the exchange of volunteers." Jobs include nature protection/conservation, renovation of historic sites, construction, archaeology, forestry and social work.

CIEE sends volunteers to work on two- to three-week stints during July and August, and in December and January for African camp sites. Generally, volunteers work a five-day, 40-hour week and receive free room and board. Participants live together in accommodations ranging from student hotels to tents. Volunteers may be assigned to ongoing projects, or jobs to be complete within the three-week service.

Volunteers must be 18 years old. Those people going to France and Germany must have working knowledge of the local language. There is a $125 application fee, and volunteers must arrange and pay for their travel to the camp. Participants need their own pocket money and must pay for any additional travel they choose to do.

CIEE negotiates placements based on individual country preferences stated on the initial application. In April or May, applicants get a listing of site locations and dates, at which time they select preferred sites. They're then notified, within four weeks, of their workcamp assignment. As CIEE says in its International Workcamp brochure, "the type of experience you will have is not defined as much by the *where, when* and *what* you will be doing as much as by *you.*"

Peace Corps
1990 K St. NW
Washington, DC 20526
800-424-8580

The Peace Corps is one of the best known volunteer organizations and today has 6,500 volunteers in more than 90 countries. Americans are sent on community-chosen projects with the mission of helping to teach local people skills and methods that aid in their lives. Volunteers are not sent to *fix* things, but to give knowledge and training that helps people manage their environment and social system better. The Peace Corps was formed as a United States government agency in 1961 by President John F. Kennedy to promote peace and friendship through the training of local people in developing countries.

For the past 30 years the Peace Corps has been known for its work in rural areas throughout the developing world, sending participants to distant villages in Senegal or to outposts on the island of Fiji. Project assignments have focused on health care, food, shelter and education.

Starting in the 1990s, the Peace Corps has been moving into the urban centers of Eastern Europe, and in 1992 the first volunteers left for the former Soviet Union. Instead of the rural-development aid traditionally offered, new recruits are providing support in areas of banking, accounting and finance, and find themselves sleeping on German-made beds in high-rise apartments. There are currently 670 volunteers, and still more are needed. The countries are requesting recruits to consult for business management experience, environmental education and English education. Since English has become the worldwide language for business, these countries are eager to be able to participate.

While the Peace Corps keeps pace with the changing needs of developing countries, it still maintains its high standards of recruit training, project administration and supervision. When you sign on as a Peace Corps worker, you agree to a two-year placement. Participants must be at least 18 years old, U.S. citizens, and have a bachelor's degree or at least three years of full-time work experience in a field related to the organization's work. Before the two-year tour of duty, recruits receive three months of language and cross-cultural training, either in the U.S. or in the host country.

Applicants have the opportunity to indicate preferred countries of service. While volunteers will not be sent to areas they do not want to serve, specific assignments are made on need. The Peace Corps pays for all travel, health care, insurance and living expenses. Volunteers receive two days of vacation per month, a living allowance in the currency of the country (unless it makes more sense to use dollars) and $200 U.S. dollars per month of training and service. Pay is held until the service is completed.

Youth Ending Hunger
The Hunger Project
1388 Sutter St.
San Francisco, CA 94109-5452
415-928-8700

Youth Ending Hunger (YEH), organized by The Hunger Project, works toward a world without hunger. Achieving such a goal is a monumental task when 35,000 people die each day from chronic hunger. YEH is supported by a worldwide network of more than 25,000 young people in 15 countries working to raise public awareness about world hunger, and influence government leaders to take effective action to end hunger.

In America, YEH is a rapidly growing network of local volunteer groups that work independently and collectively. Groups conduct educational projects to raise public awareness of world hunger and to place the ending of hunger as priority for both the public and the policy makers. YEH volunteers work to influence policy locally by meeting with elected officials and community leaders, and nationally by encouraging the U.S. government to support national legislation and international conventions, such as the 1990 U.N. Convention on the Rights of the Child.

YEH offers coordination and support for the development of individual grassroots groups. The central YEH office in San Francisco provides guidelines for forming and running the clubs, for organizing education, local action and fundraising projects. Administration and organization, including the development of goals and projects, are led at the local level within each group. New volunteers are welcome, and new local chapters can form when there are at least five members.

WorldTeach
Phillips Brooks House
Harvard University
Cambridge, MA 02138
617-495-5527

This internship is mentioned in the book *Alternatives to the Peace Corps* for good reason. Instead of being closely linked to the U.S., the volunteer is employed by the host country essentially as a professor. WorldTeach takes college graduates from any major to countries around the world: Kenya, Namibia, South Africa, Thailand, Costa Rica, Ecuador and Poland. While they have a summer internship program in Shanghai, the rest of the programs are for at least one year. In most cases they teach English, buy may also teach subjects such as math, science and sports.

While no formal teaching experience is required, volunteers must take a course in teaching English as a second language or must have spent 25 hours teaching or tutoring English. Foreign language skills are not needed, although encouraged. Applicants do not have to be US citizens, but they must be fluent in English. There are no age restrictions for this program. Recommendations, resume, interview and school transcripts are also used to determine acceptance.

While people tend to go their first year after college, there are many who work here for a year and then have anxiety attacks and decide to go teach. According to one intern, those volunteers who do go over after having worked previously often extend their stay. WorldTeach is a good door to other employment in your host country, so if you want an excuse to be somewhere and a reason to stay, this is a viable route.

At the beginning of the program, volunteers pay a fee for travel, health insurance, placement, orientation, field support and program administration. The fee is around $3,500, depending on your country destination. Once in your host country, you have no expenses. Volunteers are given enough money to live comfortably in the standard of their country of residence. If you tend to be a big spender, and/or you want to do a lot of extra traveling, it's a good idea to bring extra funds.

Adventure Careers

Big Brothers/Big Sisters of America
230 N. 13th St.
Philadelphia, PA 19107
215-567-7000

Big Brothers/Big Sisters are unpaid volunteers paired with a child or teenager to form a relationship that offers support and guidance. Both parties often find these relationships mutually supportive and fulfilling. It is suggested that the pair spend four hours a week together doing activities that they agree on.

You must be over 21 to apply for a Big Brother/Big Sister position. There is a careful screening process. After review, volunteers are matched with children or teens, who have also been screened by the organization. Each volunteer is briefed by a staff caseworker and offered support throughout the experience, but no specific training or group exercises are provided. There are currently 70,000 adults matched with children and teenagers. In most locations, the demand for Big Brothers/Big Sisters exceeds the supply.

The American Red Cross
430 17th St. NW
Washington, DC 20006
202-737-8300

There are 1.2 million trained Red Cross volunteers working in different capacities to help their communities prevent, prepare for and cope with emergencies. The American Red Cross has been providing aid and relief since 1881. American Red Cross services, governed and directed by volunteers, range from blood drives to the distribution of food at disaster sites, to AIDS education at local work sites. Service volunteers are matched with jobs based on previous skills or ones they are taught by the Red Cross. Volunteers are not paid.

Institute for International Cooperation and Development (IICD)
P.O. Box 103-B
Williamstown, MA 01267
413-458-9828

IICD offers the chance to work with indigenous people around the world. There are either six-month or 12-month stints with the current cost being $3,300 and $4,500 respectively. This includes everything, even travel expenses. The programs they offer vary year to year depending on the teams. While they have specific countries and people to work with, each team has to come up with its group goals before leaving. Groups do construction projects in Nicaragua and Brazil, and in Zimbabwe and Mozambique they work with street kids, oversee rural education and plant trees. Currently, there is also a travel team being organized to go to Zambia, Zimbabwe, South Africa and Botswana. This team will be doing research before IICD decides on a program to pursue. In fact, each of the programs are the result of similar team research. The team decides on a research focus, and then they travel through the country to do research and then set up programs.

The IICD program is based on a Scandinavian folk education idea that combines theory and practice and the means for learning. The volunteer program is intended for the "purpose of gaining knowledge and experience, not for fame or credit." The IICD work is done in groups and the focus is on cooperation and common actions. Specific programs are termed "solidarity projects" and are done in cooperation with organizations already working in each country to provide "direct and long term benefits for the community."

Cost of the programs are paid through fundraising, as well as by the participants. The fee covers training expenses, room and board, international health insurance and air fare. Participants are responsible for fundraising activities during the preparation period. Applicants must be 18 years old. No specific skills or academic training is required.

Additional listings

The National Park Service
Volunteers in the Parks (VIPs)
P.O. Box 37127
Washington, DC 20013
Contact: Service-Wide Volunteer Program Manager Bob Huggins
202-523-5270

The National Park Service organizes a nationwide program to encourage people to work in the national parks. Opportunities range from trail upkeep to projects that protect endangered species. Specific assignments and work hours are worked out between each individual and the officials at the specific park. The national office can lead applicants to parks in your area, or you can apply directly to the park where you wish to work. Volunteers are not paid. At some larger parks, free campsites are exchanged for longer-term volunteer positions such as campground host.

Amigos de las Americas
5618 Star Lane
Houston, TX 77057
713-782-5290

Sends people on four- to eight-week summer volunteer programs to Brazil, Costa Rica, the Dominican Republic, Ecuador, Mexico and Paraguay. There is a four- to six-month preparation period before leaving the States.

Australian Trust for Conservation Volunteers
Box 423
Ballarat, Victoria, Australia 3350
61-53-327-490

Six-week programs in New South Wales, Victoria and South Australia planting trees, constructing fences and working on erosion control.

Adventure Careers

Dartmouth Alumni College
6068 Blunt Alumni Center, Rm. 309
Hanover, NH 03755
603-646-2454

One- and two-week summer programs; an educational travel program.

Fourth World Movement
7600 Willow Hill Drive
Landover, MD 20785
301-336-9489

This organization sponsors 10-day work/information camps in Belgium, Canada, France, Great Britain, the Netherlands, Switzerland and the U.S., with volunteers giving time to help poor families.

Frontier Nursing Service
Courier Program
Wendover, KY 41775
606-672-2317

This is an opportunity to find out what being a rural nurse and/or midwife is all about. Interns need to be able to drive in order to chauffeur the midwives or deliver supplies. It's a great way to avoid busywork and get a close look at being a frontier nurse.

Higher Education Consortium for Urban Affairs, Inc.
Internship Director/Program Associate
HECUA at Hamline University
Mail 36, Hamline University
1536 Hewitt Ave.
St. Paul, MN 55104-1284
612-646-2986; Fax 612-659-9421

Volunteer internships in a city arts program, metro urban studies and a community program; possibility of full-time employment; placement assistance provided. Duration for all positions is one semester.

International Christian Youth Exchange (ICYE)
134 W. 26th St.
New York, NY 10001
212-206-7307; Fax: 212-633-9085

Four- to six-week workcamps in Africa, Asia, Latin America, Europe and the former Soviet Union offer volunteers the chance to participate in projects including rehabilitation of schools or health clinics, development of women's health services or working in local clinics or shelters. Depending on location, fees vary from $500 to $3,000 and cover room, board, travel, insurance and training. Some scholarship money is available.

Partnership for Service Learning
815 Second Ave., Suite 315
New York, NY 10017-4594
212-986-0989

This consortium of colleges, universities and service agencies offers programs in South Dakota, Ecuador, England, France, India, Jamaica, Liberia, Mexico and the Philippines. The programs combine academic study with community service. Programs vary in length from a year to one month.

United States Forest Service-Regional Office
Northern Region, Federal Building
200 East Broadway
P.O. Box 7669
Missoula, MT 59807
406-329-3511

Volunteers work on conservation projects, campground hosting and wildlife management for U.S. Forest Service in Montana, northern Idaho, western North Dakota and part of northwest South Dakota.

United States Forest Service-Regional Office
Pacific Northwest Region
P.O. Box 3623   33 Southwest First
Portland, OR 97208-3623   Portland, OR 97204
503-326-3816

There are opportunities for volunteer work in the 19 national forests in Oregon and Washington.

Volunteers for Peace (VFP)
43 Tiffany Rd.
Belmont, VT 05730
802-259-2759

Volunteers work in 36 countries on social, environmental, conservation, restoration, archaeological and agricultural projects. Each group of volunteers includes at least three different nationalities.

National Coalition for the Homeless
1612 K St. NW, Suite 1004
Washington, DC 20006
202-775-1322

Volunteers work in several "transitional homes" for the homeless in D.C.; offers a program for the homeless to find independent housing.

Adventure Careers

Community for Creative Non-Violence Shelter
425 Second St. NW
Washington, DC 20001-1003
202-393-1909

Volunteers work in this organization's 1,400-bed homeless shelter, helping in the soup kitchen and shelter, and doing community organizing and medical work.

Community Service Volunteers (CSV)
237 Pentonville Rd.
London N1 9NJ, England
44-1-278-6601

This organization matches volunteer projects with volunteers to work in the U.K. and Northern Ireland. Approximately 10 percent of CSV's 2,000 volunteers a year come from outside England. Most projects focus on helping people, such as helping handicapped adults and children, or working with the homeless. Participants must pay their way to London, as well as room and board, until they are matched with a project. There is also a placement fee on summer projects.

Concern
P.O. Box 1790
Santa Ana, CA 92702
714-953-8575

Volunteer professionals in the fields of agriculture, community organizing, health, engineering and education work on this organization's international hunger relief and development programs in Bangladesh, El Salvador, Guatemala, Honduras, Mexico, Nigeria and Sierra Leone.

Quaker International Social Project
Friends House, Euston Rd.
London, NW1 2BJ, England
44-1-387-3601

Throughout Great Britain and Northern Ireland, these programs bring people together to work with children and mentally and physically handicapped adults. Sometimes work will include maintenance and improvement of health care facilities.

International Rescue Committee (IRC)
122 E. 42nd St.
New York, NY 10017
212-679-0010; Fax: 212-689-3459

This organization works throughout the world to help refugees who are escaping from religious, racial and political persecution in their countries. Volunteers teach English as a second language for refugees from Afghanistan, Cambodia, Ethiopia, Laos, Mozambique and other countries. Volunteers work for at least six months, usually living in group houses, and receiving a small, monthly stipend.

International Voluntary Services (IVS)
1424 16th St. NW, Suite 603
Washington, DC 20036
202-387-5533

Veterans of two years of grassroots work in the Third World can volunteer for technical assistance programs in developing countries.

Habitat for Humanity International
121 Habitat St.
Americus, GA 31709
912-924-6935

Habitat for the Humanities is an ecumenical Christian housing ministry working to construct low-cost houses to be sold at no profit to low-income people. About 100 volunteers work at the international office in Americus, Ga., and many more are placed somewhere in the network of 1,000 affiliates across the country. These positions range from three months to one year, with job assignment involving public relations, construction, fund raising, clerical work, data processing, graphic arts and general supervision of the thousands of volunteers participating in actual construction each year.

Full-time volunteers in Americus receive free housing and a $40 a week stipend (don't worry, the cost of living in Americus is very low). For college students, college credit is arranged, when possible. All participants must be at least 18 years old. Three-year international partner programs are available through Habitat projects in close to 30 developing countries. After a short training period at the international headquarters, these international partners are sent off to share the "economics of Jesus" and their construction, administrative and bookkeeping skills.

Habitat pays for the transportation to the countries where the international partners will work. Once there, a monthly stipend sufficient for the cost of living is provided. At this point, Habitat serves in over 36 countries in the Developing World.

---

2. Social change organizations with career opportunities

American Arab Anti-Discrimination Committee (ADC)
4201 Connecticut Ave. NW
Suite 500
Washington, DC 20008
202-244-2990

American Civil Liberties Union (ACLU)
132 W. 42nd St.
New York, NY 10036
212-944-9800; Fax: 212-730-4652

Adventure Careers

American Foundation for the Blind
Dr. Susan Jay Spungin
Associate Executive Director of
Program Services
15 W. 16th St.
New York, NY 10011
212-620-2031, Fax: 212-727-1279

Volunteer internships in human services and research, including one to two blind handicapped interns. Possibility of full-time employment; placement assistance provided.

Amnesty International, USA
322 Eighth Ave.
New York, NY 10001
212-807-8400; Fax: 212-627-1451

Center for Auto Safety
2001 S St. NW, Suite 410
Washington, DC 20009
202-328-7700

Center for Community Change
1000 Wisconsin Ave. NW
Washington, DC 20007
202-342-0519

Center for Ecological Technology, Inc. (CET)
112 Elm St.
Pittsfield, MA 01201
413-445-4556

Center for Women's Studies and Services
Ms. Sue Kirk, Internship Coordinator
2467 E St.
San Diego, CA 92102
619-233-8984

Women's center providing education and services to meet women's needs and improve the status of women. Many varied volunteer positions; placement assistance provided.

Common Cause
2030 M St. NW
Washington, DC 20036
202-833-1200

Housing Assistance Council (HAC)
1025 Vermont Ave. NW, Suite 606
Washington, DC 20005
202-842-8600

Lambda Legal Defense and Education Fund, Inc.
666 Broadway, 12th Fl.
New York, NY 10012
212-995-8585

Legal Aid Society of San Francisco Employment Law Center
1663 Mission St., Suite 400
San Francisco, CA 94103
415-864-8848

NAACP Legal Defense & Educational Fund, Inc.
99 Hudson St., 16th Fl.
New York, NY 10013
212-219-1900

National Alliance for the Mentally Ill
200 N. Glebe Rd., Suite 1015
Arlington, VA 22203-3754
703-524-7600

National Family Planning and Reproductive Health Association
122 C St. NW, Suite 380
Washington, DC 20001-2109

Overseas Development Network
1675 Massachusetts Ave.
Box 1430
Cambridge, MA 02238

United Farm Workers of America, AFL-CIO
P.O. Box 62
Keene, CA 93531
805-822-5571

World Policy Institute
65 5th Ave., Ste. 413
New York, NY 10003
212-219-5808

World Resources Institute
1709 New York Ave. NW, 7th Fl.
Washington, DC 20006
202-638-6300

World Wildlife Fund/ The Conservation Foundation
1250 24th St. NW, Suite 500
Washington, DC 20037
202-293-4800

---

3. Organizations providing career referrals

American Youth Work Center
1200 17th St. NW, 4th Fl.
Washington, DC 20036
202-785-0764

Referrals: city youth worker coalitions; Washington, D.C. organizations serving youth.

Association for Community Based Education
1805 Florida Ave. NW
Washington, DC 20009
202-462-6333

Referrals: community groups in adult and community education.

Association of Community Organizations for Reform Now (ACORN)
845 Flatbush Avenue
Brooklyn, NY 11226
718-693-6700

Referrals: local ACORN chapters and other local community

Center for Community Change
1000 Wisconsin Ave. NW
Washington, DC 20007
202-342-0519

Referrals: community-based social service groups; national and regional technical assistance agencies.

Citizens for Tax Justice
1311 L St. NW, Suite 400
Washington, DC 20005
202-626-3780

Referrals: national citizen groups and labor unions.

Clean Water Action Project
1320 18th St. NW
Suite 300
Washington, DC 20036
202-457-1286

Referrals: environmental groups.

Community Information Exchange
1029 Vermont Ave. NW
Suite 710
Washington, DC 20005
202-628-2981

Referrals: grassroots community development organizations, environmental groups.

National Association for Public Interest Law (NAPIL)
P.O. Box 34103
Washington, DC 20043-4104
202-466-3686

Referrals: law student organizations and public interest law centers. Offers grants and other assistance to students and recent graduates engaged in public interest employment. Publishes the *NAPIL Directory of Public Interest Legal Internships* and the *NAPIL Fellowships Guide*.

National Association of Neighborhoods
1651 Fuller St. NW
Washington, DC 20009
202-332-7766

Referrals: neighborhood associations, city-wide coalitions and community development corporations.

National Coalition Against Domestic Violence
P.O. Box 34103
Washington, DC 20043-4104
202-638-6388

Referrals: grassroots shelter and service programs for battered women.

National Congress of Neighborhood Women
249 Manhattan Ave.
Brooklyn, NY 11211
718-388-6666

Referrals: women's organizations. Training in job development and fundraising.

National Council of La Raza
810 First St. NE
Suite 300
Washington, DC 20002
202-289-1380

Referrals: Hispanic organizations. Funding source for Hispanic organizations.

National Organizations for Women
1000 16th St. NW
Suite 700
Washington, DC 20036
202-331-0066

Referrals: NOW's more than 700 offices and chapters, and other women's groups.

Nuclear Information and Resource Service
1424 16th St. NW
Suite 601
Washington, DC 20036
202-328-0002

Referrals: national antinuclear power organizations. Information and resources for energy activists.

Office of Special Learning Opportunities
University of Minnesota
Johnson Hall
St. Paul, MN 55108
612-624-7577

Referrals: league members and projects. Campus service projects facilitate student involvement in community problem-solving efforts.

Public Media Center
466 Green St.
Suite 300
San Francisco, CA 94133
415-434-1403

Referrals: energy organizations, environmental groups, media fairness and media access groups, and San Francisco-based community action organizations.

Sane/Freeze: Campaign for Global Security
1819 H St. NW
Suite 1000
Washington, DC 20006
202-862-9740

Referrals: more than 250 chapters and affiliate groups nationwide.

United States Public Interest Research Group (USPIRG)
215 Pennsylvania Ave. SE
Washington, DC 20003
202-546-9707

Public Interest Research Groups (PIRGs) are nonprofit, nonpartisan organizations directed by students. Serves as a national office for a number of the state Public Interest Research Groups that have been formed throughout the country.

United States Student Association (USSA)
1-12 14th St. NW, Suite 207
Washington, DC 20005
202-347-8772

Provides technical information and publishes student organizing manuals.

4. Reading and references

Alternatives to the Peace Corps: A Directory of Third World and U.S. Volunteer Opportunities
Edited by Annette Olson. Food First Books, San Francisco. Orders: 800-274-7824.

The Peace Corps and More: 114 Ways to Work, Study and Travel in the Third World
Medea Benjamin. Global Exchange, 2411 Mission St., Suite 202, San Francisco, CA 94110.

Volunteer! The Comprehensive Guide to Voluntary Service in the U.S. and Abroad
Published by CIEE, 4th Edition. Call 800-349-2433, or write to CIEE, Publications Department, 205 East 42nd Street, New York, NY 10017-5706.

Work, Study, Travel Abroad: The Whole World Handbook
Compiled by CIEE, available through above address or in bookstores.

Adventure Careers

Survival Kit for Overseas Living
L. Robert Kohls. Intercultural Press, Box 700, Yarmouth, ME 04096.

The International Directory of Voluntary Work
Roger Brown and David Woodsworth. Vacation-Work, 9 Park End Street, Oxford, England.

Taking Off: Extraordinary Ways to Spend Your First Year Out of College
Lauren Tarshis, New York: Fireside Book, 1989.

How Can I Help?
Ram Dass and Paul Gorman. Random House, 400 Hahn Road, Westminster, MD 21157.

The Overseas List
David M. Beckmann and Elizabeth Anne Dobbelly. Augsburg Publishing House, 426 South 5th Street, Minneapolis, MN 55440.

Chapter 5

Adventure-Preneurship

Adventure Careers

Don't discount the value of entrepreneurship. Starting your own business is a guaranteed ticket to adventure. Here are some of the many options that are practical for people under 30—or for anyone, of any age—who have limited capital to invest (all you need are appropriate background skills). They are actual examples of businesses started and run by people in their teens and 20s:

- Back-country tours (canoeing, backpacking, horseback riding, etc.)
- Dance school for children
- House or office cleaning service
- Landscaping/gardening service (provides and cares for potted plants in office buildings)
- Translating business
- PR/communications service for businesses
- Recycling services for businesses
- Women-owned carpentry/construction business
- Crafts import business
- Baby sitter referral network

- Christmas tree farm (on borrowed land)
- Tutoring services/network (located college-student tutors for parents of grade-school children in the local community)
- Summer sailing school for adults

Despite the existence of many successful businesses started and run by people in their 20s and 30s, there is a general perception that entrepreneurship is inadvisable for people in this age group. This perception is based on some common myths about entrepreneurship. It is assumed, for example, that a certain personality profile is required. Entrepreneurs must be attracted to high risk, be very pushy and driven, and be willing to gamble high stakes (their own and others') on wild ideas. They sound more than a little off center when you read about them in the popular magazines and books on the topic.

The idea of a wild-eyed gambling entrepreneur flows from the belief that most new businesses fail. Almost everyone can quote the well-known statistic that 9 out of 10 new businesses will fail. But nobody can cite the study that produced this statistic—perhaps there never was one. In fact, the statistics are a lot better than that, and entrepreneurship (if pursued with caution) presents no higher risk of failure than the average employee's risk of losing his or her job.

Exploding the myths

Because these myths get in the way of many an entrepreneurial adventure, it is useful to describe some of the findings of one of the most extensive long-term studies of entrepreneurs. It was commissioned by American Express Travel Related Services, which has an interest in small businesses (it wants them to use and accept American Express Cards—but not if 90 percent of them are going to fail).

Researchers at Purdue University conducted extensive interviews with 2,944 owners of new businesses, and followed up with interviews one year and two years later with all the businesses that had survived. Here are some of the results that are especially relevant to our discussion and to under-30 entrepreneurs.

First, what information did the successful entrepreneurs in this study rely on? Those entrepreneurs who made it to the third-year interview were asked to rank various sources of information and assistance in terms of their importance. Here are the percentages for respondents who ranked the following sources as very important.

Accountant	45%
Franchisers/suppliers	25%
Books, etc.	16%
Bankers	15%
Business owners	14%
Courses/seminars	14%
Friends/relations	11%
Trade organizations	10%
Lawyers	8%
Government	3%

The most striking point about these statistics, aside from the obvious importance of good accounting, is that none of the sources was ranked as very important by a majority of the successful entrepreneurs! Do not expect these conventional sources of information to be of any great help. Research is important, but not nearly as important as your own experience and your willingness to go out and get some orders. You will learn much more from your customers than from any of the sources of information entrepreneurs are usually referred to.

Youth is no handicap

Another interesting statistic for our readers is that of the 2,944 business owners in the sample, 26 percent were under 30 when they started their businesses. That's a large percentage. Most people do not think of entrepreneurs as young. Yet *more than a quarter of new businesses are apparently founded by young adventurers.*

Further, the survival rate for businesses started by under-30 entrepreneurs is about the same as the survival rate for over-30 entrepreneurs. Of businesses started by the under-30 crowd, 75 percent survived the three-year study period, compared with 77 percent for entrepreneurs of all ages. *Age is not a handicap in entrepreneurship. Adios* to another long-held myth.

And what about the old saw that only one in 10 new businesses succeed? If that wisdom is true, why did this study come up with a 77 percent survival rate? Because the conventional wisdom is wrong on this score, too. It may well be that only 10 percent of heavily-capitalized, traditional startups (like a venture capital-backed computer manufacturer) survive. They are high-risk ventures by definition.

But most of the startups in the American Express study were *not* patterned on this model. Only 1 percent of them used venture capital funding! Don't ask us why most books and most advisers still push the venture capital model of entrepreneurship. To avoid the 1-in-10 level of risk and, instead, put yourself in a group that has a 3-out-of-4 chance of success, consider using the *organic* model of entrepreneurship instead.

What is the organic model? This is a concept first popularized by Paul Hawken in his public television show, "Growing a Business." He is a founder of Smith and Hawken, an enormously successful garden catalog. He did not use venture capital, or take out big bank loans, or invest money before he earned it. Instead, he let the business grow at a natural, conservative rate. To him, a business is like a living creature, to be nurtured much as a gardener nurtures a plot of vegetables, and to be harvested only on the business's schedule. A lot of entrepreneurs instinctively follow this model, and that may be why the American Express study found much lower failure rates than expected.

The organic model

Interestingly, there is not much literature on the organic model, but much of the literature on how to run a mature business in a conservative manner applies quite well. In many cases, the organic concept leads to conclusions that are contrary to traditional entrepreneurship, so it is important to define the approach by what *not* to do as well as what to do.

The fundamental concept is to start small, with a simple, self-financed business that builds on existing skills and capabilities. Let the business grow organically, or naturally. That means you reinvest some, not all, of the profits in inventories, new equipment, marketing and the other things you need to grow. And, also, follow these "don'ts."

- Don't spend most of your time writing business plans.
- Don't spend most of your time trying to raise money from bankers, venture capital firms or relatives.
- Don't work for free or take money out here and there; give yourself a steady paycheck, however small.
- Don't expect others to work for free or for vague promises of "a piece of the action."
- Don't take on any work that loses money.
- Don't commit to doing anything you are not qualified to do. If you have cleaned houses for years, start a cleaning business; but *don't* start a building maintenance business.
- Don't go into partnership with a friend, or anyone for that matter. Seriously. Most partnerships fail, and when they do, each partner feels cheated by the other. Try to find a business that you can do on your own. Or, if you must work with someone else, demarcate clearly what each of you does, how each of you makes and spends money, and how you will split up, should you wish to later.
- Don't fail to write down what you do, what you spend and what you earn. You will need to learn bookkeeping. We suggest a course or a short stint as a bookkeeper for a similar business (even as a volunteer or intern if need be to gain the experience). But for now, it is sufficient to say that every dollar you spend or get must be recorded. No matter how you create this record, as long as it is clear to you, you will be able to interpret it to a professional book-keeper and tax preparer later.
- Don't mingle your personal finances with those of your business. If you run your personal life and your business out of the same checking account, wallet or cigar box, you will never be able to figure out what you make or what taxes you owe.
- Don't pretend you are in business unless you *have* business. You have not started a business until you have orders or

sales. Period. Anything that is not producing sales is a waste of time, and is burning up the money and other resources you ought to be spending on finding sales (this includes decorating your office, designing brochures and shopping for anything, whether it be capital or a PC).

If you cannot find sales after trying hard for some time, *give up*. Your business won't work in its current form. In fact, the first thing to do when you are considering starting a business is to *go talk to some potential customers*. Ask them if they will give you their business. Get them to write their answer down, no matter how conditional it may be (a purchase order would, of course, be preferable to a "maybe"). Then you know where you stand and what the potential is before you spend any time and money on the startup.

- Don't spend money out of your cash flow that is not really profit.

These may seem like simple, obvious rules. And they are. Most established, successful businesses follow them. But many new businesses don't. We just spent a day scouring library and bookstore shelves for references about the organic business model, and came up almost empty-handed. Few offered any of these simple rules of entrepreneurship. Most stuck to the party line of "write a business plan, show it to investors, and risk lots of other people's money." Most entrepreneurs, and certainly all entrepreneurs under 30, simply have not had sufficient experience in starting and running businesses to succeed with the old model. Stick to the organic approach instead.

The importance of supporting experiences

The most critical success factor, aside from a willingness to stick within your business's organic growth rate, is your own competence and expertise. We made this point in the beginning of the chapter, but we want to point out in conclusion that *you can and should use educational experiences, internships, volunteer work and regular jobs as preparation for starting your own business.*

Adventure Careers

If you like the idea of being in charge, make it your mandate to obtain an entrepreneur's education. Learn the basic skills of book-keeping, sales and marketing, and business management through a number of educational or work adventures drawn from other chapters of this book or from your current employer (ask to be transferred at the same pay level—most employers support initiative and are pleased to see employees take an interest in learning on the job). The entrepreneurial strategy can be used to turn *any* job into an adventure, no matter how dull or demeaning it appears at first.

Personal Account

Alex Hiam is, in addition to being one of the authors of this book, an experienced entrepreneur. In fact, in his current work as a management consultant, he often helps new businesses. For this reason his editor and coauthor have grudgingly agreed to allow him to carry on about his previous experiences in entrepreneurship:

If you wish to pursue a business adventure, you should give entrepreneurship serious consideration. *But you ought to go about it quite the opposite of the way I did.*

My first experience as an entrepreneur was in the early '80s when I started a biotechnology company with some friends and business associates. I was in my early 20s at the time, and had only two years of experience in business. We wrote a business plan, recruited a group of expert molecular biologists, decided what research and development they would do, and set about raising money to fund the work. At first everything went wonderfully well. We wrote a brilliant (to us at least) business plan, paraded it in front of well-known investors and venture capital firms, and to our great surprise, some of them gave us money.

A couple years—and almost $1 million later—we went out of business.

Why? Because we failed to finish the development of our products. Although we had raised and spent a huge sum of venture capital, we had sold nothing and made not a single penny.

Were we stupid? Criminally insane? I don't think so—but we did make a big mistake. Of the companies that followed the same path as ours (and there were many), about a fifth have gone on to a series of refinancings and, finally, have started to generate revenues from product sales. It was possible to make money, lots of money, from that

113

approach to entrepreneurship. However, it was *difficult* to make money by following that path. We may not have been insane, but neither were we lucky. And you better be *very* lucky if you go into business with one-in-five odds.

Years later, after earning an MBA and working as a manager at several companies, I started another business. This time I picked a strategy that required only a few thousand dollars of investment, and I provided it all myself. No business plans. No chasing venture capital companies and making fancy presentations. I just rented a small office, furnished it with used office equipment, and started working. Within weeks I was earning money—not a lot of money, but enough to more than cover my minimal overhead. I could pay my rent, phone bill and office supplies, and even take a little money out of the business.

And I was doing something I already knew how to do. Having worked in marketing and planning for companies, I now consulted and wrote on these topics as an independent contractor. I had learned my business on someone else's nickel, not my own.

The risks were lower, and so were the potential returns. Now, four years later, I have a steady income from my consulting work and the series of business books I wrote. I am not a millionaire, as I might have been had my early efforts at entrepreneurship succeeded. But that was not my goal the second time around. Instead I was looking for better working conditions, more flexibility and freedom, and the opportunity to choose projects that would allow me to learn and develop at a faster rate than I could in a big company. (The latter is the best reason to pursue entrepreneurship—it's what makes it *adventure*-preneurship.) And because my business has stayed small, never borrowed large sums of money and never had to spend large sums of money, it has never come anywhere near to failing. It is as robust as the healthiest big company could be. As long as I am alive to perform the work, the business will survive.

Women Entrepreneurs

Trying to make it in corporate America is an adventure career for women. Although we've made great strides, we've just begun the journey. In a poll of more than 500 top female executives at large companies (*Working Woman*, Nov. 1994, p. 40), some of the following results were noted: Only 49 percent rated their company as a pretty good place for women executives to work, 54 percent find that a male-dominated corporate culture is an obstacle to success and 51 percent have observed a glass ceiling beyond which women never seem to advance. About a third of the women have encountered a reluctance to give women the same responsibilities, assignments and compensation for equal work as men and have suffered from a failure to recognize women's family needs. But don't get discouraged! This section is about finding ways to make it despite the odds, whether within or without the system.

America has experienced a shift in attitude over the last decade. Where the priority of the '80s was money, the goal of the '90s is fulfillment—whatever it may mean for you. Success can have many facets: loving what you're doing, constantly learning, making a difference in the world, having the freedom to do what you want, seeing instant results—the list is potentially endless and highly personal. More and more women (and men) are finding that they need to rethink their definition of success as companies continue to downsize and the economy remains dormant. Many women are seeking out smaller companies to work for or are becoming entrepreneurs in order to achieve their personal goals and benefit from the efficiency, friendliness, balance and support they find lacking in large corporations.

If you're interested in going into business for yourself, there are some things you should know: About 30 percent of all businesses in this country are owned by women, their growth rate is five times that of other small firms and their failure rate is about half that of male owned businesses (*Woman to Woman*, Geraldine A. Larkin, p. 1). How's that for good news?! And there's more! According to Larkin (based on a 1989 survey of entrepreneurs by Avon Products), the two things that women need to make it are perseverance and optimism.

Adventure Careers

Not a certain educational level, not an MBA, not marital status, not children or lack thereof, not a particular ethnicity. An article in *Working Woman* (March 1994, pp. 37-43) also gives the 10 best cities for women entrepreneurs, based on a special report from the Census Bureau: Boston, New York, Columbus, San Francisco, Philadelphia, Chicago, Indianapolis, Los Angeles, Baltimore and San Diego. They were rated for total number of women business owners (or WBOs), WBOs as a percentage of all firms, gross WBO revenues, WBO revenues as a percentage of all revenues, five-year growth in WBOs and 5-year WBO revenue growth.

Another important aspect of succeeding in your business is networking. Larkin cites the Ten Commandments of Networking, originally from Ivan R. Misner's *Networking for Success*. These are:

1. Carry your tools at all times: a name tag, a card holder full of business cards and a card file to carry other people's cards.
2. At a given event, set a goal regarding how many people you'll meet, and don't leave until you've met your goal.
3. Act like a host, not a guest. In other words, don't hang out by the punch bowl with a shy smile; be friendly, meet people, remember their names, talk about what you love (hopefully, your work is one of them).
4. Exchange business cards with the people you meet; give them the chance to remember you *and* call you.
5. Listen and ask the five "W" questions—who, what, where, when and why. "A notable networker has two ears and one mouth and uses both of them proportionately." So, be a nice 'host' and actually listen to your 'guests.'
6. Write comments on the back of the business cards you collect. Otherwise, you won't remember anything in the morning.
7. Give a lead or referral whenever possible. If you freely give business to others, they will be more likely to give business to you.
8. Learn to describe your product or service in less than 60 seconds. Yes, it sounds like a line, but we live in an MTV world—no one has a long attention span.

9. Spend 10 minutes or less with each person you meet, and don't linger with friends and associates. Try not to get caught up in too much idle chatter.
10. Follow up with the people you meet. A simple follow-up letter or telephone call can mean the difference in making the time valuable. If you promise to get back to someone, do it.

Although networking is important for all business owners, women especially need to put effort into making those connections. To grossly generalize, we didn't receive as much encouragement as men to be aggressive, persistent, self-confident and self-reliant—qualities necessary for building networking skills and for running a successful business. If you feel you are lacking in these and/or other skills, I suggest you work on trying to acquire them. As a first step you might want to just read about the experiences other women have had in business. In fact, even if you never want to own a business, but you *do* want to follow your own path in life, it can be incredibly helpful and uplifting to read about the lives of women you admire, who do the kinds of things you've dreamed of. It's an easily attained kind of mentor. For starters, here's a short list of books I've been inspired by:

Composing A Life, by Mary Catherine Bateson (Atlantic Monthly Press, 1989). Written by the daughter of Margaret Mead (a pioneering female anthropologist) and Gregory Bateson, this book tells us about the remarkable lives of six women, including the author. It's a wonderful account of the strength and necessity of flexibility in making our life choices.

Woman to Woman, Street Smarts for Women Entrepreneurs, by Geraldine A. Larkin (Prentice Hall, 1993). Great advice for women starting a business, written in a clear, friendly manner. Includes a chapter called "Don't Postpone Joy," which addresses such concerns as knowing yourself, exercise, emotional and sexual vulnerability, taking time off and more. I really recommend looking at it because it contains more detailed information about everything I'm writing here, plus a whole lot more.

Also useful is *Working Woman,* a monthly magazine. To order:

Working Woman
P.O. Box 3276
Harlan, IA 51593-2456
800-234-9675

Here's a list of Women's Business Associations that you may want to contact:

National Association of Women Business Owners
600 S. Federal St., Suite 400
Chicago, IL 60605
312-922-0465

Coalition of Women in National and International Business
1900 L St. NW
Washington, DC 20036

Association of Black Women Entrepreneurs
c/o Corita Communications
P.O. Box 49368
Los Angeles, CA 90049
213-559-2375

National Council of Career Women
3222 N St. NW
Washington, DC 20007
202-333-8578

That's only a sample of the many business organizations that exist for women. The nice thing about getting involved in a women's group is that, on the whole, women want to help other women—it's likely to be a good place to get support, understanding and advice. Also, call your local chamber of commerce to ask about groups in your area.

Adventure-Preneurship Directory

While most of the successful entrepreneurs in the American Express study cited in this chapter did not find government resources very important, you still should investigate the available programs. Of course, you should go out to your market first—your customers know best what you can and can't sell them. But in addition to talking to customers, see whether any of the following may be of use.

U.S. Small Business Administration
1441 L St. NW
Washington, DC 20416

SBA Hotline: 800-368-5855

Small Business Development Center: 202-653-6768

Answer Desk: 800-368-5855

Hotline for import/export questions: 800-424-5201

Information on venture capital for minority-owned businesses: Office of Investment, 202-653-6584

The SBA is a huge federal bureaucracy designed to help entrepreneurs and small businesses. Its hotline, when you manage to get through, proves to be little more than an order desk for a variety of pamphlets. Oh, well. At least the pamphlets will explain what the agency's current programs are and how to use them.

The Small Business Development Center does not offer much help either, at least not from the Washington office. But it does coordinate the operations of dozens of regional SBA offices, more than one in most states. Call to find out what facilities are near you, then call or visit them to learn how to obtain free or low-cost consulting (Warning: You get what you pay for!), and to apply for SBA-guaranteed loans through a local bank.

The loan program is designed to help you obtain a business loan after banks have turned you down. Work with a local *preferred lender*—the national or local SBA office can give you some names—because preferred lenders are familiar with the application procedures and will give you the most support.

Adventure Careers

The SBA also funds independently run Small Business Development Centers, usually staffed by knowledgeable people from local government offices and universities. There are more than 500 offices providing consultation and assistance to entrepreneurs through this program, and its services are available in about 80 percent of the states.

Rather than list hundreds of addresses here, we suggest you call the SBA hotline for the names of the nearest facilities. However, if you have trouble getting through on that number, you could try calling one of these centers, which are among the largest and best-staffed in the country (and have also been chosen to represent the country's various regions), for referrals:

SBDC of Washington DC
6th & Fairmount St. NW
Room 128
Washington, DC 20059
202-636-5150

SBDC of Florida
University of West Florida
College of Business, Bldg. 8
Pensacola, FL 32514
904-474-2908

Illinois SBDC
Department of Commerce and
Community Affairs
620 E. Adams St., 5th Fl.
Springfield, IL 62701
217-785-6267

SBDC
University of Massachusetts
203 School of Management
Amherst, MA 01003
413-549-4930, ext. 303

SBDC
State University of New York
Central Administration S-523
SUNY Plaza
Albany, NY 12246
518-473-5398

SBDC of Texas
University of Houston
University Park, 127 Heyne
4800 Calhoun
Houston, TX 77004
713-749-4236

Computers: Opportunities and internships

One of the fastest ways to start a business and make money in the 1990s is through computers. In fact, the market is no longer quite as optimal as it was five years ago. As more people grow comfortable with computers and there are more business available to help, a computer business needs to be high quality and needs to research the proper market niche. One way to break into the field is through the internships listed below. Most of them are either for undergraduates or recent grads. You should be quite computer literate (and able to prove it) to get these internships. Also, use your on-line sources to do random surveys and other research.

Hewlett-Packard
SEED Program
3000 Hanover St.
Mail Stop 20-AC
Palo Alto, CA 94304-1181
415-857-2092

Microsoft
Attn: Recruiting Dept.
CA 171-0693
One Microsoft Way
Redmond, WA 98052-6399
206-882-8080

Intel Corporation
Staffing Department
FM4-145
P.O. Box 1141
Folsom, CA 95763-1141
916-356-8080

Raychem
College Relations Manager
M/S 111/8202
300 Constitution Drive
Menlo Park, CA 94025-1164
415-361-4999

Additional listings

American Association of Exporters and Importers
11 W. 42nd St.
New York, NY 10036
212-944-2230

American Home Business Association
60 Arch St.
Greenwich, CT 06830
203-661-0105

Chamber of Commerce USA
1615 H St. NW
Washington, DC 20062
202-659-6000

A business incubator provides low-cost space, equipment, consulting and help with financing for new businesses.

The Direct Marketing Association
6 E. 43rd St.
New York, NY 10017
212-689-4977

A great resource for selling products or service through the mail, whether through a catalog or other vehicle.

Inroads, Inc.
100 South Broadway
P.O. Box 8766
Suite 700
St. Louis, MO 63102

Inroads trains minorities for management positions. Students may join as early as their junior year in high school, or as late as their sophomore year of college. There are internships in business, science and engineering, and the compensation ranges from $170-$750 per week.

Manufacturers' Agents National Association
P. O. Box 3467
Laguna Hills, CA 02654
714-859-4040

This association can give you leads to sales representatives in your industry and can also give you information if you are thinking of becoming a rep yourself.

Adventure Careers

National Association for the Cottage Industry
P.O. Box 14460
Chicago, IL 60614
312-472-8116

National Association of Export Companies
17 Battery Place
Suite 1425
New York, NY 10004
212-809-8023

National Association for the Self-Employed
P.O. Box 612067
Dallas, TX 76118
800-433-8004

National Business Incubation Association
114 North Hanover St.
Carlisle, PA 17013
717-249-4508

National Electrical Manufacturers' Representatives Association
222 W. Chester Ave.
Suite 330
White Plains, NY 10604
914-428-1307

National Minority Supplier Development Council
1412 Broadway, 11th Fl.
New York, NY 10018
212-944-2430

National Association of Small Business Investment Companies
1156 15th St. NW
Suite 1101
Washington, DC 20005
202-833-8230

National Venture Capital Association
1655 N. Fort Myer Dr.
Suite 700
Arlington, VA 22209
703-528-4370

Manufacturers' Agents Newsletter
23573 Prospect Ave.
Farmington, MI 48024
313-474-7383

If you can't find the agent or rep you need, you can advertise for one in this newsletter.

Manufacturers Representative Educational Research Foundation
P.O. Box 8541
Rolling Meadows, IL 60008
312-991-8500

Representative Resources, Inc.
P.O. Box Drawer A
Thorndale, PA 19372
215-383-1177

Sponsors for Educational Opportunity
23 Gramercy Park South
New York, NY 10003
212-979-2040

Internships with investments banks, corporate law, management consulting, accounting and asset management for minority college students. Earn $400 to $500 a week while interning with various businesses in New York City (if you want to shoot for Wall Street, might as well do it in style.)

Reading and references

While you do need to be aware that many of the books on starting a business promote the (high-risk) venture capital model—not the organic model—there are still a number of books you may find handy. Especially helpful are books that focus on practical advice about the various jobs needed to run a business, such as bookkeeping or hiring employees:

101 Best Businesses to Start. Sharon Kahn and The Philip Lief Group (Main Street Books, Doubleday, New York, 1994).

Includes sections on business services, childcare and education, computers, the environment and many other topics. Seems to have good down-to-earth advice.

101 Home Office Success Secrets. Lisa Kanarek (Career Press, 1994).

The Best Companies for Minorities: Employers Across America Who Recruit, Train and Promote Minorities. Lawrence Otis Graham (Plume, The Penguin Group, 1993).

Beyond Entrepreneurship: Turning Your Business into an Enduring Great Company. James Collins and William Lazier (Prentice Hall, Englewood Cliffs, NJ, 1993).

The Black Manager: Making it in the Corporate World (revised ed.). Floyd Dickens, Jr., and Jacqueline Dickens (AMACOM, New York, 1991).

The Closet Entrepreneur. Neil Balter (Career Press, 1994).

The Complete Small Business Loan Kit. Arnold Goldstein, Consumer Law Foundation (Bob Adams Publishers, Holbrook, MA, 1990).

Do What You Are. Paul Tieger and Barbara Barron-Tieger (Little, Brown and Co., Boston, 1992).

Entrepreneurship: Starting Your Own Business. Dr. Roger Hutt (Southwestern Publishing, Cincinnati, OH, 1994).

Free Money for Small Businesses and Entrepreneurs (3rd ed.). Laurie Blum (John Wiley and Sons, Inc., New York, 1992).

Adventure Careers

Guerrilla Marketing: Secrets for Making Big Profits From Your Small Business. Jay Conrad Levinson (Houghton Mifflin Co., New York, 1993).

The Heart Aroused: Poetry and the Preservation of the Soul in Corporate America. David White (Currency Doubleday, New York, 1994).

I'll Work for Free: A Short-term Strategy for a Long-term Payoff. Bob Weinstein (Henry Holt & Co., New York, 1993).

Mid-Career Job Hunting. E. Patricia Birsner (Prentice Hall, New York, 1991).

Small Business Management Fundamentals (6th ed.). Dan Steinhoff and John Burgess (McGraw-Hill, Inc., New York, 1993).

The Small Business Test. Collin Ingram (Ten Speed Press, 1990). Orders: P.O. Box 7123, Berkeley, CA 94707.

This workbook is used to evaluate the likelihood of success for a new business.

Small Time Operator. Bernard Kamoroff (Bell Springs Publishing, 1994). $14.95. Orders: Box 640, Bell Springs Road, Laytonville, CA 95454, 707-984-6746.

This is *the* classic practical manual for entrepreneurs, and if you don't find it at the bookstore, have them order it or contact the publisher yourself.

The Smart Woman's Guide to Starting a Business. Vickie Montgomery (Career Press, 1994).

Starting and Operating a Business in (Your State). Entrepreneurial Services Group of Ernst and Young. (The Oasis Press. The year varies by state. If you can't find it through your local bookstore, try 503-479-9464.)

This series of books, one per state, focuses on the formal legal requirements a startup ought to comply with. Some businesses will be so small and informal that they will not have to fill out very many forms, and others may have more requirements. In either case, it is best to know what the requirements are.

This series gives you all the information you need to start a business in your state, including copies of any forms you ought to file.

Start Up: An Entrepreneur's Guide to Launching and Managing a New Business. William J. Stolze (Career Press, 1994). Orders: 800-CAREER-1.

The author is a successful entrepreneur who also advises, invests in and directs numerous startup companies. He offers sound advice to new entrepreneurs, focusing on the key issues that can make or break a new company.

Success at Work: A Guide for African-Americans. Anita Diggs (Barricade Books, New York, 1991).

This is a great book for someone thinking about entering the work force; it has humorous personal anecdotes and good advice.

To Build the Life You Want, Create the Work You Love. St. Martin's Press, New York, 1995.

Woman to Woman: Street Smarts for Women Entrepreneurs. Geraldine Larkin (Prentice Hall, 1993).

Work of Her Own: A Woman's Guide to Success Off the Career Track. Susan Wittig Albert, Ph.D. (A Jeremy D. Tarcher/Putnam Book, New York, 1994).

Magazines

Black Enterprise
for subscription info:
P.O. Box 3009
Harlan, IA 51537-4100
800-727-7777

Entrepreneur: The Small Business Authority
Subscription Department
P.O. Box 58808
Boulder, CO 80321
800-274-6229

Hispanic Business
For subscriptions 800-334-8152

One of the best publications for any entrepreneur is the local yellow pages, with its listings of businesses by type. Use it to find out whether there are any competitors for your new business idea, to locate potential suppliers and customers, to find out where the geographic center of your industry is, and to answer many other such questions.

Chapter 6

The Artistic Adventure

Adventure Careers

If the history of art teaches us anything, it is that great artists—no matter what genre they're working in, no matter what period they come from—create from the inside out. These artists have a true vision, a vision uniquely theirs, and they have the courage to obey its commands, no matter how unfashionable the results.
—Tom Wolfe

Art is often treated as a sideline in our educational system. Art classes are the fun ones that do not really count when your application to college or graduate school is considered. And artists are often treated as second-class citizens, and expected to live in garrets without any regular income to support them. This marginalized view of artists stands in stark contrast to the multi-million dollar prices paid for the paintings of masters at auctions, or to the millions of dollars popular artists receive from their movies or records. Is art a serious profession, at least for those of us who are not superstars? Can a fulfilling and financially viable career be created on the basis of an interest in art? Yes.

Artists can find ways to support themselves comfortably and spend their lives pursuing their art. Many artists do succeed both artistically and professionally—contrary to popular belief, art can provide financially as well as personally rewarding careers!

Your family and your education may push you in other directions, but if your art is important to you, it is up to you to push back. Use the directory in this chapter to find organizations and positions that will support your art and help you both to develop your skills and to find work that will allow you to practice those skills. There are many ways to work as an artist. In fact, the majority of artists do not live solely by selling their art; many teach, do commercial art on the side or work with one of the many artists' organizations listed here in order to allow them to continue perfecting their own art and to find a paying audience for it.

Personal Accounts

It may be helpful for you to listen to what several young artists have to say about their work and their careers. In this chapter we let artists speak for themselves.

Tanya: Actress and Director

Tanya Kane-Parry exemplifies the committed working actress—as her story hints, she has considerable experience in her art around the world. Tanya tells of her study, work, experience and adventures in France and in Russia a few years ago.

Two large bags, one large suitcase, a shopping bag, backpack, boom box, a winter coat, snow boots...

"You're going where?"
"To Moscow."
"Moscow! For how long?"
"The work contract I've been given is for three months, but I hope to stay maybe a year."
"A year?!"

I have just been hired as an actor, choreographer and teacher for a new theater company in Moscow. People from this company saw me perform last year, liked my work and my technique, and wanted me to come work with them. My work will be to use my training in avant-garde theater—to take experimental performance techniques to this closed society. I want to go learn firsthand about this world that has always been presented to me as "The Evil Empire." I want to learn about communication and expression in this world where Freud has not yet even been published. I want to meet the challenge of teaching people to express, in the theater, their unconscious mind, when they had no other way to express it.

There's nothing keeping me in Paris any more. I've spent two wonderful years here, I've learned a lot and now it's time to move on.

The two things I love the most: travel and acting—for me they are adventuring and working. But what do these things have in common? For me, it comes down to the basics of communication. When I travel I prefer to go someplace where they *don't* speak English. Now the challenge begins: facial expressions, hand gestures, vocal intonations, rhythms and stresses. Body language. These are the symbols and signposts to pass through a whole new world. These are the tools that I use on my traveling adventures and these are the tools I use in my work in theater—the tricks of my trade.

Theater, as in all art forms, is a means and form of expression that incorporates and thus affects the public in a conscious and unconscious manner. As a performer, writer and director, I have always been fascinated by the unconscious level of communication, both in our daily lives and how it is expressed artistically, whether through text, sound, movement, images or symbols.

...Food. There will be no food in the Soviet Union. There's not even coffee. What will I do? I'm so addicted to my café au lait. How will I survive without my 10 cups a day? How will I adjust?—Kick the habit.

So a week before leaving my old home and theater company in Paris for my new work in the USSR, I threw out the coffee mug, the spoon, the milk, the artificial sweetener and the coffee pot! Three days I was in bed in withdrawal, shaking, crying, listless and restless, with headaches and chills.

Russian language tape plays over and over again, trying to distract myself from the pain...

"*Gye metro?*...Where is the subway?"

"*Skolka stoit?*...How much does it cost?"—a useless question to learn to ask since there isn't anything to buy, unless, of course, you have dollars. Then you can buy almost anything.

Adventure Careers

My friends and I congregate at the station for my departure. Gare du Nord, in the slimier section of Paris, now crowded with elegant African immigrants who have come from former French colonies. The men tall and slender, finely dressed. The women round and fertile, wrapped in traditional African prints, a baby tied to the back and a child at each hand.

My eight bags are unloaded from the van—the van in which we had all shared the past year, working together in our moving theater company. Performing all over France—twice a day, five days a week. We became the classic dysfunctional family. Lisa, the dominant mother; Hussar, the placating father. The children: Jean, the drunk and the womanizer; Bill, the brooding, angry young man; Chris, the baby brat; and myself, the lost child. I'll never forget how angry I was the day we were returning to Paris after performing in Lyons for a week. From the road, I pointed out a tall steeple. It was the great Cathedral of Chartres, known for having one of the most beautiful stained-glass windows in Europe. I begged Hussar (who was driving) to take a small detour so we could visit the cathedral, but he and the rest of the group dismissed my request, and he kept driving. I was baffled how everyone could simply pass up the opportunity to witness one of the world's great pieces of artistry—one passenger's dream adventure, another's needless detour.

Now on the train bound for Moscow—cued by symbols that pass before my eyes and many that float through my mind as memories—I reflect back to my life a year ago. I had just graduated from New York University's Drama Department with a BFA in Theater. I was living in Paris that whole year, studying experimental theater with a New York University program. On graduation day, all of us (in Paris) from the NYU program gathered at a friend's house in a suburb of the city. One by one, we walked up to the fireplace to receive our diplomas, wearing silly black capes we had made hastily out of paper and staples. I would choose to stay in Paris, to work with my roaming troop of theater performers—knowing there was more to learn and much more work to be done. That feeling rides with me on the train to Moscow.

Moscow—the work is so rigid and chaotic. I am in the world of Old Russia, the spiritual culture that still lives there so powerfully. Questing to break into the heart of the Russian soul, this is a world to which I would always remain an outsider. Then the everyday things: It always snows and it is always cold; crying at the stores because there is never any food; taking endless baths to try to keep warm; the people, their heart and their spirit.

Carrying home with me to America a full Russian Army suit, the symbol, knowing I could never wear it on the streets. I could never parade along the streets of New York's Lower East Side, in front of the old Russian ladies with their handkerchiefs and their memories, in this symbol of death and fear.

And now, back in New York, kicking the crack addicts out of the front vestibule of my apartment building; passing homeless people; dodging a speeding bike messenger on my way to visit a friend who is dying of AIDS. What is the meaning of theater and traveling to me today? What is the meaning of my continuing career and my current adventures? Still the same search for the truth—the inner truth, and my own desire to communicate with the inner truth of other people.

The way I know to do this work is through conversation, and the "un-conversation" of the stage. The stage is a place where human symbols are framed and given more power...this view of importance, the potency of the moment of delivery and performance. What I end up recreating there often resembles the feeling of the 6 o'clock news brief—flashes of events: A child is run down and killed by a hit-and-run driver; the live video tape reveals a sneaker lying in the curb. Masses topple a huge statue of Lenin in Moscow. Michael Jackson is ceremoniously crowned king in Africa. Symbols—local and international. All criss-crossed, juxtaposed and fused, thus created gives new meaning. This is my world, my work and my adventure.

Reneé: Singer and Songwriter

Reneé Cologne is a singer, songwriter and performer who combined traditional and creative paths to design her own personal career.

Music is my way of life. I've realized that everything I do and am is part of a life-long development process, musically and personally.

Adventure Careers

Each gig, no matter how big or small, is part of my career. The blockages and problems I encounter are also important, if not easy. My work is to become more aware and alive, and carry that aliveness through my music.

I was in the third grade when I bought my first guitar for $32. I would walk to school before classes to take lessons. I would try multilayer recording with my Fisher Price cassette tape decks—recording back and forth from one to the other. When I was a kid, my father would listen to all types of music, everything from jazz to flamenco guitar to Loretta Lynn. Listening to that music helped me develop my early repertoire, which I would perform to my brownie/girl scout troop, for people at the local "old folks" home or for anyone who would stand still and listen.

I left my home town, Cary, N.C., to attend East Carolina University in Greenville, N.C. Studying classical theory and harmony, I learned old standards and how to stand correctly. I didn't know until years later how stifled, musically and personally, I was there. I felt frustrated, uncomfortable and not good at what I was doing. The lesson I learned from that experience was that when things feel bad, it means they are bad.

My whole world opened up when I transferred to the Berklee College of Music in Boston after three semesters at East Carolina. I started writing more at this point. It was a creative, explosive time. For the first time, I was really playing with other musicians and hearing them play my songs. I was working on a degree in music production and engineering, getting experience in studio recording and learning to operate the studio—making the knobs work. During this time, I laid the groundwork for my continuing development as an artist.

For the last five years I've lived in New York City. Last year I spent a good bit of time in Europe: six months writing and performing in London, and touring in Yugoslavia with the well-known European artist, Alexander Mezek. But living in New York I've been forced to focus and sharpen my career. It is here that I have found my strengths and weaknesses. I've had to learn about the business side of music. Let me tell you, it's tough and it's not pretty.

I obsess about it. I'll lie in bed at night, not able to sleep. But some of my best songs have come from those times that I'm half awake and half in my dreams. I'm the most vulnerable at this time, the most honest. When I hear honesty in other people's music, I am inspired. It is the quality I want in my music and in my life.

Andrew: Author and Art Critic

Andrew Solomon, in his "Coup Story" that follows, tells of his experiences in Moscow while there researching his recently published book, The Irony Towers: Soviet Artists in a Time of Glasnost. *He is a contributing editor for* Harper's & Queen *and* HG, *and a regular contributor to* Artforum, The Spectator *and other American and British publications.*

While in high school he was accepted to the Metropolitan Museum of Art internship program. After graduating from Yale University magna cum laude with a B.A. in English, Andrew was awarded a Yale Conservation Project Fellowship for travel to Pompeii to work on the restoration of the House of Menander. He then traveled to England to continue his studies at Cambridge University where he received the Mrs. Claude Beddington Prize for the top first-class degree and the Quiller-Couch Prize for the best original English composition—the only student ever to win both prizes.

He now divides his time between London, Moscow, Berlin and New York, developing his career and planning his next adventure.

In the Spring of 1988, I heard about a sale of contemporary Soviet art that was taking place in Moscow and persuaded an editor to send me to cover it. I was 24 years old, less than a year out of a master's program at Cambridge and eager to become a writer. In the years that followed that original visit, I befriended the artists and went to their exhibitions in the East and in the West, writing magazine articles and catalogue essays to pay my way.

I spent a lot of time in Moscow, living in the desperate squats where the artists of the Soviet vanguard were based, and I spent a lot of time in the cities in the West where their work was shown to great critical acclaim. The artists' discovery of the values and social structures of the West was parallel to my own discovery of the values and social structures of the East; as the artists came to understand capitalism and the art market, I came to see the creation of works of art as more than a pleasant diversion or an intellectual exercise.

These men and women had worked to give meaning to life in a country where ideology had destroyed ordinary pleasures. They saw themselves as the guardians of the truth in a world in which truth itself had been systematically annihilated, first by Stalin, and then by his inheritors. My friendship with them became the basis of my book, *The Irony Towers*, in which I chronicled our experiences together.

In the summer of 1991, I was in Moscow when the coup took place. For the first time I had the opportunity to see these people put into practice the convictions they had so eloquently articulated in their work and in our conversation. More than that, I was invited to take active part in the moral battle about which I had written at such length. "Now it is a moment of real crisis," one artist said to me. "It is up to you whether you want to stay and fight by our side and help in the resistance, or to go back on a safe flight to your own country. We will understand, whatever you do." At the time it did not seem to be a choice; as a holder of a Western passport, I thought that I was not placing myself in much danger (this later seemed untrue), but I felt, in any event, that I could not abandon my friends.

So I helped to build the barricades, camped outside the Russian Parliament at night, joined in the protest marches during the day. On what was to be the last day of the coup, I went with friends to the spot where shootings had taken place the previous evening, and found there perhaps 100 people speaking of tragedy. A man who looked like the student from a Chekhov play—wire-rimmed spectacles, needing a shave, tatty cap clutched in a pale hand—ran over, cried through a megaphone that there were tanks approaching the barricade, and appealed to us to defend it. Without discussion or question, all of us followed him to the outer limit of the many-tiered system of defenses we had built and ranged ourselves along it. We were prepared for anything, though there had been too many rumors of tanks, and none of us really expected to see one.

In fact, they arrived within minutes. The soldier in the first explained that they had come to destroy the barricade, and ordered us to move, adding that they would have to run us down if we did not give way. The man with the megaphone responded that we were holding our ground not in aggression, but to defend the rights of the people. "We are only a few, but there are tens of thousands at the Parliament, and across all this country," he said. He spoke of democracy, pontificated on the nature of freedom, reminded the men in the tanks of the terrors of the past. Others joined in; my artist friends all called up to the drivers. We emphasized that the orders that had been given were orders no one could force on them. "If you do this, it is because you have chosen to do it," said the man with the megaphone.

The soldiers looked at each other and then they looked at us. We were so wet, so cold, so impotent in all but the courage of our convictions—so entirely persuaded that we spoke in the name of righteousness, but so transparently lacking in material defenses— that the soldiers might easily have laughed. But instead, the driver of the front tank shrugged as though he were doing nothing more than giving way to the inevitable course of destiny, said, "We must bow to the will of the people," and instructed us to move aside so the tanks could make U-turns. It takes a lot of space and some time for a tank to make a U-turn. "Why do you think they are really going?" I asked one of my friends. "Because of us," he replied. "Because we are here, and because of what we've said." All of us—friends and strangers—embraced each other, then stood and cheered until we were hoarse.

The moral points, which we had so often discussed in the abstract, had finally to be carried through in reality. What is the will of the people? And how does it form itself? The will of the people can be robust only when the understanding of the people is strong. So dialogue became the key to a popular resistance; it was the moral honesty of the arguments against Yaneyev that made them so compelling, the vigor with which they were spoken that made them accessible. Seldom outside of TV drama has there been a war in which the course of right against wrong seemed so manifestly clear.

Ghandi-like, the men and women of the Soviet intelligentsia stood their ground without any weapon more powerful than their belief in their own words. "You see, these soldiers were educated with lies, and we are only telling the truth," a film maker said to me one night as we shivered beside a spluttering fire. How astonishing it was to see the power of that truth, eloquently expressed, overtake one of the most powerful military machines in the world, in a country that was for almost 70 years ruled by fear.

For me, as a writer, there could be no greater moment of truth. In the course of those three fateful days in Soviet history, I came to understand anew the enormous power of language. Confronting the tanks was, in the end, at least as much a verbal as an active experience, and it demonstrated for me all the real reasons for being a writer.

The Artistic Adventure Directory

This directory offers something for the whole spectrum of artists: those that are 100 percent committed to a career in the arts; those that fancy the idea but are not yet convinced; and those shy artists who suspect working in the world of artistic expression may be the path to their personal fulfillment.

We offer listings that range from professional training in fine arts to poetry-writing workshops you can take while vacationing on Cape Cod. Many offer internships or other nonpaid positions that range from one-month seasonal stints to permanent positions. Because the length of commitment can vary greatly, you'll need to contact the organization directly for specifics.

It's a big directory, so it is divided into five sections: 1) Visual arts, 2) Writing, 3) Music, 4) Dance, and 5) Dramatic arts.

1. Visual arts

The New York Academy of Art
The Graduate School of Figurative Art
419 Lafayette St.
New York, NY 10003
212-505-5300

This studio art program devotes its curriculum to figurative and traditional art while offering reinterpretations of traditional methods with a contemporary twist. Emphasizing the study of the human figure, the program's goal is "to provide students with sufficient conceptual knowledge of anatomy, perspective, geometry and the effects of light on form, to draw the human figure from imagination, as well as from life, and to utilize such figurative skills in their early development as painters, sculptors and teachers."

The two-year graduate program leads to a master's in fine arts and qualifies graduates to teach at university level. Of the 63 credits needed to graduate, 51 are received by completing studio art classes. Students must complete a Diploma Project—a painting, sculpture or drawing with a description of the artist's intent and methods.

The Pennsylvania Academy of the Fine Arts
118 N Broad St.
Philadelphia, PA 19102
215-972-7600

The Academy has been providing classical training in figurative art since 1805. "The people who come to study at the Pennsylvania Academy are people who know they want to be fine artists." Academy programs include a four-year certificate program, bachelor of fine arts degree offered in cooperation with the University of Pennsylvania or the University of the Arts, and a new master of fine arts degree. The certificate program focuses on the study of drawing, painting, sculpture and printmaking.

European Summer Art Program
University of Massachusetts
Department of Art/Fine Arts Center
Amherst, MA 01003
413-545-1902 or 6939

For two months every other summer, this program takes 36 students and six instructors on a six-to-eight week artistic journey to France. Most of the trip is spent at a 900-year-old castle on the French Riviera. The group uses the castle, the large gardens and seashore, and surrounding towns as its artistic inspiration. For five-and-a-half weeks the group works and lives in the chateau, dines on food prepared by their own chef and explores the inspiration of the French Riviera. Daily critiques of each student's work are conducted by the group. Throughout the day, students work independently, with instructors available for consultation and instruction.

A study trip is taken to Italy, where the group gets to view Italian art—both in the museums and in the streets. Artistic journals are kept by the students. The trip includes a bus tour through Provence, Burgundy and the Loire Valley and a final four days in Paris. Participants receive nine college credits. A $3,800 fee covers all expenses except for airfare.

Scuola Internazionale d'Arte
Laboratorio Grafia e Pittura
La bottegga dell'Acquaforte
Via Chiantigiana 3r, Badia a Ripoli
50126 Florence, Italy
055-6810268

Private art school offering courses in graphic and painting techniques.

Art Institute of Florence
"Lorenzo de' Medici"
Piazza Pallottole, 1
50122 Florence, Italy
055-283142

Study center with experimental laboratories, offering courses in drawing, painting, etching, sculpture, photography, ceramics and restoration.

Note: The Italian Institute of Culture provides an expanded list of private art schools in Italy: 686 Park Ave., New York, NY 10021.

Castle Hill
Truro Center for the Arts
P.O. Box 756
Truro, MA 02666
508-349-7511

Summer workshops in painting, drawing, photography, printmaking, image making, sculpture, metal, fiber work and ceramics.

University of Delaware & Winterthur Museum
Art Conservation Program
303 Old College
University of Delaware
Newark, DE 19716
302-831-4330; Fax: 302-831-2479

This three-year course leads to a master of science degree in art conservation. The master's program is a 10-course curriculum, with an 11-month internship and two eight-week summer work projects. According to the school, "practical work in conservation techniques is stressed and emphasis is placed on connoisseurship and the understanding of chemical and physical properties of art materials and the scientific techniques used to characterize them."

Institute of Fine Art
1 E. 78th St.
New York, NY 10021
212-772-5800

Artists Foundation—Massachusetts Artists Fellowship Program
860 Harrison #309
Boston, MA 02127
617-859-3810

This nonprofit organization is set up to serve Massachusetts artists. It supports the "Commonwealth's best artists." The Foundation has the MA Artists Fellowship Program, and offers internships with the Foundation in public relations, panel research, archive management, program assistance and slide registrar.

Association of Hispanic Arts, Inc.
173 E. 116th St., 2nd Fl.
New York, NY 10029
212-860-5445

Internships with varying stipends are available in development/funding, publications/graphic services, technical assistance and accounting.

Center for Photography at Woodstock
59 Tinker St.
Woodstock, NY 12498
914-679-9957; Fax: 914-679-6337

The Center supports "excellence in photography and the related arts." Assistance internships are available for the Center-sponsored Woodstock Photography Workshops; workshops with nationally recognized artists.

Colorado Council on the Arts and Humanities
750 Pennsylvania St.
Denver, CO 80203
303-894-2617
Contact: Fran Holden, Director

Providing grants and technical assistance, the Council works to "create an environment in which the arts will flourish." There are internships in arts organization programs, individual artists programs, community programs, art in public places and media relations.

Division of Cultural Affairs, Department of State
The Capitol
Tallahassee, FL 32399-0250
904-487-2980

Paid positions in information, director's office, grants programs, touring and special projects.

G.L.C.A. New York Arts Program
305 W. 29th St.
New York, NY 10001
212-563-0255

Coordinates apprenticeships in the arts for college students.

Headlands Center for the Arts
Building 944, Fort Barry
Sausalito, CA 94965
415-331-2787; Fax: 415-331-3857

This residencies' interdisciplinary art center for "artists to develop unique functional spaces in its quarters" offers public programs. Internships are available.

Interlochen Center for the Arts
P.O. Box 199
Interlochen, MI 49643
616-276-9221; Fax: 616-276-6321

Nonpaid internships are available for the special events office at this "world-renowned fine arts boarding school."

Oregon Arts Commission
835 Summer St. NE
Salem, OR 97301
503-986-0082

The Commission, which supports the arts in Oregon through grants to individuals and organizations, administration of public art programs, performing arts touring and arts education, offers two unpaid internships.

Utah Arts Council
617 E. South Temple
Salt Lake City, UT 84102
801-533-5895

This state agency working in support of the arts, offers both paid and unpaid positions.

Wyoming Council on the Arts
2320 Capitol Ave.
Cheyenne, WY 82001
307-777-7742

Through programs, grants and technical assistance, this state agency fosters the growth of art in Wyoming. One paid internship is available in community arts development/rural arts development.

Visual Arts Internships

Gensler and Associates Architects
Intern Coordinator
600 California St.
San Francisco, CA 94108
415-433-3700

Internships (paid) at this well-respected firm are open to both beginners and those with experience. Gensler has offices in New York, Washington, D.C., San Francisco, Los Angeles, Denver and Houston. Interns learn such skills as creating scale models and construction drawings.

Adventure Careers

Hill, Holliday, Connors, Cosmopulos Advertising, Inc.
Internship Coordinator
200 Clarendon St.
Boston, MA 02116
617-572-3418

An advertising internship.

Lucasfilm
Human Resources-Intern Department
P.O. Box 2009
San Rafael, CA 94912
415-662-1999

Yes, with the Star Wars crew. Here's a great chance to learn about film-making, but that's not all—there are also internships available in computer graphics and art. There are even business internships for those so inclined. The work involved depends entirely on the department you end up in, but it tends to be substantial. This is for upper-class undergrads and grad students.

Marvel Comics
Internship Program
387 Park Ave. South
New York, NY 10016
212-696-0808

Love comics? Want to figure out how they fit into an "adult" world? Get in here and get hooked up with an editor. You end up gofering a lot, but you get to look over the shoulder of the editors and see what's involved in making a comic. Plus, they'll send you down to research in the archives (that's the stacks of comics.) As the editor trusts you more, you'll get more interesting assignments.

Arts Administration

It's not as glamorous as being the artist, but arts administration can be a good field to get into in order to network. Most art internships expect you to work like a slave for free (just because you love art). Well, when the passion fades and the rent is due, arts administration can be a viable option.

Butterfield & Butterfield
Internship Program
220 San Bruno Ave.
San Francisco, CA 94103
415-861-7500

Fine art and antique auctioneers. This internship will teach you the repair and handling of fine art. It's a terrific educational opportunity if you want to learn about a type of art or antique.

The Cloisters
College Internship Program
Fort Tryon Park
New York, NY 10040
212-923-3700

International Society of Performing Arts Administrators (ISPAA)
2920 Fullar Ave. NE
Suite 205
Grand Rapids, MI 49505
616-364-3000; Fax: 616-364-9010

This membership association of nonprofit, independent, university and for-profit art organizations presents cultural events, manages performance facilities and represents performing artists. General administration internships are available.

Lincoln Center for the Performing Arts, Inc.
Internship Coordinator
70 Lincoln Center Plaza
New York, NY 10023-6583
212-875-5000

The Metropolitan Museum of Art
1000 Fifth Ave.
New York, NY 10028-0198
Attn: Education Dept., Internship Program
212-570-3710

New York Foundation for the Arts
155 Ave. of the Americas, 14th Fl.
New York, NY 10013
212-366-6900

This public foundation supports the arts throughout New York state, with an open number of internships available.

North Carolina Arts Council
Department of Cultural Resources
Raleigh, NC 27601-2807
919-733-7897; Fax: 919-715-5406

Three internship positions are available for people interested in community arts administration.

San Francisco Arts Commission Gallery
155 Grove St.
San Francisco, CA 94102
415-554-9682

A municipal exhibition space operated by the City and County of San Francisco offers a few unpaid positions.

Smithsonian Institution
Internship Coordinator
Office of Museum Programs
Arts & Industries Building
Suite 2235, MRC 427
Washington, DC 20560
202-357-3102

Whitney Museum of American Art
Internship Program, Personnel Office
945 Madison Ave.
New York, NY 10021
212-570-3600

Wolf Trap Foundation for the Performing Arts
Intern Coordinator
1624 Trap Road
Vienna, VA 22182
703-255-1900

2. Writing

The Bread Loaf Writers' Conference
Middlebury College
Middlebury, VT 05753
802-388-3711

The Conference is a mid-August tradition on the Middlebury College campus in the Green Mountain National Forest. During this two-week gathering of writers, prospective writers and writing teachers, "through lectures, discussion groups, workshops, panels and reading, the craft of writing prose and poetry is discussed, together with the related topics of editing manuscripts, submission of work to publishers, author/agent/editor relationships and the teaching of writing."

The program is divided into two parts: theory and practice. The first week is filled with staff lectures on the craft of writing and small discussion groups. The second week is spent in workshops for poetry, fiction and nonfiction in which work of student contributors is considered.

Castle Hill
Truro Center for the Arts
Box 756
Truro, MA 02666
508-349-7511

Workshops in writing and literature are offered each summer.

Random House, Inc.
Internship Program
201 E. 50th St.
New York, NY 10022
212-572-2610

Get into publishing through the back door rather than by gatecrashing.

Warren Wilson College
701 Warren Wilson Rd.
Box 5115
Swannanoa, NC 28778
704-298-3325

The Warren Wilson College offers a "low residency" program for a master's of fine arts degree. This 12-year-old program opens each semester with a 10-day on-campus session of classes and conferences. For the following six months, each student works off campus, with supervision from the teacher/writer faculty through mail correspondence and manuscript critique.

Admission to this program is based primarily on the student's original manuscript of 10 pages of poetry and 25 pages of prose. Also the applicant's demonstration of commitment to working independently is taken into account.

Journalism Internships

A journalism internship. Don't sneer; journalism is the classic way for a writer to survive and learn to be clear and succinct. It's a good idea to have practical ways to keep yourself working. Trust me, the garret with rice and beans grows less appealing with every passing year.

Center for Investigative Reporting, Inc.
c/o Communications Director
568 Howard St., 5th Fl.
San Francisco, CA 94105-3008
415-543-1200

Los Angeles Times
Editorial Internships
Times Mirror Square
Los Angeles, CA 90053
800-283-NEWS, Ext. 74487

National Public Radio
Internship Coordinator
635 Massachusetts Ave.
Washington, DC 20001-3753
202-414-2000

Nightline
Intern Coordinator
1717 Desales St. NW, 3rd Fl.
Washington, DC 20036
202-887-7360

The Wall Street Journal
Internship Program
c/o Richard Martin, Assistant Managing Editor
200 Liberty St.
New York, NY 10281

The Washington Post
Internship Program
1150 15th St. NW
Washington, DC 20071-5508
202-334-6000

3. Music

Berklee College of Music
1140 Boyleston St.
Boston, MA 02215
617-266-1400

Approaching the teaching of music from the "American tradition," Berklee offers a four-year bachelor of music degree. The schools teaching foundation of contemporary music stems from a jazz background, working into pop/rock.

BMG (Bertelsmann Music Group)
Alternative Marketing Program
Manager of Recruiting and Development
1540 Broadway, 38th Fl.
New York, NY 10036
212-930-4000; Fax: 212-930-4862

An internship that provides the chance to work within the recording industry. Get the low-down on how to get your CDs out.

Chamber Music America
545 Eighth Ave., 9th Fl.
New York, NY 10018
212-244-2772

Chamber Music America (CMA) is a membership organization of professional chamber musicians working to "promote professional chamber music and to make chamber music a vital part of American cultural life."

Connecticut Opera Association, Inc.
226 Farmington Ave.
Hartford, CT 06105
203-527-0713

Fulton Opera House
Box 1865
Lancaster, PA 17608-1865
717-394-7133

This performing arts center produces professional theater, internationally acclaimed dance, music and special entertainment series, and offers unpaid positions in production and administration.

Greater Miami Opera Association
1200 Coral Way
Miami, FL 33145
305-854-1643

Presents 35 performance and five grand operas each season, and offers 13 paid positions (eight vocalists, one coach-accompanist, one stage management, one costuming, etc.)

The Handel & Hayden Society
300 Massachusetts Ave.
Boston, MA 02115

Presents a 14-concert season in Boston's Symphony Hall, and offers three paid positions—two in Marketing and one in Development.

Adventure Careers

The Juilliard School
60 Lincoln Center Plaza
New York, NY 10023
212-799-5000

Juilliard was established in 1905 as a music academy that would rival the European conservatories. Today it is known for training some of the most gifted young classical musicians. In the six major American orchestras, more than 20 percent of the musicians have studied at Juilliard.

The Lower Manhattan Cultural Council
One World Trade Center, Suite 1717
New York, NY 10048
212-432-0900

The Council, which produces more than 100 free lunchtime music, dance and performance events per year, offers one paid position.

Lyric Opera of Chicago
20 N. Wacker Drive
Chicago, IL 60606
312-332-2244

Classical opera company offering unpaid positions in production, education, public relations, tickets and development.

Metropolitan Opera Association
Lincoln Center
New York, NY 10023
212-799-3100

The association hires two paid assistants to work on the "Met in the Parks" concert series.

Minnesota Orchestral Association
1111 Nicollet Mall
Minneapolis, MN 55403
612-371-5600

This nonprofit corporation operates the Minnesota Orchestra and Orchestra Hall, and offers a few unpaid internships.

The New England Conservatory of Music
290 Huntington Ave.
Boston, MA 02115
617-262-1120

The New England Conservatory offers undergraduate degrees and graduate degrees in musical areas of concentration ranging from the bassoon to vocal performance. The Conservatory's teaching is based in classical theory with an outstanding faculty that is complemented by guest artists such as Yo-Yo Ma. The bachelor of music degree combines studio instruction, with music history instruction, music theory, humanities and performance opportunities. The School of Graduate Studies offers a master's of music degree and a doctor of musical arts.

Pittsburgh Civic Light Opera
719 Liberty Ave.
Pittsburgh, PA 15222
412-281-3973

Presents "Broadway-scale" summertime musicals, offering two to four paid positions.

Sony Music Entertainment, Inc.
Credited Internship
550 Madison Ave., 2nd Fl.
New York, NY 10022-3211

Sony is more than electronics—it also operates CBS Records. Doesn't sound familiar? They produce Michael Jackson, Bruce Springsteen, Pearl Jam, Mariah Carey and others. This internship is for undergraduates and graduate students who can work for credit at their school (no money). The departments that place interns include Promotions, Artists and Repertoire, and Video Production, just to name a few.

Sony Music Entertainment, Inc.
Minority Internship
550 Madison Ave., 13th Fl.
New York, NY 10022-3211
Attn: Department 13-5

Similar to the credit internship but with special perks. Each week the interns have lunch with a senior level executive. They are also given the chance to meet and network with former interns that now work for Sony.

Summer music festivals

Alfred University Summer Chamber Music Institute and Festival
26 N. Main St.
Alfred, NY 14802-1232
607-871-2219

Aspen Music Festival and School
P.O. Box AA
Aspen, CO 81612
303-925-3254

Banff Festival of the Arts
Banff Center for the Arts, Box 1020
Banff, AB, Canada TOL OCO
403-762-6100

Bar Harbor Music Festival
59 Cottage St.
Bar Harbor, ME 04609
212-222-1026

Adventure Careers

Festival of the Sound
Box 750
Parry Sound, ON, Canada P2A 2ZI
705-746-2410

Interlochen Arts Festival
P.O. Box 199
Interlochen, MI 49643
616-279-9221

L'Ensemble Chamber Music in the Barn
11 North Pearl St.
Albany, NY 12207
518-436-5321

Midsummer Mozart Festival
World Trade Center, Suite 233335
San Francisco, CA 94111
415-781-5931

Mohawk Trail Concerts
P.O. Box 843
Greenfield, MA 01302
914-679-7558

Mostly Mozart
Avery Fisher Hall, Lincoln Center
New York, NY 10023
212-877-1800

The Newport Music Festival
P.O. Box 3300
Newport, RI 02840
401-846-1133

Norfolk Chamber Music Festival/ Yale Summer School of Music
96 Wall St.
New Haven, CT 06520
203-542-5537

Olympic Music Festival
P.O. Box 45776
Seattle, WA 98145
206-527-8839

Rockport Chamber Music Festival
Box 312
Rockport, MA 01966
508-546-7391

Santa Fe Chamber Music Festival
P.O. Box 853
Santa Fe, NM 87504
505-983-2075

Southeastern Music Center
P.O. Box 8348
Columbus, GA 31908
706-568-2465

Summerfest Chamber Music Festival
Box 23181
Pittsburgh, PA 15222
412-361-5525

Swannanoa Chamber Festival
Box 5062, 701 Warren Wilson Rd.
Swannanoa, NC 28778
704-298-3325

Tanglewood Music Festival
Lenox, MA 01240
413-637-1600

Vancouver Chamber Music Festival
P.O. Box 35605, Postal Station E
Vancouver, BC, Canada V6M 4G9
604-736-6034

Viennese Sommerfest
1111 Nicollet Mall
Minneapolis, MN 55403
612-371-5600

Yellow Barn Festival
RD 2, Box 371
Putney, VT 05346
802-387-6637

4. Dance

The Juilliard School
60 Lincoln Center Plaza
New York, NY 10023
212-799-5000

Juilliard, located at Lincoln Center in New York City, has for many years been known for its excellence in education in the arts. Structured as a conservatory, Juilliard offers three main divisions: dance, music and drama. Standards are high and practice schedules rigorous.

Most students of the Juilliard dance division go on to professional careers as performers, choreographers and heads of dance companies. This program is designed to prepare students for the world of performance. Juilliard offers many opportunities for students to perform, with fall and spring concerts, workshops, the contemporary music festival, tours of New York area schools and festival appearances in Europe and Asia.

Admission to the school is based on performances at competitive auditions held at the Juilliard School and in cities selected around the country. While there are no age restrictions for admissions, students in the "formative stages of their performance careers" are given preference by the Committee on Admissions. The school's admissions office provides information on audition schedules. Tuition and fees for the nine-month academic year are just over $10,000.

Jacob's Pillow Dance Festival & School
P.O. Box 287
Lee, MA 01238
413-637-1322

Jacob's Pillow has been a center for contemporary dance-training, performance and creation for 60 years. Its schedule of summertime workshops and 10-week festival events offers a wonderful environment for "both established and aspiring professionals."

Workshops ranging from one week to many weeks, have their own daily schedules. Workshops offered include Choreography Workshop with Bessie Schonberg, the Ballet Project and Modern/Jazz Workshop.

Students must fulfill audition requirements, must be over 16 and demonstrate a high level of technique when applying for Etudes, the Ballet Project and Modern/Jazz Workshop. Fees for weekly tuition, room and board are $500, with varying additional costs for each workshop.

Jacob's Pillow offers an internship program in the specific areas of development, marketing/press, business and operations, school administration and technical theater/production. The internships extend from June 1 through August 31. Full room and board with a small stipend is provided.

Adventure Careers

The American Dance Festival
P.O. Box 9097 College Station
Durham, NC 27708
919-684-6402; Fax: 919-694-5459

The American Dance Festival (ADF), billed as "the Most Important Summer of Your Life," offers a six-week summer school, workshops in jazz for teachers and intermediate/advanced dance, and a summer internship program. ADF is held on the Duke University campus. Full tuition, which includes four classes a day, five days a week, is $1,150.

About 300 students who have "sufficient dance training and maturity to ensure that they receive maximum benefit from the program" are admitted to the summer school. Internships are offered from the end of May to the end of July in the areas of development, school administration, marketing/dance touring, finance, community development, merchandising, press, performances, special projects, international choreographers workshops, house management, box office, space and equipment management, etc. Interns receive an $850 stipend, fee attendance to one class, one complimentary ticket to performances of visiting companies, and access to discussions, seminars and lectures.

The Atlanta Ballet
477 Peachtree St.
Atlanta, GA 30308
404-873-5811

Community organization supporting ballet/art, two nonpaid positions in development and marketing.

Boston Ballet
42 Vernon St.
Newton, MA 02158
617-964-4070

Internationally renowned ballet company offering three unpaid internships in marketing.

Dance Theater of Harlem
247 W. 30th St.
New York, NY 10001
212-967-3470

World-class, "neo-classical" ballet company and school with a number of unpaid internship positions.

DANCEASPEN, INC.
Box 8745
Aspen, CO 81612
303-925-7718

This nonprofit agency that coordinates professional level dance performances, has three paid positions available in public relations, box office, administration or development.

DANCECLEVELAND
611 Hanna Bldg.
1422 Euclide Ave.
Cleveland, OH 44115
216-861-2213

There are three nonpaid internships, one in development and fundraising, one in contracts and management and one in promotion and PR at this nonprofit agency which presents modern dance performances, and organizes dance workshops, master classes and dance therapy seminars.

Foundation for the Advance of Dance, Inc.
55 Bethune St., Studio 630A
New York, NY 10014
212-989-2250

The Foundation raises funds and plans bookings to support dance companies. Two part-time internships.

Gus Giordano Jazz Dance Chicago
614 Davis St.
Evanston, IL 60201
708-866-6779

This American jazz dance company performing locally, nationally and internationally, has four paid positions per year.

Minnesota Dance Alliance
528 Hennepin Ave., Suite 600
Minneapolis, MN 55403
612-340-1900

An organization offering service to dance artists in Minnesota and upper Midwest regions, occupational internships in dance production, program development, bookkeeping and accounting and arts administration.

National Dance Association
1900 Association Drive
Reston, VA 22091
703-476-3436

This association for people interested in dance education in schools, studios and community, offers an unpaid internship.

North Carolina Dance Theater
200 South Independence
Charlotte, NC 28204
704-372-0101

This professional, not-for-profit performing arts organization, has a number of paid and nonpaid internships in operations, production, development, marketing and accounting.

Pittsburgh Ballet Theater
2900 Liberty Ave.
Pittsburgh, PA 15201
412-281-0360

This professional ballet company performing classical and contemporary works, offers six unpaid internships.

5. High Glamour/High Busywork

Each of these looks great on a resume, but in reality, they're full of photocopying and fetching coffee.

The Walt Disney Studios
Internship Program Administrator
500 South Buena Vista St.
Burbank, CA 91521-0880
818-560-6335

Forty Acres and a Mule Filmworks, Inc.
124 Dekalb Ave.
Brooklyn, NY 11217
718-624-3703

Spike Lee's film company.

155

Adventure Careers

The Kennedy Center
Internship Program Manager
Washington, DC 20566
202-416-8800

Late Show with David Letterman
Internship Coordinator
1697 Broadway
New York, NY 10019
212-975-5300

MTV
MTV Networks Internship Program
Human Resources
1515 Broadway, 22nd Fl.
New York, NY 11036
212-258-8000

Rolling Stone
Editorial Department
1290 Ave. of the Americas
New York, NY 10104
212-484-1616

---

6. Dramatic arts

The Acting Studio
29 E. 19th St.
New York, NY 10003
212-228-2700

Professional workshops, such as scene study, monologue or voice production are continually offered. Acceptance into this program, intended for serious beginners and actors with previous training and experience, is by interview only. Prices for classes and workshops vary.

American Academy of Dramatic Arts
120 Madison Ave.
New York, NY 10016
212-686-9244
and
2550 Paloma St.
Pasadena, CA 91107
818-798-0777

A renowned training program for professional actors, the American Academy of Dramatic Arts offers a two-year professional training program and summer program. Founded in New York in 1884, this school has a long tradition of training "stars" for the stage, film and television. Some alumni include Grace Kelly, Spencer Tracy and Danny DeVito.

The six-week summer program is offered each year in New York City and in Pasadena, Calif. The core curriculum includes acting, voice and speech, singing and movements, with electives of fencing, mime, makeup, musical theater and dance for actors. This program is for beginning actors and for those who want to test their ability and aptitude for professional training. Core tuition is $800, with electives being additional.

The Juilliard School
60 Lincoln Center Plaza
New York, NY 10023
212-799-5000

The newest division at the Juilliard school offers training in classical and contemporary acting styles. More than 80 percent of the drama division's students go on the work in professional theater organizations, Broadway productions, films and television.

Juilliard School Stage Department
144 66th St.
New York, NY 10023
212-799-5000, ext. 215

The Department is responsible for the production of all technical elements of Juilliard's Drama, Dance and Opera productions, and offers 16 paid positions in costumes, electrics, properties scenery, scene painting, and sound and stage management.

Alliance Theater Company
Robert W. Woodruff Arts Center
1280 Peachtree St. NE
Atlanta, GA 30309
404-733-4650

One of the nation's top 10 producing regional theaters offers a professional intern program for individuals with university training or professional experience, who have professional goals in acting.

American Conservatory Theater
Internship Program
450 Geary St.
San Francisco, CA 94102
415-834-3200

ACT offers about nine to 13 internships each year, for about eight months, in many aspects of theater production. All internships are paid and are open to undergrads and college grads of any age. It's a lot of hard work and is considered an excellent experience.

Adventure Careers

American Repertory Theater
64 Brattle St.
Cambridge, MA 02138
617-495-2668

Company offers unpaid positions in artistic management, fund raising, stage management, wardrobe, voice coaching, etc.

American Stage Festival
Box 225
Milford, NH 03055
603-673-4005

Close to 25 positions in acting, stage management, administrative and technical areas.

Berkeley Repertory Theater
2025 Addison St..
Berkeley, CA 94704
510-845-4700

Internships with small stipend offered in scenic painting, scenic construction, consumes, properties, sound, stage electrics and directing.

Body Politic Theater
2261 North Lincoln Ave.
Chicago, IL 60614
312-348-7901

Equity theater putting on seasonal productions that "emphasize thought and language," offers about a dozen unpaid positions in theater production and theater administration.

Center Theater and the Training Center for the Working Actor
1346 W. Devon
Chicago, IL 60660
312-508-0200

Professional theater and training for acting, voice and movement, has flexible number of internships.

Center Theater Group/Mark Taper Forum
135 North Grand Ave.
Los Angeles, CA 90012
213-972-7353

Major nonprofit theater offers unpaid internships in administration, audience development, casting, press, production, artistic administration, management and fund raising.

Cincinnati Playhouse in the Park
P.O. Box 6537
Cincinnati, OH 45206
513-345-2242

A number of acting positions available each year for performance in the Playhouse's intern productions and in daily training classes.

Circle in the Square Theater
1633 Broadway
New York, NY 10019-6795
212-307-2732

Nonprofit Broadway theater has five unpaid positions in marketing, play development, administrative assistance and theater school.

Playhouse on the Square
51 South Cooper
Memphis, TN 38104
901-725-0776

Professional theater company offering six to 10 paid internships in acting, administrative and technical positions.

Creative Faires, LTD: New York Renaissance Festival
134 Fifth Ave., 3rd Fl.
New York, NY 10011
212-645-1630

A medieval-style arts and theater festival in August and September offers a few paid positions in public relations and special events.

Dorset Theater Festival/American Theater Works, Inc.
Box 519
Dorset, VT 05251
802-867-2223

Paid internships available with professional theater company producing summer performances with companion writers' colony. They also publish the *Summer Theater Directory,* listing more than 400 opportunities, the *Regional Theater Directory* and the *Directory of Theater Training,* which lists 350 programs for grads and undergrads.

The Drama League
165 W. 46th St., Suite 601
New York, NY 10036
212-302-2100

Organizes programs to support "best young theater talent," sponsors educational seminars and hosts the Annual Distinguished Performance Awards—

the oldest theater award in the States. Unpaid positions available in arts administration, programs and production, and press/public relations.

Florida Shakespeare Festival
2304 Salzedo
Coral Gables, FL 33134
305-446-1116

Festival presenting full season of classics, offers seven to 10 paid positions in acting, technical production, stage management, box office and public affairs.

Florida Studio Theater
1241 N. Palm Ave.
Sarasota, FL 34236
813-366-9017

This theater, presenting a season of contemporary plays, has 10 paid positions in production, administration and children's education.

Goodspeed Opera House
Box A
East Haddam, CT 06423
203-873-8664

Housed in a restored Victorian theater on the banks of the Connecticut River, the Opera House performs American musicals and new works. It offers a dozen positions in electrics, property construction, scene painting, public relations, general development and production, etc.

The Gutherie Theater
725 Vineland Place
Minneapolis, MN 55403
612-347-1100

The repertory theater, offers nonpaid positions in company management, costume, directing, publicity, administration, etc.

Idaho Shakespeare Festival
P.O. Box 9365
Boise, ID 83707
208-336-9221

Festival presenting one contemporary and three Shakespeare productions per season, offers internships in all areas.

Los Angeles Theater Center
514 S. Spring St., 2nd Fl.
Los Angeles, CA 90013
213-627-6500; Fax: 213-847-3169

A professional theater presenting contemporary works to the local community, offers one unpaid position to work in technical theater and theater management.

Main Street Theater
2540 Times Blvd.
Houston, TX 77005
713-524-3622

Offers two unpaid positions—production and arts administration.

Maine State Music Theater
Box 656
Brunswick, ME 04011
207-725-8769

Committed to the training of young theater professionals, this theater offers 35 paid positions: 16 for performers and 16 for technical workers.

Manhattan Theater Club
453 W. 16th St.
New York, NY 10011
212-645-5590

Professional theater devoted to developing new works offers as many as 40 internships each season in marketing/press, finance, casting, company representative, data systems, development, literary, production, general management and technical.

New Dramatists
424 W. 44th St.
New York, NY 10036
212-757-6960

Working since 1949 to produce "playwrights rather than play," New Dramatists offers four stipend, full-time internships.

New Jersey Shakespeare Festival
36 Madison Ave.
Madison, NJ 07940
201-408-3278

Equity theater offering stipend internships, usually in acting.

Organic Theater Company
3319 N. Clark
Chicago, IL 60657
312-327-2427

Offers nonpaid internships in literary management, public relations/marketing, development, artistic administration and technical theater.

Pennsylvania Stage Company
837 Linden St.
Allentown, PA 18103
610-434-6110

Maintains intensive internship program for actors and stage managers preparing for professional theater work. Paid internships in acting, stage management, wardrobe, electrics, props, and marketing and development.

Pepsico Summerfare/Purchase College Performing Arts Center
735 Anderson Hill Rd.
Purchase, NY 10577
914-251-6222

International opera, theater, concert, dance and arts festival, offering 50 paid internships for stage electronics, stage carpentry, costumes, properties, company management, production management, and more.

Playwrights' Center
2301 Franklin Ave. East
Minneapolis, MN 55406
612-332-7481

Center supports development of playwrights and offers five unpaid internships in development, theater programs, educational outreach, etc.

San Diego Repertory Theater
79 Horton Plaza
San Diego, CA 92101
619-231-3586

Repertory theater presenting contemporary, world premier and new interpretations of classic plays, has nine internship positions: administration, artistic, costume, lighting, scenic design and props.

Spoleto Festival USA
Box 157
Charleston, SC 29402
803-722-2764

The famous arts and chamber music festival has paid positions in the areas of production and technical, administration, development, merchandising, public relations, box office and business office.

Stagewest
1 Columbus Center
Springfield, MA 01103
413-781-4470

Professional theater and not-for-profit organization has 16 paid positions in acting, costumes, electrics, sound, marketing, development, etc.

TADA!
120 W. 28th St.
New York, NY 10011
212-627-1732

Children's ensemble company, offers high-quality theater and dance productions performed by and for children, and has five stipend positions.

Theatervirginia
2800 Grove Ave.
Richmond, VA 23221
804-367-0840

Professional equity theater, offering about a dozen paid positions in electrics, stage management, properties, costumes, production management and administration.

Theaterworks Shakespeare Festival
University of Colorado
Box 7150
Colorado Springs, CO 80907
719-593-3232, 719-520-7069

Summer festival with a number positions in technical theater, marketing/development and acting.

Adventure Careers

Three Rivers Shakespeare Festival
University of Pittsburgh
617 Cathedral of Learning
Pittsburgh, PA 15260

Festival producing classical Shakespeare offers paid and nonpaid positions in administration, performance, design, costume and scene construction, front-of-house and box office.

Virginia Stage Company
Box 3770
Norfolk, VA 23514
804-627-6988

This professional regional theater offers a dozen paid positions in administration, costume construction, stage design, properties, scenic construction, lighting/sound and stage management.

Williamstown Theater Festival
Box 517
Williamstown, MA 01267
413-597-3377

Summer theater with unpaid positions in design, production, box office, general management, sets, costumes, cabaret, props, electrics and stage management.

Chapter 7

Work in the Political Arena

Let the word go forth from this time and place, to friend and foe alike, that the torch has been passed to a new generation of Americans...

And so my fellow Americans, ask not what your country can do for you. Ask what you can do for your country.
—John F. Kennedy, The Inaugural Address, Washington, D.C., Jan. 20, 1961

What do Earth First!, Amnesty International and the United Negro College Fund have in common? Despite their disparate focuses, they all express the vision Kennedy expressed many years ago. They represent some of the many ways individuals choose to "carry the torch," to get involved in the political events that shape policy and our lives. Environmental activists, human rights crusaders, civil rights workers, school board members, even (we hope) elected officials, represent some of the many ways people participate in the political process.

This chapter is about work in the political arena. The type of political career you will pursue is of your choosing, whether you work as a grassroots activist or as a professional lobbyist in

Washington. As an adult member of a democratic society, your political work can be undertaken in many ways: staying informed, making your own decisions regarding voting, speaking out and taking action to defend what you believe in. Such activities can provide valuable steps in an adventure career, they can enliven an otherwise pedestrian career through part-time or volunteer efforts, or they can be the primary focus of work and career. There are opportunities for participation at any level. This chapter is designed to support you in developing your political career, whether you're working 9 to 5 or on weekends, and whether you are in the streets or in the White House.

Many of the career opportunities described in the directory that follows represent different forms of activism. This word is defined in Webster's as "a doctrine or practice that emphasizes direct vigorous action (as a mass demonstration) in support of or opposition to one side of a controversial issue." The term came into common use during the '60s, but of course, the concept of political activism provides the foundation for the United States itself:

> *We hold these truths to be self-evident, that all men are created equal, that they are endowed by their Creator with certain unalienable Rights, that among these are Life, Liberty and the pursuit of Happiness. That to secure these rights, Governments are instituted among Men, deriving their just powers from the consent of the governed, that whenever any Form of Government becomes destructive of these ends, it is the Right of the People to alter or to abolish it, and to institute new Government...*
> —The Declaration of Independence, July 4, 1776

Activism created the country, and activism continues to renew it over the generations. Nowadays it rarely takes on the violent form it did during the American Revolution, and we have not included any organizations that promote or perpetrate violence in the directory for this chapter. But activism still expresses the idea that people have the right to change their government when it is not functioning properly. As a result, the governing institutions of this country undergo constant evolution, responding to prods from both within and without. Elected politicians, their appointed staffs and lobbyists of all denominations dash madly about the capitals, both state and federal.

And thousands of citizens' organizations and groups work to change or improve policies and programs through education, lobbying, voter registration, protests, marches, media events, civil disobedience, fund raising, membership drives, and many other activities.

These citizens' groups constitute an informal but important vehicle for individual participation in politics, one that interacts with and informs the official political apparatus at every level. It is most often in this informal political system that young people find a role, although there are also many opportunities for involvement in the official world of government and politics. Perhaps people in their teens and 20s find the slow and sometimes self-contented world of formal politics frustrating, and the informal political sector more direct, action-oriented and, most important, open to them. How many elected officials do you know of who are under 30?

But regardless of the reasons, the informal political sector offers the majority of the opportunities for political involvement for younger adults, and as a result we have focused on it in the following directory. All the organizations listed offer many opportunities for people of all ages, including (and sometimes predominantly) people in their teens and 20s.

What's more, they have an almost endless variety of causes and missions. Despite the political achievements of the country, everyone, of every political viewpoint, has a lengthy agenda for improvement and change. For example, a recent report in *The Nation* finds that:

> *One out of every five infants is born into poverty, 30 million Americans are living below the poverty line, major cities in the United States are experiencing a 20 to 25 percent rise in hunger and homelessness, some 32 million Americans have no health coverage and more than 5 million children go to bed hungry every night. (The Nation, June 17, 1991.)*

Think about your own agenda before reading the following directory or trying to select a political experience for your next adventure. What issues trouble you? Are there any problems or ideals that surfaced in the exercises of Chapter 1, that might now guide you toward a position in the political sphere?

We sometimes forget (especially when exposed to too much national politics) that political action is rooted in personal conviction. The listings in the directory are sources of jobs, internships, volunteer or part-time work. Less obviously, they are vehicles through which you can pursue your own vision, allowing you to grow as you try to improve your society.

Alternative sources of political information

Many people follow political events and issues through the mainstream media—television news programs, local newspapers, news magazines like *Time, Newsweek* and *U.S. News & World Report*, and *The New York Times* and *Washington Post*. All are readily available in any community and can provide access to considerable detail about events throughout the country and the world.

However, there are a great many other publications that provide alternative voices, covering news that is not picked up by the majors or covering stories from a different perspective. These often have limited circulation and can be hard to find on newsstands. For this reason, readers may find the following, a partial list of alternative publications, helpful. They can often be found at larger public and college libraries and are good sources of opposing views on "hot" issues in the realm of politics. In addition, they can be used to locate smaller and less well-known political organizations that may offer jobs or experiences of interest to you. Check them for classified ads:

The Progressive	*The Guardian*
Nation	*Public Citizen*
Mother Jones	*Against the Current*
Ms.: The World of	*New Politics*
Women	*New Age Journal*
Utne Reader	*LA Weekly*
Dollars and Sense	*Whole Earth Review*
Earth First!	*Dissent*
-Z- Magazine	

Personal Account

Nick on Activism

New York City resident Nicholas D. Wolfson believes in direct action as effective political activism. Note his effective use of research skills to locate interested organizations and the way he involved them in his cause to implement a large-scale solution. This kind of approach is often employed by organizations such as those in the directory that follows.

When I can, I go running in Central Park in New York City. Some days your eyes, nose and lungs tell you that the air is completely unbreathable. While on other days the air is, if not great, at least minimally acceptable. I care more about what's in the air than what temperature it is or if it is going to rain. But the weather report rarely, if ever, reports air quality. I think air quality should be reported in every weather report. So here is what I did.

I called Joanne Allen at WNYC Radio in New York, who said that WNYC broadcasts weather and air quality information when it comes to the station over the news wire from AP. She said the only time AP puts out air quality information is when there is an air pollution danger alert. If a daily air quality report came over the wire from AP, she said, they would happily run it on the radio.

I called Rich Mendelson at the AP City Desk (50 Rockefeller Center, NY 10020 621-1670). He said, if they were to receive daily air quality information from a reliable source they would put it out over the wire every day. He said the State of New Jersey provides air quality information to local AP desks in New Jersey, and that AP in New Jersey sends that information out over the wire regularly.

I spoke to Mr. Luis Lim at the New Jersey Air Monitoring Service of the State EPA in Trenton (609-846-4224). He said that the New Jersey Department of Environmental Protection's automated sensors all over New Jersey gather data on levels of ozone, carbon monoxide, nitrogen dioxide and sulfur dioxide. The data is telemetered to Trenton continuously. On the basis of the previous day's information, and the current day's meteorology, they make educated forecasts for today and for the next day ("good, moderate, unhealthful"). They give this data to their EPA Press Officer and the press office distributes it. In addition, the Air Monitoring Service telephones the information to the Delaware Valley Clean Air Council (Philadelphia area) and to the AP in Newark. In the afternoon the Air Monitoring Service issues an update, which they send directly via fax to all TV, radio and newspapers.

A few days later, I spoke to Carol Ash, Regional Director of the New York State Department of Environmental Conservation (718-482-4949). Her department is charged with gathering air quality data in New York City. She said that during the summer months, the media telephones her office, on an irregular basis, to obtain air quality data. She thought there was no harm in attempting to "ritualize" the dissemination of air quality information to the media. I gave her Mr. Mendelson's and Mr. Lim's telephone numbers. She said she would ask her press person, Mr. Bill Hewett, to call Mr. Mendelson and see what could be done to get the air quality reports in every weather report. So, tune in for future updates and for the air quality report.

171

Work in the Political Arena Directory

This section includes environmental groups, causes for minorities or women, international organizations working against discrimination and injustice, and more. They can lead you to many job opportunities, whether you are interested in working as a grassroots activist, intern, volunteer or for the government.

ACT UP
AIDS Coalition to Unleash Power
ACT UP, N.Y.
135 W. 29th St.
New York, NY 10001
212-564-AIDS

ACT UP has declared war on AIDS, the neglect of those who are sick and the social complacency in addressing the problem. Since its formation in 1987 at the Lesbian and Gay Community Service Center in Greenwich Village, the Coalition has been effectively organizing mass demonstrations and acts of civil disobedience to focus attention on this issue.

There are dozens of autonomous ACT UP chapters in North and South America, Europe, Australia and South Africa. Its activities have changed public policy. Improvements and success include the price reduction of the AZT drug used in AIDS treatment, the active participation of patients in experimental treatment programs, and the formation of coalitions with health care workers, environmentalists, patient advocates and other groups.

There are nine ACT UP chapters in the U.S. The New York office can provide information and contact numbers. Note: The AIDS Treatment Data Network provides information, counseling, case management, referral and outreach services on treatment, research and resources for people with AIDS. 259 W. 30th St., 9th Floor, New York, NY 10001. Call 212-268-4196 (English or Spanish).

Amnesty International
National Student Program
1118 22nd NW
Washington, DC 20037
Janice Christanson
202-775-5161

Amnesty International works throughout the world to end the torture and mistreatment of prisoners, to abolish the death penalty and to release prisoners of conscience. In the U.S., there is a large network of high school and college chapters that work at the grassroots level as human rights activists. There are roughly 2,000 to 2,500 of these groups in the U.S. They are active in local campaigns, such as letter writing and public education.

Grassroots activism is coordinated with the national and international work. The national office coordinates nationwide campaigns that the chapters execute at the local level. The national office also provides resources to support the basic workings of local chapters. General administrative frameworks and resource manuals are provided along with specific guides for setting up letter-writing and outreach. Regional offices then work directly with the chapters, offering training, instruction and support. New chapters are formed under the guidance of regional Amnesty offices. People interested in forming a new chapter or in joining an already existing group can phone the national office for a regional contact.

The Brookings Institution
Internship Coordinator
(Name of Program)
1775 Massachusetts Ave. NW
Washington, DC 20036-2188
202-797-6050

Volunteer internships with "one of America's most prestigious think tanks." A medium amount of busywork, interns are paired with Senior Fellows in a program researching American government functions.

The Carter Center
Internship Program
One Copenhill Ave.
Atlanta, GA 30307
404-420-5151

Volunteer interns choose to work in one of the many programs offered by the center related to international public policy: protecting human rights, promoting democracy, resolving conflicts. Daily activities depend on program and involve researching specific issues.

Adventure Careers

City of New York
Department of Personnel
(Name of Program)
2 Washington St., 15th Fl.
New York, NY 10004
212-487-5698

The Coro Fellows Program
Northern California Center
One Ecker St., Suite 330
San Francisco, CA 94105
415-546-9690

College graduates find these internships (you have to pay to be there!) rigorous and challenging. In nine months, a series of five internships, each approximately four weeks in duration, offers "hands-on" experience with five different fields of public service. The program is also located at offices in the regions that are listed as follows.

Regional Offices:

Southern California Center
609 South Grand Ave., Suite 550
Los Angeles, CA 90017
213-623-1234

Eastern Center
95 Madison Ave.
New York, NY 10016
212-683-8843

Midwestern Center
1730 South 11th St.
St. Louis, MO 63104
314-621-3040

The Green Party USA
Box 30208
Kansas City, MO 64112
816-931-9366

The Green Party USA is an alternative political party and a social-change movement. It works in the public arena to shift the power and control of community policy back into the hands of the citizens. It works for peace and nonviolence, social justice, a safe, healthy environment and grassroots democracy. The theoretical foundation is "post-patriarchal values," respect for diversity, personal and global responsibility and community-based economics.

There are more than 400 local Green groups in 46 states throughout the country. The Green Party is now the fourth largest party in the State of California and had qualified for ballot status in California's 1992 primary and general elections, and secured statewide ballot access in Alaska. There are more than 30 elected Green officials now in public office.

Grassroots Green groups are encouraged to function independently and working in cooperation with the party for social change. The Green Organization Packet contains all official documents to start a new local group, organizing manual, process manual on meetings and decision making, a national Greens directory and Green publications.

Internships on Capital Hill
Congressional Intern Program: 202-226-3621

People interested in internships on the Hill must contact their local representatives. These positions are only arranged through the offices of specific representatives. As many as 4,000 interns work on the Hill in every given year, so there are many slots to fill. The length and terms of each internship vary depending on each situation.

Once an internship has been set up, the Congressional Intern Program office can provide some support information. This office organizes a lecture series, offers housing information and compiles a guide book to help orient interns to their new setting. Again, this office cannot aid in setting up an internship and has no information on availability.

The Nation
The Nation Publishing Internships
72 Fifth Ave.
New York, NY 10011
212-242-8400

Practical and comprehensive internships in magazine journalism and publishing are offered at *The Nation* through The Nation Institute. This internship offers participants hands-on experience at the country's oldest magazine, which for 125 years has been a journal covering foreign and domestic policy, civil liberties and literature.

Seven positions are available at the main office in New York and one in Washington. The internships are three to four months long and rotate three times a year. These are full-time positions with office hours Monday to Friday, 10 a.m. to 6 p.m. Each intern receives a stipend of about $75 per week. There are no specific requirements for this placement. Applicants are evaluated based on their resumes, writing samples (two are required with application along with two letters of recommendation) and interviews.

National Organization of Women (NOW)
1000 16th St. NW, Suite 700
Washington, DC 20036
Amy Tracy
202-331-0066

NOW, founded in 1966, is the largest women's rights organization in the country. The organization is made up of 250,000 women and men working for women's legal, political, social and economic equality. NOW works toward these goals through mass action, intensive lobbying, direct action and litigation on the grassroots, state, regional and national levels. "NOW strives to eliminate discrimination and harassment in the workplace; secure abortion and birth control rights for all women; stop all forms of violence against women; eradicate racism; and ensure and promote lesbian and gay civil rights."

Local NOW chapters consist of at least 10 members. Chartered by the national office, the chapters work on local action programs and community-based activities. State organizations, defined by their members and chapters, coordinate statewide activities, such as lobbying state legislators. State offices are a coordinating body for their chapters' grassroots work. The national office is the organizer of NOW mass action campaigns, such as the Abortion Rights Marches in Washington, D.C., in 1989 and 1992.

New York Public Interest Research Group Inc. (NYPIRG)

9 Murray St.   Legislative Office: 184 Washington Ave.
New York, NY 10007   Albany, NY 12210
212-349-6450   518-436-0876

The PIRGs are lobbying organizations that address issues of solid-waste management, government accountability and consumer protection. Based on the ideas of Ralph Nader, they operate on college campuses to strengthen student activism, often upset by the graduation exodus from year to year. The PIRGs are mostly state-based. Groups function in approximately 23 states, with USPIRG conducting federal lobbying efforts.

NYPIRG is typical of the state PIRGs. It operates on 19 campuses throughout the state. It works to train students and the community about policy issues, to support and empower citizens to be a force that affects public policy and to win policy victories through lobbying efforts. Hundreds of students work as NYPIRG volunteers, organizing, leafleting, fund raising. There are a number of internships available in the NYPIRG Albany office.

The Sierra Club

730 Polk St.
San Francisco, CA 94109
415-776-2211

The Sierra Club—yes, the people who make the beautiful calendars—functions as a national network to protect the environment. From its lobbying group in Washington, D.C., to the smallest grassroots group of volunteers, it works to influence government on the legislative, administrative, legal and electoral levels.

Each state has at least one chapter, as well as numerous working groups. It is through the charters and the groups that most people volunteer. There are more than 5,000 volunteers in leadership positions throughout the national network of the Sierra Club.

Local groups work on projects such as public awareness regarding the environment and coordinate local and statewide conservation projects. But some of the major work is designed and coordinated through the national office, such as working for the election of Club-supported political candidates, letter-writing campaigns and petition-signing drives.

Supreme Court of the United States
Judicial Internship Program
Office of the Administrative Assistant to the Chief Justice
Room 5
Washington, DC 20543
202-479-3374

Volunteer internships, with available scholarships, offered to college juniors, seniors and recent grads who have studied Constitutional law. Work primarily with the Judicial Fellow who oversees the daily activities, which require a medium level of busywork.

Times Mirror
Minority Editorial Training Program
Los Angeles Times
Times Mirror Square
Los Angeles, CA 90053
213-237-5000

Times Mirror, publisher of *The Los Angeles Times* and *The Hartford Courant,* has a two-year career-entry program for minorities. The program is aimed at "diversifying the ranks of reporters and photographers at the nation's metropolitan daily newspapers." African-Americans, Asian-Americans, Latinos and Native Americans are encouraged to apply. All applicants must be U.S. citizens. Those with college degrees are preferred. Participants are reviewed by a Times Mirror editorial panel, which bases its decisions on essays, written work or photographs, college transcripts, recommendations, writing tests and personal interviews.

During the first 11 months, trainees move from the classroom to police and court beats, then to working on *The Los Angeles Times* daily regional edition. A stipend and housing is provided during this period. After successful completion (determined through ongoing evaluations), the trainee is assigned to work at one of the Times Mirrors newspapers. Trainees then receive compensation and benefits applicable at the newspaper to which they are assigned.

United Nations Association of the USA
Intern Coordinator
485 Fifth Ave.
New York, NY 10017
212-697-3232

Volunteer internships with nonprofit organization dedicated to fostering participation in the U.N. Daily activities depend upon the department chosen. Exposure to comprehensive information about the U.N. and international affairs.

Adventure Careers

United Nations Headquarters Internship Programme
Internship Programme Coordinator
Room S-2500E, United Nations
New York, NY 10017
212-963-1223

Graduate students work in selected departments or offices within the United Nations Secretariat, in fields such as economics, international law, internal relations, journalism, political science, population studies, public administration, social affairs and translation and terminology. The program offers participants the opportunity to learn about the immediate issues, dynamics and problems confronting the world and to learn about the United Nations' role in working to provide solutions to international problems.

This is a two-month nonpaid placement, with three periods offered yearly: mid-January to mid-March, mid-May to mid-July, and mid-September to mid-November. Interns are supervised by a professional staff member. Work assignments range from research on political or economic issues to servicing the General Assembly.

In the past, between 200 and 250 students have participated per year. Forms completed by the applicants and their graduate school must be submitted six months prior to internship. Grade transcripts or lists of courses taken and an essay stating the participant's purpose for enrolling in the internship are required. A sample research paper is requested. People with second-level university degrees are not considered. Other programs for interns are available at offices away from headquarters or through specialized agencies, such as UNICEF. These agencies should be contacted directly.

U.S. Department of State
Office of Recruitment
Student Programs
P.O. Box 9317
Arlington, VA 22219

Director
Department of State Foreign Affairs Fellowship Program
The Woodrow Wilson National Fellowship Program
Box 2437
Princeton, NJ 08543-2437
703-875-7490

The State Department takes on as many as 350 nonpaid interns per year. The majority of interns work in the Washington, D.C., office as junior professionals. Assignments vary from work in the Department of Public Affairs to cataloguing historical documents. Interns are sometimes sent to work in overseas posts. They are assigned as junior foreign service officers working in an embassy. Overseas interns are chosen by foreign bureau managers on the basis of grades, experience, language skill and general match of skills with job available.

There are three internship periods that last three-and-a-half to four-and-a-half months: summer, fall and winter. For interns posted overseas, accommodations are provided. Washington interns must find their own housing. All program participants must pay their own travel costs and living expenses.

United States Student Association (USSA)
815 15th St. NW
Washington, DC 20005
202-347-4769

The 350 student governments representing 3.5 million students focus on access to higher education, organizing grassroots movements to broaden the financing for higher education and lobbying for increased access to higher education for minorities. USSA also offers skill training programs for organizers. Student governments elect to join the Association as members for a yearly fee ranging form $400 to $1,000.

The White House
Intern Program
Office of Presidential Personnel
Old Executive Office Building, Room 151
Washington, DC 20500
202-456-6676

Volunteer internships during one of the summer sessions chosen from 22 White House offices. While daily activities vary as related to the particular office, interns will have a high level of busywork.

Additional listings

American Indian College Fund
21 W. 68th St.
New York, NY 10023
212-787-6312

Development Group for Alternative Policies
1400 I St. NW, Suite 520
Washington, DC 20005
202-898-1566

Food & Water Incorporated
225 Lafayette St., Suite 612
New York, NY 10012
212-941-9340

Works to halt water pollution and food irradiation through public awareness, lobbying and educating.

Food First/Institute for Food and Development Policy
145 9th St.
San Francisco, CA 94103
800-888-3314

Works to end hunger through public education.

Human Rights Advocates
P.O. Box 5675
Berkeley, CA 94705
415-841-2928

Works with the UN and OAS on human rights issues.

Adventure Careers

Human Rights Watch
36 W. 44th St., #911
New York, NY 10036
212-840-9460

International Indian Treaty Council and the American Indian Movement
710 Clayton St., #1
San Francisco, CA 94117
415-566-0251

International Women's Rights Action Watch
Humphrey Institute of Public Affairs
University of Minnesota
301 19th Ave. S.
Minneapolis, MN 55455

Monitors implementation of UN Convention on the Elimination of All Forms of Discrimination Against Women.

Mobilization for Survival
853 Broadway, #2109
New York, NY 10003
212-533-0008

Works to ban nuclear weapons and power through coalition of local peace, disarmament, safe energy, and community organizations.

National Abortion Rights Action League (NARAL)
1101 14th St. NW, 5th Fl.
Washington, DC 20005
202-408-4600

National Clean Air Coalition
503 7th St. SE
Washington, DC 20003
202-797-5446

National Gay Rights Advocates
540 Castro St.
San Francisco, CA 94114
415-863-3624

Challenges laws, policies and discrimination against lesbians, gay men and people infected with the HIV virus.

Oxfam America
26 West St.
Boston, MA 02111
617-482-1211

International funding agency for self-help development projects and disaster relief in Africa, Asia and Latin America.

Planned Parenthood Federation of America
810 7th Ave.
New York, NY 10019
212-541-7800

Provides sex education and the availability of birth control devices around the world. In U.S., family planning, medical aid and counseling.

The United Negro College Fund
500 E. 62nd St.
New York, NY 10021
212-326-1100

Women Strike for Peace
145 S. 13th St.
Philadelphia, PA 19107
215-923-0861

World Health Organization
Global Programme on AIDS, CH-1211
Geneva 27, Switzerland

UN agency coordinates international AIDS reporting and assists countries with AIDS programs.

Reading and references

Newsletters and magazines

Public Citizen
2000 P St. NW
Washington, DC 20036
202-833-3000

Public Citizen is the magazine by the organization of the same name, founded by Ralph Nader in 1971. The group is a nonprofit citizen research, lobbying and litigation organization working for consumer rights in the marketplace, for safe products, for a healthy environment and workplace, for clean and safe energy sources and for corporate and government accountability.

The Green Party USA puts out the following publications:

Green Bulletin	*Green Notes*
Green Synthesis	*Green Letter*

These can be obtained through The Green Clearinghouse, P.O. Box 30208, Kansas City, MO 64112, 816-931-9366.

Reports and publications

The American Civil Liberties Union (ACLU), defends citizen's civil liberties. Through legislative lobbying, litigation and public education, it works to defend freedom of expression, equal protection of the laws, due process, privacy and other rights guaranteed by the Constitution. The ACLU maintains three publication lists:

1. The National Office in New York maintains a long list of ACLU handbooks (*Candidates and Voters, Employment*), briefing papers (*Freedom of Expression, Racial Justice*), reports and civil liberties books. Write ACLU Literature Department, 132 W. 43rd St., New York, NY 10036.

2. The Washington Office puts out publications of the Center for National Security Studies, the ACLU Newsletter, *Civil Liberties Alert*, public policy reports and general civil liberties information. Write ACLU Washington Office, 122 Maryland Ave. NE, Washington, DC 20002.

3. The Prison Project in Washington reports: Write The National Prison Project, 1875 Connecticut Ave. NW, Suite 410, Washington, DC 20009.

Development Reports—a forum for scholars and activists to publish works in progress.

Policy Briefs—analysis of contemporary issues.

Action Alerts—publications about various problems in the world and actions that are being taken or need to be taken. Subjects range from alternative agriculture to organic farming in Cuba.

Call **Food First** for their great book selection and publication series. They can be reached via Subterranean Company in Monroe, OR; 503-847-5274; Fax: 503-847-6018. Here is a summary of their publications:

United Nations Environmental Programme
North American Regional Office, DC2-803
#2 United Nations Plaza
New York, NY 10017
212-963-8093

UNEP publishes studies and general information reports on many environmental topics, including the ozone layer and global warming.

Books

Bridging the Global Gap: A Handbook to Linking Citizens of the First and Third Worlds. Medea Benjamin and Andrea Freedman. Cabin John, Maryland. (Seven Locks Press, 1989). Copies can be obtained through Global Exchange, 415-255-7296.

Education for Action: Where to Go for Undergraduate and Graduate Studies that Focus on Social Change. Edited by Sean Brooks and Cory Wechsler. ISBN 0-935028-64-1. (Food First, San Francisco.) Orders: 800-274-7826.

A guide to progressive programs in agriculture, anthropology, development studies, economics, ethnic studies, history, law, management, peace studies, political science, public health, sociology, urban planning and women's studies.

The 20-Something American Dream: A Cross-Country Quest for a Generation. Michael Lee Cohen (Plume, published by the Penguin Group, 1994).

Features a series of interviews that reveal more than the "slacker" myth about the twenty-something generation. It's a good source for ideas of how other people in their 20s are living out their ideals.

The Call of Service: A Witness to Idealism. Robert Coles (Houghton Mifflin Corp., New York, 1993).

The Moral Dimensions of Public Policy Choice: Beyond the Market Paradigm. John Martin Gillroy, Maurice Wade, ed. (University of Pittsburgh Press, Pittsburgh, 1992).

The Quickening of America: Rebuilding Our Nation, Remaking Our Lives. Frances Moore Lappe & Paul Martin DuBois (Food First, San Francisco). Orders: 800-274-7826.

A book about the grassroots approach to problems and how it's working in the U.S. today.

Chapter 8

On the Road: A Guide to Travel and Adventure

In the '60s, all you needed was a thumb to explore the world and discover adventure and opportunity. At least that is how we remember it. The Merry Pranksters crossed the country in an old school bus, the infamous Ken Kesey at the wheel. Before that, Jack Kerouac went *On the Road* and made a mint on the book about his adventures. In fact, there is a long literary history of hitting the road. In Hemingway's generation, they went to Europe, landing down-and-out in Paris (or fighting in Spain). In the '50s, the beat generation hitchhiked across America and fetched up in colorfully impoverished neighborhoods to write bestselling novels. No longer.

Maybe would-be authors still crisscross the globe by thumb. But there are far better ways to experience the world, ways that offer more discovery and excitement with less risk. They take more planning than hitchhiking, but work a whole lot better.

As you consider travel in general, it ought to be intimately related to your personal and career development. Travel is often the vehicle for creating an adventure. A job in a foreign country or in another part of the U.S. offers a dimension lacking in jobs back home. And travel is not only a good way to gain exposure to the diversity of ideas and cultures, it is also, at times, the only way to go deep into a particular area of interest. Many adventure careers focus on a narrow field of interest for which there is no critical mass of jobs, internships and so forth in any one location. But when you consider the entire world as your workplace, it becomes possible to put together a rich collection of experiences in any field, no matter how obscure.

Educational travel, short and long

One of the best alternatives is a preplanned educational trip utilizing one of the many organized programs available around the world. Educational travel is not an interlude in your personal and career development—it is an integral, often critical, part of it. The word "vacation" is from a Latin root meaning freedom or exception, and we traditionally think of a vacation as freedom from our routine, humdrum lives and careers. There are many things wrong with this concept of travel. Perhaps it is easiest just to describe the alternative: A life that is routinely exciting and engaging, in which vacations are an integral part rather than an exception. In fact, the vacation ought to be a catalyst, used to jumpstart our routine lives and turn them into more exciting and rewarding journeys in their own right.

For example, you might use your summer or vacation time to learn a new skill—how to rock climb, how to speak Italian, how to excavate archaeological ruins—then pursue your new interest via an internship, a year of specialized study abroad, a job teaching the skill at a camp, or whatever. This might lead you to other adventures, and eventually even to a full-blown career in which you work your way up through jobs in the field, go back to school to obtain an advanced degree in the field or create your own entrepreneurial job in it. Or maybe you will go on to other adventures and other educational trips before settling on a career—but you will always benefit from the knowledge and experience gained from an educational trip, whether you go on to specialize in that field or not.

Undertake travel for experience and wisdom, but do not underestimate the possibility of practical career development through travel as well. Travel, properly pursued, is a form of learning, and learning can lead to interesting work opportunities, which in turn can lead to more learning, which in turn...you get the idea. Now get moving!

In the "Personal Accounts" section of this chapter is an interesting anecdote from one woman who filled a year between college and graduate school with a trip to Japan. Actually, the trip was less than a month long. But the planning took time, and her preparations included an intensive Japanese language course and sufficient work to save the money needed for her trip. In this sense, the trip did fill a year—and it certainly *enlivened* the year. A trip like this is never over—this woman will more than likely return to Japan, and her experience and knowledge of the Japanese language and culture will probably shape her graduate studies and career as well.

Meredith's trip involved air and train travel, as well as the use of various hotels—some quite hard to find! Obviously the logistics of travel and lodging can be important, whether you head out behind the wheel of a car or in the seat of a bus, train or plane. Travel can be difficult or easy. And it can be cheap or outlandishly expensive. In fact, the difference between the cheapest and most expensive tickets, hotel rooms and the like can be huge. If you know what you're doing, you can often pay half price or less on airline tickets, for instance. Chapter 12 includes practical advice on the logistics of travel, and is recommended for anyone planning a trip of *any* sort.

We want to add a general observation about travel, however: In travel, unlike most services, you get what you *don't* pay for. What we mean is that people generally pay more in order to see, do, experience and learn *less*. Expensive travel options insulate the travelers and protect them from the very environment to which they have traveled.

The most expensive hotels create an environment in which the traveler feels right at home—English is spoken, the other guests are American, and even the food is American. This is *anti*-travel—travel for people who are afraid of the unfamiliar and are avoiding novel experiences that might contribute to adventure careers. In many cases, you get a lot more by traveling for a lot less.

Take a train, subway or bus, and you have a unique opportunity to experience local culture and meet locals (please read the travel books of that veteran train traveler, Paul Theroux, if you don't believe us). Stay at a local bed and breakfast, camp in a national park or exchange homes with a local resident (check Chapter 12 for networks), and you will experience and learn far more than the person who stays at a large, luxurious hotel. This means you should feel good about feeling cheap when it comes to travel. The more research and thinking you do, the lower the cost of your trip and the more you will get out of it.

Personal Accounts

Meredith on life and foreign travel

Meredith H. Sherter, a recent graduate of the University of Massachusetts at Amherst, is a native of nearby Greenfield, Mass. She was 22 at the time of her great adventure and is currently the manager of an Amherst cafe. She will pursue a master's degree in the impractical field of speech communication at Pennsylvania State University.

Practicality is really a four-letter word, it just seems to have more letters. Perhaps it only *evokes* four-letter words. Whatever the case, practicality is the catchword that the older generation directs toward the younger in an attempt to maintain a hold on the elusive "good ole days." Its manifestation is as follows: Going to college is the only practical move to make, but be sure to choose a practical major in order to get a practical job. Once this has occurred the next practical step is to own a practical car and, when practical, to start a family. But be sure to pick a practical spouse!

It may appear that we, the younger generation, are simply rebelling, as we are prone to do. After all, James Dean memorabilia sales are on the rise. The reality is, however, that for the moment this brand of practicality is unattainable and may not be what we need in the first place.

I went to college, but the practical majors such as business and engineering simply didn't hold my attention. After four years, I graduated with a double major in English and communications. Make that a triple major—*impracticality*. I went from the safety of

188

college into a recession and even though I had no loans to pay, practical jobs remained scarce. Aside from this, I knew I wanted to continue my education through graduate school in hopes of someday becoming a college professor. I had, however, for reasons I can't even comprehend, neglected to apply to graduate school during my senior year. Thus, I had a year off with no definite plans—except for graduate school applications.

The pile of applications and an increase in my work hours at a local cafe soon produced that queasy claustrophobia of dissatisfaction. My life was not only impractical, it was stagnant! It was at this point I learned that my older brother and an old friend of mine had both gotten work teaching English in Japan (my brother in Ikaruga, my friend in Hiroshima).

Why shouldn't I go to Japan, too? I had two different people to see with whom I could stay for free. Why, this seemed quite *practical*. I decided to begin planning a trip, and I enrolled in an intensive Japanese language class. Suddenly I had a goal: I studied hard, worked more to save money, sent my applications in early and boarded a plane to Osaka on Dec. 23, 1991, with the majority of my savings in traveler's checks and a 24-day Japan Rail pass. It was my first trip out of the country.

The notes on my trip fill half a notebook, but here are a few of the highlights:

The book that went whap in the night

My friend and I boarded an overnight train from Aomori to Sapporo at 11:30 p.m., already exhausted from days of hard travel. We walked through eight cars before we found two empty seats together. Actually, they were inhabited by a bag and a pair of legs. In the facing seat was a Japanese man in his middle 20s. I asked him if we could sit and he grudgingly moved his bag and feet. We squeezed in and fell asleep immediately.

Around 2 a.m., I woke up to find my friend wide awake, too, and looking annoyed. While asleep, my friend's knee had drifted into our neighbor's territory, whereupon my friend had been awakened by a swift crack upon the knee from the man's book. As we talked about this in English, the man woke up again and hit us both on the forehead with his book. With a loud "Ssssshh!" he returned to his slumber, a sour look fixed on his face. We were horrified but also amused. What happened to the stereotype of Japanese courtesy and unassertiveness?

Karaoke samaritans

In general, however, people were remarkably friendly. That was the only time anyone hit me over the head with a book. At another point in our train travels, we arrived in Nikko at 11:30 p.m. to cold, bare streets and had no idea where to spend the night. As we walked we passed a few hotels, but their lobbies were darkened and their doors locked. The first life we found was in a karaoke bar (where the guests sing to canned music), filled with neighbors and regulars. It was here that two tall, disheveled young *gai-jin* (foreigners) became stars. We were ushered into the bar with warm smiles, friendly handshakes and an assortment of phrasebook English, and were given free food and coffee.

The owner of the bar set to work calling hotels while another, a young woman named Tamiko, came over and sang the Beatles' "Yesterday" to us. (The only other English-language song available there was Elvis' "Love Me Tender," which I was later compelled to sing to the group.) Finally, the owner claimed success and Tamiko led us, along with a large group of the guests, to a nearby hotel. The hotel owner greeted us in the dark lobby, half-awake, and checked us in. When he handed us our room key, our escorts from the bar broke into loud applause!

I think my most interesting experience overall was the experience of being a minority. For the first time in my life I stuck out from the rest, I was automatically different and was responded to on the basis of this difference. Everyone would stare at me as I passed by and sometimes I noted that people would avoid contact on trains. Knowing that people were talking about me was the perfect accompaniment to my discomfort.

I was struck by the cultural differences between Japan and the U.S. You need to know a lot more than the language to understand and fit into Japanese society. For example, I was in Japan during President Bush's visit (he led a trade delegation to Japan to pursue concessions for the U.S. auto makers). It wasn't so bad that he got sick and passed out at a formal dinner. This was excusable to the Japanese because he couldn't help it. However, he committed a major *faux pas* when he blew his nose in public—and on television, no less! In Japan, this is viewed as urinating on television would be in America. Apparently, no information about Japanese culture and customs had been prepared for Bush by his aids. The nose-blowing incident played on Japanese television as often as a commercial while I was there.

All in all, my trip to Japan was a much-needed adventure. Experiencing a new culture and being a stranger in a strange land helped me realize much about myself. Removing myself from the everyday concerns of practicality actually helped me mature and I returned knowing that I can survive and thrive because I am capable and responsible. I know that I want to experience more, learn, travel and maybe even return to teach in Japan after I receive my master's degree. The experience provided me with vitality—I can't wait for my next adventure, and I'm excited about my future.

The most important advice I can give to people in their 20s, and to all, is to travel somewhere by yourself. Even if it is to visit friends, it is important to spend time alone in an unfamiliar environment where the focus is not on the everyday. This unattached perspective is an important one for coming to terms with self and situation. Oh, yes—and a bit of practical advice: If you happen to travel to Japan, please don't blow your nose in public.

Laurae: A career in eco-tourism

Laurae Lister's career path, to date, epitomizes the adventure career concept. She has changed directions repeatedly, but each new direction has built upon skills, interests and qualifications developed in previous experiences.

Laurae, who majored in Chinese and minored in anthropology, first taught English in Taiwan. She worked as a travel agent in New York. Trips to Greece led to a new direction: She opened and operated a ceramics and art gallery in collaboration with a Greek family in Athens.

Adventure Careers

Laurae returned to the U.S., and to travel and tourism, and became interested in the impact of tourism on the local society, economy and environment. So it was natural to go back to school to study eco-tourism. (She obtained funding in the form of a merit award from the Office of Minority Graduate Student Recruitment at the University of Massachusetts.) She is now studying for her master's, focusing on eco-tourism, and has opened a travel agency specializing in eco-tourism.

As a long-time travel agent, and a latent naturalist, a point came recently in my career when I could no longer ignore the unspoken priorities of the travel industry. The distribution network now in use has a clear hierarchy: the supplier at the top, the client next, and lastly if at all—the destination. It is the goal of eco-tourism to change that order: to the destination first, next the client and lastly the supplier. Eco-tourism puts the destination first by turning the destination into the supplier.

Loosely defined, eco-tourism is the principle of traveling with minimal negative impact on host environments—both natural and cultural.

An example will make this clearer: You are taking a trip to Jamaica. You may have chosen it for the price, after investigating the rates for other "sun" destinations. Your package includes airfare on a U.S. carrier, a Holiday Inn reservation on the beach and vouchers for transfers. This is not an eco-tourist trip. Why? First, you need to look at where your money goes: a U.S. carrier, a U.S. hotel chain, various fees to arrangers in the U.S. who set up the package. So far, very little for the host, Jamaica. All right, but won't you be spending money for food, tips, souvenirs while you are there?

Here are some questions about that: Will you eat Jamaican food, or will you be eating food imported from home? In many developing nations dependent on tourism, the money spent on imports of food, as well as other familiar amenities, largely offsets the income from selling it. When tipping service persons: Is that person sacrificing his or her dignity in exchange for your currency? Has the staff altered its cultural patterns to accommodate yours? In purchasing souvenirs: Was the artisan making them for tourists, or are they authentic to the culture? In other words: Has tourism created a market that inhibits or discourages authentic culture?

Some environmental questions: Is your beach front room on a strip of hotels that bisect a natural area? Where are wastes being disposed? Does your hotel offer unlimited water use while citizens are rationed fresh water? In short, what impact are *you* having on your destination?

So. Now I have taken the fun out of your vacation. Why must even spring break be full of decisions? For myself, eco-tourism is not a matter of taking the fun out of travel—it is bringing the true point of travel back into it. I travel to see the world, and be part of the world. I want to be affected by my experiences, and the only way to really do that is to take responsibility for my own impacts. I want to meet real people, see real things and have real experiences—not be provided things that have been contrived for me.

Well, there are alternatives if we are willing to see ourselves as not simply one person, but as a large, powerful lobbying group with a huge bankroll. Here are some steps we can take to be part of a responsible movement:

- **Stay at a locally owned bed & breakfast.** It is cheaper, you will meet people who actually live at your destination and you will be contributing financially to the real community. Think of it as the "trickle up" economic theory. The money you save by using inexpensive lodgings will more than make up for telephone calls to track down bed & breakfasts. The more adventurous traveler may want to "wing it" by arriving without any reservations, but an intermediate idea would be to make a reservation for at least one night at a traditional hotel, then spend the first day wandering and inquiring about local B&Bs. Many smaller operations neither list themselves internationally nor do they advertise—frankly, those will be the best finds! The more people seek out such accommodations, though, the easier it gets—and the message to the travel industry is clear: We want this option.

- **Don't stay on the beach.** The travel industry is a major contributor to marine ecosystem pollution because it centers around waterfronts. You can decrease demand for that kind of development by not using it. Walk to the beach, use public transportation or try inland tourism. Getting away from traditionally tourism-oriented areas will also mean lower accommodations, food and other incidental costs. Best of all, people who are not weary of tourists are more likely to treat you as a guest, rather than a necessary evil.

- **Use mass transportation when traveling.** This is not always easy. The comfort and sanitation level of some public transportation systems discourage travelers out for a good, convenient and familiar time. The environmental advantages are self-evident, but there is also the element of experiencing a destination as its "natives" do. This will also be the cheapest way to get around.

- **Respect the local environment.** Consider whether you are treating your surroundings like a resident or a visitor. Taking cues from the residents rather than other tourists can often be helpful.

- **Choose your destination carefully.** Countries like Belize are using tourism dollars to decrease the need for nonrenewable uses of land, like large-scale export agriculture that destroys rare tropical forests and the sale of products made from rare species of animals and plants. Many countries have policies that involve local citizens in decision-making and policy implementation in tourism: You can "vote" for such policies with your choice to travel there.

Before taking any trip, it helps to educate yourself on the social system and culture. My experience has made me increasingly skeptical of second-hand information, and I have little faith in third-hand reports. I now rely heavily on a strategy of collecting every bit of information I can get, and then being prepared to be surprised. Knowing a lot before you go does not mean predictability, it means getting the most potential from your experience.

Travel with the conscious purpose of expanding your horizons, rather than exploiting a cheap destination for the creature comforts that cost too much at home. Use travel to learn more about your own culture through comparison with others.

Accept a little inconvenience, some strange foods, language barriers, new smells, a few stares, funny-looking toilets and the reality of poverty. When you do this you are also accepting your place as a world citizen—and becoming part of a global "we" instead of an "us vs. them." In the global ecology that younger generations are inheriting, travel is a classroom to learn what role each individual will ultimately play.

Some cautions. Eco-tourism has already gained a reputation for being expensive and exotic—which it can be. Many pricey, prepackaged tours to unusual places that call themselves "eco-friendly" are not necessarily so. By doing your own research you can take control of your impact as a traveler, and control your costs as well.

Another concern is the ongoing conflict between the concerns of environmentalists and indigenous populations. It is common for outsiders to lose sight of the immediate concerns of a society when ecological preservation is at issue. As one cynical associate of mine puts it: "We already destroyed our environments, but *you* cannot!"

I traveled, and was part of the travel industry, for years before I began to identify the enormity of its potential, both positive and negative. Now I am seeing an increased recognition and acceptance of eco-tourism both in and outside the industry. I look forward to working in a travel industry and a society that sees travel as a precious gift, and eco-tourism as a given.

On the Road Directory

This directory includes credit and noncredit educational travel offerings, with an emphasis on summer and vacation-length programs that feature excitement and adventure, such as traveling through Italy to study art or walking beaches to find, tag and study nesting sea turtles. One organization even offers *time* travel (the best way to learn history—providing you don't mind outhouses). At the end of this directory we have listed information sources if you want to work while on the road.

By and large, these are *not* full-time, year-long study abroad options. They are study vacations, summer schools and similar miniadventures that often lead to longer-term interests and experiences.

If you plan on traveling in Europe, one of the best guides we've seen is *The Berkeley Guide: Europe On the Loose 1995*, written by a group of Berkeley students (Fodor's Travel Publications, Inc., 1994). It's full of maps and insider's guides to the cities—jazz clubs, where to sleep and eat cheap. It's a budget traveler's dream come true. If you want to be an armchair tourist, you can skim through and talk like you've been there (like me—just ask me about Lapland). There are numerous *Berkeley Guides* written for individual countries, so if you want to get specific, it's a fun way to go.

As you leave to traverse the planet, keep in mind your responsibility to "take only photographs and leave only footprints." (Well, maybe we'll let you buy a souvenir for your grandmother...) Seriously, though, one of the growing fields in the tourist industry is eco-tourism, also called "nature tourism." It is designed to aid conservation efforts around the world. So, instead of sitting in a bus with 30 people being carted around from market to market, one is given the chance to "walk lightly on the earth" and buy responsibly (no ivory or tortoiseshell, for example). Eco-tours can range from safaris to snorkeling to being a gofer for a research team for a couple of weeks. We have included a section on nature tourism agencies and organizations in this chapter; refer to the Chapter 9 directory for additional listings of these organizations according to the specific types of activities they offer. A great resource for eco-tourism is *Eco-tours and Nature Getaways* by Alice Geffen and Carole Berglie (Clarkson Potter Publishers, New York).

Adult Education Study Tours
Granville House, 49 The Mall
Faversham, Kent ME13 8JN, England
44-759-539744

Two-day to three-week tours from art and archaeology to wildlife ecology.

Andover Foundation for Archaeological Research
1 Woodland Rd.
Andover, MA 01810
508-470-0840

Archaeological expeditions in Central and South America, approx. $1,200/wk. and $2,200/mo. including room and board.

Appalachian Mountain Club
P.O. Box 298
Gorham, NH 03581
603-466-2727; Fax: 603-466-2720

Workshops, travel for ecology.

Appalachian State University
Office of International Studies
Boone, NC 28608
704-262-2046

Summer art studies in Switzerland and an English travel program, "Bards and Balladeers of Brittania."

The Archaeological Conservancy
5301 Central Ave. NE, Suite 1218
Albuquerque, NM 87108
505-266-1540

Archaeological Tours
271 Madison Ave., Suite 904
New York, NY 10016

Archaeology Field School
University of Vermont
Anthropology Dept., Williams Hall
Burlington, VT 05401
802-656-3884

These three organizations offer a variety of archaeological tours and expeditions throughout the world.

The Art Institute of Chicago
Michigan Ave. at Adams St.
Chicago, IL 60603
312-443-3917

One- to three-week art tours to domestic and foreign destinations.

The Athens Centre
48 Archimidous St.
11636 Athens, Greece
30-701-5242

Summer sessions in Greece, with credit available through affiliated U.S. colleges.

Center for Global Education
Augsburg College
2211 Riverside Ave.
Minneapolis, MN 55454
612-330-1159

Travel seminars around the world on poverty and injustice.

Adventure Careers

Alumni Association Travel Program
Passport Travel
Clemson University Alumni Office
P.O. Box 345603
Clemson, SC 29634
803-656-2345

Year-round program, with tours led by university facility.

Denver Museum of Natural History
Public Programs Dept.
2001 Colorado Blvd.
Denver, CO 80205
303-370-6307

Wide variety of educational tours led by museum staff.

Dillington College for Adult Education
Ilminster, Somerset TA19 9DT
England

More than 100 short courses year-round; reasonable room and board costs.

The Dylan Thomas School
The University College of Wales
Aberystwyth, SY23 2AZ, U.K.

Two-week course on poet Dylan Thomas.

Earthwatch
680 Mount Auburn St.
Watertown, MA 02172
617-926-8200

Volunteers work on field research projects worldwide.

Edinboro University Oxford Experience
Edinboro Univ, Doucette Hall, Rm. 102
Edinboro, PA 16444
814-732-2884

A two-week program at Exeter College, Oxford, in England.

Edinburgh University Summer Schools
Center for Continuing Ed.
University of Edinburgh
11 Buccleuch Place
Edinburgh, EH89LW, Scotland
44-31-677 1011, ext. 6686

Several-week courses and study tours, including film, music and drama festival courses.

Fairfield University Study Tours in Italy
School of Continuing Ed.
Fairfield University
Fairfield, CT 06430
203-254-4220

Ten-day and one-month programs in Florence. Studio arts, art history, archaeology, Italian language, cooking.

Gallatin Division
New York University
715 Broadway, 6th Fl.
New York, NY 10003
212-998-7370

Four-credit summer program in Florence, Italy, with lodging. Italian Renaissance art and literature.

School for Summer and Continuing Education
Georgetown University
Washington, DC 20057
202-687-5942

Summer travel courses to Europe and South America.

Insight Travel
602 South High St.
Yellow Springs, OH 45387
513-767-1102

Buddhist pilgrimage/study tour to India and Nepal. Lectures, monasteries and meditation.

Institute for Scholars and International Studies in Europe (ISISE)
142 Woody Creek Plaza
Woody Creek, CO 81656
Attn: Susan Johnson

College courses available—maximum of 10 weeks.

International Summer School in Irish Studies
Department of Education
University College
Cork, Ireland
44-353-21-276871

Journeys Into American Indian Territory
P.O. Box 929
Westhampton Beach, NY 11978

Lamar University Summer Study Program
Division of Public Services and
Continuing Education
P.O. Box 10008
Beaumont, TX 77710
409-880-8431

For-credit international trips usually last three weeks.

Los Angeles World Affairs Council
Diplomatic Tours
911 Wilshire Blvd., Suite 1730
Los Angeles, CA 90017
213-628-2333

Travel that features diplomatic briefings at U.S. embassies and foreign ministries.

Mexi-Mayan Academic Travel, Inc.
125675 Knoebel Drive
Lemont, IL 60439
708-972-9090

Museum of American Folk Art Explorer's Club
61 W. 62nd St., 3rd Fl.
New York, NY 10023
212-977-7170

The one-week Santa Fe trip is a must, plus other offerings as well.

National Trust for Historic Preservation
Special Programs
1785 Mass. Ave. NW
Washington, DC 20036
202-673-4138

Historical tours and trips.

National Wildlife Federation
1400 Sixteenth St. NW
Washington, DC 20036
800-432-6564

One-week summer conservation summits at a variety of locations.

The New York Botanical Garden
Travel Program
Education Dept.
Bronx, NY 10458
718-817-8705

Reasonably-priced foreign garden trips.

New York University
International Programs
School of Continuing Ed.
331 Shimkin Hall
50 W. 4th St.
New York, NY 10012-1165
212-998-7133

Tours to Egypt, France, Holland and Belgium and elsewhere. Non-credit summer program at Emmanuel College, Cambridge, England.

Adventure Careers

Norlands Living History Center
Washburn-Norlands, RFD 2
Livermore Falls, ME 04254
207-897-2236

Time travel! Adult live-in weekends put you in rural Maine in the 1870s.

Office of International Studies
School of Visual Arts
209 E. 23rd St.
New York, NY 10010
212-679-7350

Three-week summer program on archaeology in Greece.

Summer Programs
Office of Special Programs
Parsons School of Design
66 Fifth Ave.
New York, NY 10011
212-741-8975

Month-long programs in France, Italy, England, Israel, Japan and West Africa teach participants about topics, from graphic design to art history. All-inclusive fees from $3,000 to $5,000.

Collegiate Program
People to People International
501 East Armour
Kansas City, MO 64109
816-531-4701

Programs for college and graduate students offered in Europe, Asia, Latin America.

Pitt's Informal Program
University of Pittsburgh
3804 Forbes Ave.
Pittsburgh, PA 15260
412-648-2560

San Diego Natural History Museum
Education Department
P.O. Box 1390
San Diego, CA 92112
619-232-3821 (press 5)

Natural history trips to Baja and other West Coast destinations.

San Diego State University
Extended Studies Travel Programs
5630 Hardy Ave.
San Diego, CA 92182
619-594-5154

For-credit trips from the Galapagos Islands to Greece.

Semester at Sea
University of Pittsburgh
811 William Pitt Union
Pittsburgh, PA 15260
800-854-0195

For-credit sea travel on the ocean liner *S.S. Universe.*

Smithsonian Study Tours and Seminars
1100 Jefferson Dr. SW
Rm. 3045
Smithsonian Institution
Washington, DC 20560
202-357-4700

Summer College and Travel/Study Programs
Stanford Alumni Association
Bowman House
Stanford University
Stanford, CA 94305
415-723-2027

Eco-tourism

Amazon Outreach
1500 WE 3rd Court
Deerfield Beach, FL 33441
305-698-6302

Company run by a Peruvian Indian, Ney Pinero, who builds his own rafts for each trip and then donates them to the Amazon Indians at the end of the run.

Arctic Edge/TransSiberian Tours
P.O. Box 4850
Whitehorse, Yukon Territory
Canada Y1A 4N6
403-633-5470; Fax: 403-633-3820

Arctic Edge offers a range of boating trips, from rafting to canoeing, as well as trekking and dogsledding in the Yukon. As conservationists, they offer "eco-tours," trips that allow you to see the wilderness off the beaten path. Prices vary according to length of trip and comfort level. TransSiberian Tours, their Russian partner, offers natural history and cultural trips (including diving in Lake Baikal and birdwatching).

Baja Expeditions
2625 Garnet Ave.
San Diego, CA 92109
619-581-3311; Fax: 619-581-6542

Sea kayaking off the Baja Peninsula, run by both American and Mexican guides. Outfits the Sierra Club and the American Cetacean Society.

The Dream Team
P.O. Box 033271
Indialantic, FL 32903-0271

Dive with the dolphins. It's good diving in a friendly atmosphere, without the frills.

Four Corners School of Outdoor Education
East Route
Monticello, UT 84535
800-525-4456

An expensive, but exciting, adventure. Leave from Minneapolis, MN, to study and track wolves and visit the Canadian Rockies. Essentially a wolf study trip guided by the Audubon Center and the International Wolf Center.

Grand Canyon Expeditions
P.O. Box O
Kanab, UT 84741
800-544-2691

Raft trips on the Colorado. They offer some special interest expeditions, including astronomy, geology and photography.

Hawk, I'm Your Sister
P.O. Box 9109
Santa Fe, NM 87504-9109
505-984-2268

Canoe trips through the Everglades. Some trips are for women only.

Inuit Adventures
19950 Clark Graham
Baie d'Urfe, Quebec H9X 3R8
Canada
800-465-9474; Fax: 514-457-4626

Trips led by the Inuit into their own land in Arctic Quebec in an effort to preserve their cultural heritage and their land by sharing them with others.

Adventure Careers

Eco-travel resources

Contact these organizations for information about opportunities and eco-tourism agencies in your area.

The Responsible Tourist
P.O. Box 827
San Anselmo, CA 94979
415-258-6594

Travel Links, Co-op America
2100 M St. NW, #403
Washington, DC 20036
202-872-5307

Sierra Club
Outings Department
730 Polk St.
San Francisco, CA 94109
415-776-2211. ext. 6884

The World Wildlife Fund
1250 24th St.
Washington, DC 20037
202-778-9683

The National Audubon Society
613 Riversville Rd.
Greenwich, CT 06831
203-869-5272

One World Family Travel Network
Lost Valley Center, Inc.
81868 Lost Valley Lane
Dexter, OR 97431
503-937-3351

Reading and references

The Au Pair and Nanny's Guide to Working Abroad. Susan Griffith and Sharon Legg. (Vacation Work, Oxford.)

Bridging the Global Gap: A Handbook to Linking Citizens of the First and Third Worlds. Medea Benjamin and Andrea Freedman. (Seven Locks Press, Cabin John, Maryland, 1989.)

The Complete Guide to America's National Parks. (National Park Foundation.)
Provides detailed information on the 367 national parks—fees, mailing addresses, seasons, facilities, etc.

Directory of Alternative Travel Resources. Dianne G. Brause. (One World Family Travel Network, Dexter, OR, 1988.) $7.50.

Directory of International Internships: A World of Opportunities. J. Roberts, C. Gliozzo and J. Shingleton, Eds. (Michigan State University, East Lansing, MI 48824, annual, $20.)

Directory of Overseas Summer Jobs. David Woodworth, Editor. (Writer's Digest Books, annual, $10.95.)

EarthTrips: A Guide to Nature Travel on a Fragile Planet. Dwight Holing. (Living Planet Press, Venice, CA, 1992.)

Eco-tours and Nature Getaways: A Guide to Environmental Vacations Around the World. Alice Geffen and Carole Berglie. (Clarkson N. Potter, Inc., New York, NY, 1993.)

Eco-Vacations: Enjoy Yourself and Save the Earth. Evelyn Kaye. (Blue Penguin Publications, Leonia, NJ, 1991.)

Fodor's Healthy Escapes. Bernard Burt. (Fodor's Travel.)
Covers health and fitness resorts throughout the U.S., Canada, Hawaii and the Caribbean. Not cheap, but maybe you can try for a job at one of the resorts.

Going Places: The High School Student's Guide to Study, Travel and Adventure Abroad. Compiled by Council on International Educational Exchange (CIEE). (St. Martin's Press, 4th ed.) Orders: 800-349-2433.

Handle with Care: A Guide to Responsible Travel in Developing Countries. Scott Graham. (Food First, San Francisco, CA.) Orders: 800-274-7826.

Insight Guides: Native America. Edited by John Gattuso. (Houghton Mifflin Co., Boston, MA.)
Written by various authors, including a number of Native Americans. Provides a guide to the people, groups and culture, as well as a travel guide for visiting tribes around the country.

International Directory of Voluntary Work. Roger Brown and David Woodworth. (Vacation Work, 9 Park End Street, Oxford, England.)

International Workcamp Directory. (VFP International Workcamps, 43 Tiffany Road, Belmont, VT 05730.) $10.

Overseas Development Network Opportunities Catalog. (IIE Books, 809 U.N. Plaza, New York, NY 10017.)

The Sierra Club National Traveler: Wild France. Douglas Botting. (Sierra Club Books, San Francisco, CA.)

Student Travels—magazine for international travel, study and work. (Published bimonthly by CIEE, 205 East 42nd Street, New York, NY 10017; 212-661-1414.)

Adventure Careers

Summer Jobs in Britain. Emily Hatchwell, Editor. (Vacation Work, annual, $12.95.)

Transitions Abroad. Subscriber Services, Dept. TRA, P.O. Box 3000, Denville, NJ 07834.

USA: The Rough Guide. Samantha Cook and others. (Rough Guides Ltd., London.)
Part of a series of rough guides from Amsterdam to Zimbabwe. A down and dirty guide from an English perspective.

Volunteer! The Comprehensive Guide to Voluntary Service in the U.S. and Abroad. (CIEE, 4th edition.) Orders: 800-349-2433.

Women Travel: Adventures, Advice and Experience. Miranda Davies and Natania Jansz. (Rough Guides, London.)

Work Abroad. (CIEE Publications, 205 East 42nd Street, New York, NY 10017.) Free annual.

Work, Study, Travel Abroad: The Whole World Handbook. Del Franz, Editor. (CIEE Publications, 205 East 42nd Street, New York, NY 10017.)

Working Holidays. (Central Bureau, London). Distributed by IIE Books, 809 U.N. Plaza, New York, NY 10017.

Chapter 9

Go Wild: Wilderness Experiences and Careers

In the late '70s, biologist E. O. Wilson (he was never referred to by his first name; students held him in awe) was making headlines worldwide for his controversial views on sociobiology.

Today he is better known for his advocacy of a firmer moral basis on which to base the conservation movement and build a new relationship with the natural world. In his interesting book on this subject, *Biophilia*, is a remarkable little passage that casts this distant professor in a new light, recounting a personal event that touched him emotionally and helped shape his philosophy of life.

Let's cut to the chase, the chase after exotic species of ants that both Wilson and his mentor, William Mann, undertook—a generation apart—as a rite of passage as young men:

> *In his autobiography William Mann...tells of a trip he made as a young man into the Sierra de Trinidad of central Cuba. When he lifted a rock to see what animals were hiding*

underneath (there are always animals of some kind, usually
very small, under every rock), it split down the middle to ex-
pose a half-teaspoonful of metallic-green ants living in a
small cavity deep inside.

...Thirty-six years later, with his discovery a romantic
image in my head, I was climbing a steep slope in the same
mountains, another young man at the start of a career in en-
tomology. I had begun an ant-hill odyssey around the world
remarkably similar to Mann's. A rock I grabbed for support
split in my hand, exposing a half-teaspoonful of the same
glittering green species. I accepted the event as one of the
rites of passage.

A strange image, this: the young man, on a self-described odyssey far from home in a tropical mountain range, accidentally
breaks open a rock. And within that apparently dull and inani-
mate object, an incredible living treasure—a miniature colony of
green ants. This is a powerful image—might it not represent the
surprise discovery of one's own inner secrets through the journeys
of personal exploration and development? As authors, we will be
content if readers find their own magical half-spoonfuls of glisten-
ing creatures, within their own rocks, through one of the many adventures described in this book.

And it is interesting that the discovery Wilson reports was in
nature. Nature offers much that is green and surprising to the in-
trepid explorer or careful observer. Wilson went into the wilderness as an observer, to learn and explore. And the wilderness in
turn gave him this gift, this remarkable symbol of his own passage
into adulthood. You can do this on your own, of course—there are
woods and mountains all over the country. Thoreau did it by
moving to a cabin on Walden Pond. But it helps to have either a
supportive organization or a mentor to provide structure for the
experience.

In Wilson's case, the experience was structured emotionally,
rather than on a practical level. There is no organization called
Green Rock Ant Tours. Yet he had entered the wilderness with a
romantic image in his head of his teacher's initial discovery of
this rare creature. This enriched the experience and gave it continuity, continuity that in fact came down to him through many

generations of naturalists. When his teacher, William Mann, first discovered this species, it also stirred in him some inherited romantic image, for he named it in honor of *his* teacher, famous Harvard biologist William Morton. And now, two generations removed, the student E. O. Wilson is also a famous professor of entomology at Harvard. The wilderness experience can indeed be a powerful one, especially when guided by the traditions and experiences of earlier explorers.

Mentors in print

You might want to read the journals of some of the more famous early wilderness explorers. As Wilson and hundreds of others have, you may find these a good way to connect with mentors who can help structure your wilderness experiences. Try some of the classics, such as:

- Henry David Thoreau's *On Walden Pond* or one of the various editions of his published journals.
- Charles Darwin's *Diary of the Voyage of the H.M.S. Beagle, 1831-1836* (this was his formative wilderness odyssey).
- John Burroughs' *Deep Woods* and other writings.
- Any of the earlier works by John Muir about his experiences in the Sierras.
- Aldo Leopold's *A Sand County Almanac*.

For a more modern take on the wilderness experience, you might also enjoy any of the following authors:

- Cathy Johnson's *A Naturalist's Cabin* and *On Becoming Lost*.
- Tom Brown, Jr.'s *The Quest*.
- Dian Fossey's *Gorillas in the Mist* (yes, there was a book before the movie!)
- David Carroll's *The Year of the Turtle* (in which he enters the world of the turtles in his back yard—now there's an economical trip!)

- Joan Dunning's *The Loon: Voice of the Wilderness.*
- Cindy Ross's *A Woman's Journey*, about her adventures on the Appalachian Trail.

These days it is hard to be a passive observer of nature, because as soon as you take a close look at it, you become painfully aware of the daily assaults and injuries it sustains at the hands of humanity. More and more nature experiences focus on protecting and sustaining wilderness, rather than simply experiencing it. This is fine, and as a practical matter, vitally necessary. And we certainly do not want to discourage environmental activism if you are inclined in this direction. (The following chapter focuses on conservation experiences.) But don't rob yourself of the *personal* experience of nature—if you spend all your time doing telemarketing for a conservation group you will do some good for society, but you won't have found your own rites of passage through a wilderness experience.

Strike a balance—do some good for society *and* for yourself! Ultimately you do more for the conservation movement by deepening your understanding of nature and of yourself *through* nature, for this will give you strength and wisdom for a lifetime of environmental action, not just one summer. No one can be as committed to the preservation of nature in the abstract as they are to the preservation of nature on a personal level. When E. O. Wilson thinks about extinction, I have no doubt he visualizes that green colony of ants in the stone and wonders whether they are still alive in the mountains of Cuba.

Networking and learning

To prepare for an optimal experience, learn something about the natural world. This knowledge can come from many sources—a wise old Native American mentor would be a great one. But for most of us, it is more practical to draw on the knowledge and field techniques of a variety of scientific disciplines.

If you are currently enrolled in a college program (or have access to one through extension courses) you can probably pick up some natural history skills and field experience through courses in these areas. But not all such courses focus on field work—most of them probably will not. Check the description and talk to the instructor first.

Another way to get some good background knowledge is to pick up a few *field guides* at a bookstore or library. When you know what to look for, you will be surprised at how much more you see in nature. A local park or wildlife refuge is a good testing ground for your new observation skills.

Why is this important? Because the complexity and excitement of the natural world are completely hidden to the average observer. You can easily walk for a week in the woods and only see a few birds and animals, for instance, even though there are probably hundreds all around you. Field skills allow you to see into this secret world. It is almost magical—in fact, perhaps it is. To the uninitiated, there is nothing there at all. But to the initiated, there are dozens of different creatures everywhere you look.

Also, seriously consider one or more of the many wonderful adventure travel options and educational options that provide structured teachings and nature exploration (consult the directories in this chapter and in Chapters 3 and 8 for options).

It is entirely possible (and lots of fun) to be a weekend adventurer. Wherever you live, there are people who venture forth, armed with binoculars, butterfly nets, rock picks, fish nets or whatever, to spend a day or two completely immersed in nature. This is a wonderful journey of exploration and personal development—it can be done in your spare time on the outskirts of any town or city.

While most of us cannot find wilderness in the purest sense anywhere near our homes, we certainly can find plenty of land that is wild and natural. But how do you gain access to this hidden natural world? The easiest way is to find the people who already know and explore it. Contact the interpretive naturalists at nearby conservation centers and wildlife refuges. Ask them about courses in field identification and natural history, for references to local clubs and groups, and for schedules of outings or field trips. Contact the officers and trip leaders of local clubs and groups and ask if you can come on outings. They almost always say yes.

Also try the local Audubon Society—probably listed in the phone book for your area. If you strike out on all these ideas, call the nearest reference librarian and ask for help.

Safety tips

Whether you are out for a weekend hike or are kayaking around the Bay of Fundy, there will be risks (you need health insurance!). Plenty of expert advice exists on what to do in order to minimize those risks. Simple research techniques, like using the library to find publications and associations, work well—*if* you use them! But you must take some time to study the safety issue before heading out. Are there dangerous snakes where you will be camping? If so, learn to identify them and obtain the necessary equipment to treat their bites. You get the idea—an ounce of prevention is worth a pound of cure.

Many people think that the way to have a safe wilderness experience is to travel with someone who is more experienced. But in practice, the experienced buddy usually has brought an out-of-date map that doesn't mention the new dam around the next bend in the stream, or has recommended not to bother packing that heavy parka (even though he brought his), or has underestimated the amount of food and water you will need.

The first lesson nature teaches is self-reliance. Be your own expert, and don't leave home until you *are* expert. Also, take the simple precaution of having a backup plan. If you lose the trail, do you have a proper map and compass? If you don't come back on schedule, have you told someone to look for you and sound an alarm in your absence?

With the proper skills and preparations, wilderness experiences are probably safer than many things you do routinely. *The leading cause of injury and death for Americans in their 20s is other people*—people in cars, people with guns and knives, and so forth. Go wild and you will be away from humans, the most dangerous and unpredictable of species. You should feel much more secure in a canoe on a deserted lake than in your car on the freeway. If you want to see a really dangerous wilderness, ride the subways in New York at night.

Guns

By the way, some people think it is a good idea to bring "protection" with them when they go into the wilderness. Your best protection is not to be armed. Most guns are designed for the express purpose of shooting people, and if you carry one around with you for long enough, it might somehow manage to fulfill its designer's mission. If you think you might take up subsistence hunting, you should also think again. What may seem like uncharted wilderness to you is likely to be the territory of one or more law enforcement officers. Shooting animals out of season is a great way to spend the night in jail and incur fines substantially in excess of the total costs of your trip. And besides, most of us are untrained in hunting and more likely to bag a foot than a deer. Bring your own food in and out, and try to have as little impact on the wilderness as possible.

Personal Account

Dick: Agog at Umbagog

Dick Thomas, director of Camp Chewonki in Maine, claims jokingly that he has been there since he was first a camper at 12, although somewhere along the way he earned a B.A. from the University of Maine, started a family and was appointed director of the Maine Youth Camping Association.

I began my "career," although I didn't realize it at the time, at age 12 as a summer camper here. My first summer was an eye-opening one, which kindled my interests enough in the out-of-doors to come back the following two summers for some expanded wilderness trip opportunities. In 1972, I spent the summer on Lake Umbagog canoeing and hiking some pristine areas of the northern Maine-New Hampshire border. (Coincidentally, my counselor/trip leader that summer was Don Hudson, now the executive director of the Chewonki Foundation.)

I came back many times to work as a counselor, and for the past six years, I have been year-round camp director at Chewonki. Chewonki now offers a summer camp experience to some 290 youngsters, for either three-, five- or seven-week programs. I employ a staff of about 100 for the summer, so needless to say the place is hopping.

Our 400-acre peninsula, surrounded by tidal bays, inlets and salt marsh, is located in mid-coast Maine, an hour north of Portland. Called Chewonki Neck on the old maps, the meaning of the Penobscot word has been lost, but legend defines it as "the place of the turning," perhaps referring to the channel that bends around the Neck. For many, Chewonki Foundation programs mark a turning point in their attitude toward themselves, their community and the natural world.

I believe that what Chewonki has to offer is truly unique, and certainly falls under the category of "adventure career" opportunities. Students in the field of outdoor/environmental education and like careers are those who will be widely sought after in the years to come. Clearly, schools are recognizing the need for our types of programs, and more recently corporations, small businesses and even the state government are looking to Chewonki for ideas, help and resources. Chewonki is becoming widely recognized as the environmental center in Maine, and there is a growing need for the type of programs we offer.

Go Wild Directory

You may find this list helpful if you are trying to locate an experience in a particular geographic area or professional or academic field. For example, many of these organizations offer teaching and interpretive naturalist positions—an excellent field in which to build a wilderness career and one that does not necessarily require an advanced degree.

A national association is a good source of general information on a field or sport, including directories and referrals to other organizations and information sources. When in doubt, call or write organizations with a general information request and ask if they can help. Another option to keep in mind while traveling the world is eco-tourism, or nature tourism. We have included some eco-tourist opportunities here; see the previous chapter for more detail.

With great difficulty we have picked a handful of excellent programs and organizations to profile, but we hope you will use the additional listings and referenced resources to explore others as well. Go wild!

Appalachian Trail Conference
P.O. Box 807
Harpers Ferry, WV 25425
304-535-6331

The Appalachian Trail is the longest marked and maintained trail in the world, and one of the most beautiful as well. Less than 2,000 people have walked the full 2,100 miles from Georgia to Maine. It takes about six months, and is best done between April 1 and October 1.

One of the recommended readings in the beginning of this chapter is Cindy Ross's book about the trail. It is a good resource, and the Appalachian Trail Conference can send (and more likely sell) you lots of other books.

Cost varies, depending on your willingness to rough it. The bare minimum for an entire summer is probably about $2,000, including pack and boots, lots of food, and an occasional visit to towns along the way for showers, shopping and postcards. And of course you will need to make travel arrangements at both ends. The trip will be smoother if you can budget $3,000 to $4,000.

If this is too much, or (as is more often the case) the time commitment is too great, pick a shorter length and plan your own trip. Even a week or two on the trail is well worthwhile.

You might also find Edward Garvey's *The Appalachian Hiker II* a helpful guidebook in evaluating or planning your trip.

Manomet Bird Observatory (MBO)

Box 936
Manomet, MA 02345
508-224-6521

MBO runs one of the few formal training programs in field biology in the world. And it is a good one. Its Field Biology Training Program trains in field technique and the science behind its application. Students participate in varied research programs. In the past they have gone to Puerto Rico to study shorebird usage of salt flats, to the Gaspe Peninsula in Quebec to study the boreal forest, to Belize to study the nesting colonies of herons, egrets and ibises on coastal mangrove islands. And of course many students go to Manomet, in Cape Cod, where the staff of conservation biologists and many of their projects are headquartered (and dormitories are available).

Courses generally fill a semester. They typically cost the same as one semester of college tuition—ask about available programs, timing and costs.

MBO also offers the Research Apprentice Program, for an advanced apprentice experience that some students use as a follow-up to the Field Biology Training Program. Stipends are provided for research and teaching.

Dozens of colleges give credit for the program, including Boston University, Cornell University, Florida State University, Ohio Wesleyan University, Rutgers University, and the Universities of Massachusetts, Michigan, Nebraska, New Hampshire, and many other states.

Earthwatch

680 Mount Auburn St.
Watertown, MA 02272
617-926-8200

Field Offices:

Earthwatch California
11812 San Vicente Blvd., Suite 610
Los Angeles, CA 90049

Earthwatch Australia
Clarence St., Box C360
Sydney 2000 Australia
02-290-1492

Earthwatch Europe
Belsyre Ct., 57 Woodstock
Oxford OX2 6HU
United Kingdom
0865-311-600

Earthwatch offers volunteers the opportunity to "invest in the future of the planet by serving in an environmental EarthCorps," as a recent press release describes it. Some of the many experiences available to volunteers include excavating mammoth fossils in Hot Springs, S.D., studying volcanic action on Mt. Etna in Italy, discovering new species of katydids in Peruvian rain forests, and documenting through photography 14,000 paintings and petroglyphs of Australian aborigines.

You will have to cough up some money, ranging from $800 to $2,500. Costs cover your food, accommodations and all necessary field equipment and support—not transportation, however, which will add dramatically to the costs of the more remote and exotic adventures. The typical participant spends two weeks working on a project, often on one of four or five teams.

Earthwatch is quite strict about cancellations and requires payment 90 days in advance—so you'd better make firm plans before signing up!

Scholarships and financial aid are provided to teachers or students (but not others) through a fellowship program. Several hundred such fellowships are awarded every year. This experience is open to anyone over 16, and you will probably find a wide age range on your team.

How do you find out what Earthwatch is currently offering? Call the main number or write for a copy of *Earthwatch* magazine, specifying that you want the latest one to list their current projects. A recent issue, for example, listed 62 projects open to volunteers.

If you think you want to participate in a project, Earthwatch insists that you *buy* a "briefing" on it for $25. If you like the sound of an expedition, but are not yet ready to invest even $25, try calling and asking for information over the phone. Also, Earthwatch maintains a network of field representatives throughout North America. Their names and numbers are listed in the *Earthwatch* magazine, and the head office can also provide referrals. These people will be happy to talk with you for no charge.

Adirondack Mountain Club
Box 867
Lake Placid, NY 12946
518-523-3441

Contact this organization for help in planning outdoor experiences in the Adirondack Mountains. It also offers excellent internships. About 50 mostly seasonal internship positions are filled yearly by college students and graduates. Room and board is provided. Work includes maintaining backcountry hiking trails, staffing the Backcountry Information Center and two mountain lodges, and acting as interpretive naturalists. An application form is available upon request, and personal interviews are a good idea if you can make it to upstate New York. This is a well-organized program and a well-known, reputable organization.

Adventure Careers

Hobbiton-On-Hogsback Association
P.O. Hogsback
South Africa, 5312

We just *had* to include this one, although it *is* a bit off the beaten track, even for wilderness adventurers. This group's mission is to use environmental education and recreation "to promote racial interaction and harmony." The work can include training groups in environmental education, rock climbing, kayaking, orienteering and mountain climbing, technical climbing, sailing and wilderness medicine. The organization offers a certification that is apparently of some value anywhere in the world (for example, you could probably go from here to an instructor job at an Outward Bound).

Internships include a paid one-year position and are open to people from the U.S. and other countries, although minorities or anyone who has a history of political activism may have trouble obtaining a South African work permit. Only room and board are included. Longer-term employment is also possible. This group can plug you into the network of conservation and wilderness organizations in Africa, if you wish to go on to jobs in other parts of the country or continent. It will consider candidates of high-school and college age and also older candidates working on a career change or reentering the work force. It is important to have some background in "experiential education" such as in one of the activities described above.

Additional listings

Appalachian Mountain Club
5 Joy St.
Boston, MA 02108
617-523-0636

Carrie Murray Outdoor Education Campus
Ridgetop Rd.
Baltimore, MD 21207
410-396-0808

Workshops and classes year-round. Internships in teaching and other duties (full-time positions available).

Chewonki Family Adventures/ Camp Chewonki
RR 2, Box 1200D
Wiscasset, ME 04578
207-882-7323

Camp for kids, wilderness travel (experienced leaders needed) and year-round programs.

Field Studies in Natural History
Office of Continuing Education
San Jose State University
One Washington Square
San Jose, CA 95192
408-924-2680

Four Corners School of Outdoor Education
East Route
Monticello, UT 84535
800-525-4456

Green Briar Nature Center
Thornton W. Burgess Society
6 Discovery Rd.
East Sandwich, MA 02537
508-888-6870

Offers some internships.

Green Chimneys Farm
Putnam Lake Rd.
Brewster, NY 10509
914-279-2995

Demonstration farm; internships available.

Greenkill Outdoor Environmental Education Center
Huguenot, NY 12746
914-856-4382

About a dozen seasonal paid internships include room and board. Run by the Greater YMCA-YWCA of New York.

The Holden Arboretum
9500 Sperry Rd.
Mentor, OH 44060
216-946-4400

About 12 paid internships are available in landscape maintenance, conservation (they have a wildflower garden, for example) and education. Housing and possibility of college credit.

Inner Quest, Inc.
Route 1, Box 271C
Purcellville, VA 22132
703-478-1078

Offers Outward Bound-type experiences via kayaking and mountain climbing, and hires people of high-school age and up for its Apprentice Program.

International Oceanographic Foundation
P.O. Box 499900
Miami, FL 33149-9900
305-361-4697; Fax: 305-361-9306

Offers internships.

Intersea Research
P.O. Box 1667 Research
Friday Harbor, WA 98250
206-378-5980; Fax: 206-378-5911

Here's a way to check out whales without those cumbersome tourist whale-watching trips. Join a research team in Alaska (summer) or Hawaii (winter); small groups (10-14 people) accompanied by research scientists.

Little St. Simons Island
P.O. Box 1078-AG
St. Simons Island, GA 31522
912-638-7472

The outfit offers nature-oriented vacations (at more than $100/night) with naturalist guides. Ask about job openings.

National Audubon Society
700 Broadway
New York, NY 10003
212-979-3000

Provides listings of local Audubon chapters. Its publications, including the *Audubon Magazine*, are recommended.

National Parks & Conservation Association
1776 Massachusetts Ave. NW, Ste. 200
Washington, DC 20036
202-223-6722
and
National Recreation & Parks Association
2775 S. Quincy, Suite 300
Arlington, VA 22206
703-820-4940

Both are sources of information on national, state and local parks and on careers in park management.

Adventure Careers

Olympic National Park and Pioneer Memorial Museum
600 E. Park Ave.
Port Angeles, WA 98362
206-452-4501

Contact the Visitor Center Manager for information on internships there. Housing, stipends and sometimes college credit are available. Seasonal jobs in spring, summer and fall.

Pocono Environmental Education Center
R.R. 2, Box 1010
Dingmans Ferry, PA 18328
717-828-2319

A dozen paid positions give interns an opportunity to teach and develop educational programs. Room, board and a $600/month stipend are provided for up to 12 months.

Point Reyes Education Program
Point Reyes National Seashore
Point Reyes Station, CA 94956
415-663-1200

Short natural history classes.

Project Ocean Search Expeditions
The Cousteau Society
870 Greenbrier Circle, Suite 402
Chesapeake, VA 23320
804-523-9335

Riverbend Environmental Education Center
P.O. Box 2
Gladwyne, PA 19035
610-527-5234

One paid internship is available with a focus on teaching but also works with the Touch Museum, newsletters, and so forth.

Sierra Club
730 Polk St.
San Francisco, CA 94109
415-776-2211

Active in both conservation action (see Chapter 9) and in assisting hikers and other adventurers. Internships available.

Trust for Public Land
116 Montgomery St., 4th Fl.
San Francisco, CA 94105
415-495-4014

Purchases and protects land of environmental significance. Provides financing expertise and assistance. Ask about jobs and internships if you are interested in the important area of financing the acquisition of conservation lands.

U.S. Canoe & Kayak Team
201 S. Capitol Ave., Suite 470
Indianapolis, IN 46225
317-237-5690

U.S. Orienteering Federation
P.O. Box 1444
Forest Park, GA 30051
404-363-2100

Wellfleet Wildlife Sanctuary
P.O. Box 236
South Wellfleet, MA 02663
508-349-2615

Yellowstone Institute
Yellowstone National Park
P.O. Box 117
Wyoming, 82190
307-344-7381, ext. 2384

American Hiking Society
P.O. Box 20160
Washington, DC 20041
703-225-9304

American Horticultural Society
7931 E. Boulevard Drive
Alexandria, VA 22308
703-768-5700

National Gardening Association
180 Flynn Ave.
Burlington, VT 05401
802-863-1308

**Boat Owner's Association
of the U.S.**
880 S. Pickett St.
Alexandria, VA 22304
703-823-9550

**American Sport Fishing
Association**
1033 N. Fairfax, Suite 200
Alexandria, VA 22314
703-519-9691

Family Campers and RV'ers
4804 Transit Rd., Bldg. 2
Depew, NY 14043
716-668-6242

Wilderness Society
900 17th St. NW
Washington, DC 20006
202-833-2300

Outdoor/sports adventure travel

The following listings are organizations that provide structured outdoor adventures. They cater to the vacation market, which puts their prices beyond at least some of our readers. Explore them anyway, because some are surprisingly inexpensive, and even the expensive ones may be worth saving up for. Further, *all are potential sources of employment.*

Climbing experiences: Because it's there!

Adirondack Alpine Adventures
Dept. 609, P.O. Box 179
Keene, NY 12942
518-576-9881

Alaska-Denali Guiding, Inc.
P.O. Box 566
Talkeetna, AK 99676
907-733-1221

American Alpine Institute
1515 12th St.
Bellingham, WA 98225
206-671-1505

Colorado Mountain School
Box 2062
Estes Park, CO 80517
303-586-5758

**Jackson Hole Mountain Guides
& Climbing School**
Box 7477D
Jackson, WY 83001
307-733-4979

Outward Bound
Rte. 9-D, R 2, Box 280
Garrison, NY 10524-9757
800-243-8520

Sierra Wilderness Seminars Inc.
P.O. Box 707
Arcata, CA 95521
707-822-8066

Yosemite Mountaineering School
Yosemite National Park, CA 95389
209-372-1335, 209-372-0200

Cattle/horse drives and horseback

Adventure Specialists, Inc.
Bear Basin Ranch
Westcliffe, CO 81252
719-783-2519, 800-252-7899

Alaska Horseback Vacations
58335 East End Rd.
Homer, AK 99603
907-235-7850

Bar Diamond Ranch
Box 688
Hotchkiss, CO 81419
303-527-3010, 800-252-7899

Broken Skull Cattle Co.
P.O. Box 774054
Steamboat Springs, CO 80477
303-879-0090

Cameras, Horses, and Trails
P.O. Box 219
Powell, WY 82435
307-645-3173; 218-233-7249 (Apr-Oct.)

Happy Hollow Camps
Star Route Box 14-A
Salmon, ID 83467
208-756-3954

High Country Outfitters
59761 Wallowa Lake Highway
Joseph, OR 97846
503-432-9171

Mammoth Lakes Pack Outfit
P.O. Box 61
Mammoth Lakes, CA 93546
619-934-2434

Outward Bound
Rte. 9-D
R 2, Box 280
Garrison, NY 10524-9757
800-243-8520

Pace Ranch
P.O. Box 98
Torrey, UT 84775
801-425-3519, 800-252-7899

Price Canyon Ranch
P.O. Box 1065
Douglas, AZ 85607
602-558-2383

Spanish Springs Ranch
P.O. Box 70
Ravendale, CA 96123
800-272-8282, 800-228-0279

Wilderness Connection
Cinnabar Basin Rd.
Gardiner, MT 59030
406-848-7287

Cycling

Backroads Bicycle Touring
1516 5th St.
Berkeley, CA 94710
510-527-1555, 800-245-3874

BikeCentennial
P.O. Box 8308-QC
Missoula, MT 59807
406-721-1776

Carolina Cycle Tours
13077 Highway 19W
Bryson City, NC 28713
704-488-6737

Outward Bound
Rte. 9-D, R 2, Box 280
Garrison, NY 10524-9757
800-243-8520

Timberline Bicycle Tours
7975 E. Harvard, #J
Denver, CO 80231
303-759-3804

Canoeing/kayaking

Anderson Outfitters
7255 Crane Lake Rd.
Crane Lake, MN 55725
218-993-2287, 800-777-7186

Baja Expeditions
2625 Garnet Ave.
San Diego, CA 92109
619-581-3311; Fax: 619-581-6542

Hawk, I'm Your Sister
P.O. Box 9109
Santa Fe, NM 87504-9109
505-984-2268

Hugh Glass Backpacking Co.
P.O. Box 110796
Anchorage, AK 99511
907-344-1340

North American River Runners
P.O. Box 81
Hico, WV 25851-0081
304-658-5276

Northern Lights Expeditions
6141 NE Bothell Way, #101
Seattle, WA 98155
206-362-4506

Outward Bound
Rte. 9-D, R 2, Box 280
Garrison, NY 10524-9757
800-243-8520

Wilderness Outfitters, Inc.
1 E. Camp St.
Ely, MN 55731
218-365-5089, 800-777-8572

Diving

The Dream Team
P.O. Box 033271
Indialantic, FL 32903-0271
407-723-9312

River running

Amazon Outreach
1500 WE 3rd Court
Deerfield Beach, FL 33441
305-698-6302

American River Touring Assoc.
Star Route 73
Groveland, CA 95321
209-962-7873, 800-323-2782

Adventure Careers

Arctic Edge/TransSiberian Tours
P.O. Box 4850
Whitehorse, Yukon Territory
Canada Y1A 4N6
403-633-5470; Fax: 403-633-3820

Arizona Raft Adventures, Inc.
4050-A East Huntington Drive
Flagstaff, AZ 86004
602-526-8200

Cherokee Adventures
Rt. 1, Box 605
Erwin, TN 37650
615-743-7733

Dvorak Expeditions
17921 U.S. Highway 285
Nathrop, CO 81236
719-539-6851, 800-824-3795

Far Flung Adventures
P.O. Box 707
El Prado, NM 87529
505-758-2628, 800-359-4138

Grand Canyon Expeditions
P.O. Box O
Kanab, UT 84741
800-544-2691

Hudson River Rafting Company
One Main St.
North Creek, NY 12853
800-888-7238

Nantahala Outdoor Center
13077 Highway 19W
Bryson City, NC 28713
704-488-6900

Northern Outdoors, Inc.
P.O. Box 100
Rte. 201
The Forks, ME 04985
207-663-4466, 800-765-7238

Outward Bound
Rte. 9-D
R 2, Box 280
Garrison, NY 10524-9757
800-243-8520

River Runners, Ltd.
11150 Highway 50
Salida, CO 81201
800-525-2081, 800-332-9100

Sailing schools

Annapolis Sailing School
P.O. Box 3334
Annapolis, MD 21403
800-638-9192

California Sailing Academy
14025 Panay Way
Suite 201
Marina Del Rey, CA 90292
213-821-3433

Offshore Sailing School
16731-110 McGregor Blvd.
Fort Myers, FL 33908
813-454-1700, 800-221-4326

Outward Bound
Rte. 9-D
R 2, Box 280
Garrison, NY 10524-9757
800-243-8520

Windjammers

Dirigo Cruises
39 Waterside Lane
Clinton, CT 06413
203-669-7068

Discovery Charters
P.O. Box 1182
Dunedin, New Zealand
03-453-6986

Operates the S.V. Tradewind, a two-masted auxiliary topsail schooner with 12 sails. Fits 19 passengers and has naturalist guides on board. The tours are as much about subantarctic wildlife observation as they are about sailing, so be ready for long stops.

Ocean Voyages, Inc.
1709 Bridgeway
Sausalito, CA 94965
415-332-4681

Traverse Tall Ship Co.
13390 W. Bay Shore Drive
Traverse City, MI 49684
616-941-2000

Windjammer Barefoot Cruises
P.O. Box 190120
Miami Beach, FL 33119
305-672-6453, 800-327-2601

Ski touring

Balsams/Wilderness
Rte. 26
Dixville Notch, NH 03576
603-255-3400, 800-255-0600

Coffee Creek Ranch
Dept AG, HC 2
Box 4940
Trinity Center, CA 96091
916-266-3343

The Inn at Starlight Lake
Ski Touring Center
Box 27
Starlight, PA 18491
717-798-2519

North Rim Nordic Center
Box 2997
Flagstaff, AR 86003
602-526-0924, 800-525-0924

Sierra Wilderness Seminars, Inc.
P.O. Box 707
Arcata, CA 95521
707-822-8066, 800-648-5650

Skoki Lodge
P.O. Box 5
Lake Louise
Alta, Canada TOL 1E0
403-522-3555

Vista Verde Guest Ranch
Box 465
Steamboat Springs, CO 80477
303-879-3858, 800-526-7433

Hiking and camping trips

ABEC's Alaska Adventures
1304-AG Westwick Drive
Fairbanks, AK 99712
907-457-8907

Hike Maui
P.O. Box 330969
Kahului, HI 96733
800-879-5270

Innerasia Expeditions
2627 Lombard St.
San Francisco, CA 94123
800-777-8183; Fax: 415-346-5535

Rigorous hiking trips with a cultural and ecological bent.

Kootenai Wilderness Recreation
Argenta, B.C. V0G 1BO
Canada
604-366-4480

Mystic Saddle Ranch
Stanley, ID 83340
208-774-3591

Pack Creek Ranch
P.O. Box 1270
Moab, UT 84532
801-259-5505

Sierra Wilderness Seminars Inc.
P.O. Box 707
Arcata, CA 95521
707-822-8066, 800-648-5650

The Open Road
748 East Dunlap #2
Phoenix, AZ 85020
602-997-6474

Vermont Hiking Holidays
Box 750
Bristol, VT 05443
802-453-4816

Summer camps

A wonderful way to "go wild" for a summer is to work at a summer camp. An excellent source of information on camps throughout the U.S. is the annual *Peterson's Summer Opportunities for Kids and Teenagers*, published by Peterson's Guides of Princeton, N.J. The book is often carried in the career sections of bookstores.

Following is a directory of many of the best-known and best-run summer camps in the U.S. They are all known to hire a significant number of high school and college students every year. Write to some or all of them for details and application instructions.

Alford Lake Camp
17 Pilot Point Rd.
Cape Elizabeth, ME 04107
207-799-3005

Barnard's Summer in New York
3009 Broadway
New York, NY 10027-6598
212-854-8866

Beauvallon
International Camp
286, Rang de'Eglise
Henryville, PQ, Canada JOJ 1EO
514-299-2506

Belvoir Terrace
145 Central Park West
New York, NY 10023
212-580-3398

Brandeis University
Summer Odyssey
Waltham, MA 02154-9110
617-736-2113

Butterfield & Robinson
70 Bond St., Suite 300
Toronto, ON, Canada M5B 1X3
800-387-1147, 800-268-8415

Camp Atwater
Urban League of Springfield, Inc.
765 State St.
Springfield, MA 01109
413-739-7211

Camp Birchwood/Gunflint
Wilderness Camp
Box 547
St. Cloud, MN 56302
800-451-5270

Camp Cabot
Waltham, MA 02154
A YMCA camp: 617-894-5295

Counselors work with a wide spectrum of children, from inner-city kids to the emotionally and physically challenged to more traditional suburban campers. A recent business school graduate relates, "I've worked there for eight summers. I find it rewarding to work with children who need a positive male role model. It's fun to see kids come back a little better adjusted each year."

Camp Chewonki
RR2, Box 1200P
Wiscasset, ME 04578
207-882-7323

Camp Mishemokwa
P.O. Box 40-PG
Bat Cave, NC 28710
704-625-9051, 904-932-9465

Camp Nor'Wester
Route 1 Box 1700
Lopez, WA 98261
206-468-2225

Camp Quinebarge
17 Kathleen Lane
Norwood, MA 02062
617-769-1727

Camp Regis-Applejack
Paul Smith's, NY 12970
518-327-3117, 914-997-7039

Camp Robin Hood
Freedom, NH 03836
603-539-4500
Winter:
344 Thistle Tr.
Mayfield Heights, OH 44124
216-646-1911

Camp Sangamon and Camp Betsey Cox
349 South Mountain Rd.
Northfield, MA 01360
413-498-5873
Summer:
Camp Sangamon
Sangamon Rd.
Pittsford, VT 05763

Camp Tohkomeupog
Route 153
East Madison, NH 03849-9403
800-414-2267

Adventure Careers

Camp Treetops
P.O. Box 187
Lake Placid, NY 12946
518-523-9329

Camp Waziyatah
RR 2, Box 465
Harrison, ME 04040
207-583-6781
Winter:
P.O. Box 86569
Madeira Beach, FL 33738
813-391-0022

Carmel Valley Tennis Camp
27300 Rancho San Carlos Rd.
Carmel, CA 93923
800-234-7117

C Bar T Ranch
P.O. Box 158
Idledale, CO 80453
303-674-6477

Cheley Colorado Camps
P.O. Box 1170
Estes Park, CO 80517
303-586-4244
(winter) 303-377-3616

Chewonki Expeditions
RR 2, Box 1200D
Wiscasset, ME 04578
207-882-7323

Culver Summer Camps
1300 Academy Rd.
Culver, IN 46511
219-842-8207

Dvorak Expeditions
17921 U.S. Highway 285
Suite AG
Nathrop, CO 81236
719-539-6851, 800-824-3795

Eagle's Nest Camp
633 Summit St.
Winston-Salem, NC 27101
704-877-4349
*Winter address and outdoor academy
for 10th graders:*
43 Hart Rd.
Pisgih Forest, NC 28768
910-761-1040

Forest Acres Camp for Girls
RR 1, Box 48
Fryburg, ME 04037
207-935-2305
(winter) 617-969-5242

The Gow Summer Programs
Emery Rd.
South Wales, NY 14139
800-332-4691

The Hill School
717 E. High St.
Pottstown, PA 19464
610-326-1000

Indian Acres Camp for Boys
RR 1, Box 48
Fryburg, ME 04037
207-935-2300
(winter) 617-969-5242

Inner Quest
Rt. 1, Box 271-C
Purcellville, VA 22132
703-478-1078

Interlocken
RR2, Box 165
Hillsboro, NH 03244
603-478-3166

Kingsley Pines Camp
113 Plains Rd.
Raymond, ME 04071
207-655-7181
(winter) 207-773-4621

Michigan Technological University
Youth Programs Office
1400 Townsend Drive
Houghton, MI 49931
906-487-2219

Outward Bound
(For catalog listing all U.S. courses)
Rte. 9-D
R 2, Box 280
Garrison, NY 10524-9757
800-243-8520

Pathways
Academic Study Associates, Inc.
355 Main St.
P.O. Box 800
Armonk, NY 10504
914-273-2250, 800-752-2250

Perry-Mansfield Performing Arts Camp
40755 RCR #36
Steamboat Springs, CO 80487
303-879-7125

Pre-College Enrichment at Amherst
Academic Study Associates, Inc.
355 Main St.
P.O. Box 800
Armonk, NY 10504
914-273-2250, 800-752-2250

Sampson's Navajo Trails
Rocky Mountain Ranch and
Adventure Camp
Box 886-P
Los Altos, CA 94022
408-245-6789 (owner)
801-425-3469 (summer only)

Skinner Brothers
Box 859
Pinedale, WY 82941
307-367-2270, 800-237-9138

Southwestern Adventures
Admissions, Southwestern Academy
San Marino Campus
San Marino, CA 91108
818-799-5010

Supercamp
1725 South Hill St.
Oceanside, CA 92054-5319
800-527-5321, 619-722-0072

TrekAmerica
P.O. Box 189
Rockaway, NJ 07866
800-221-0596

Visions
RD 3, Box 106A
Newport, PA 17074
717-567-7313

Wilderness Southeast
711-AG Sandtown Rd.
Savannah, GA 31410
912-897-5108

The Windridge Tennis and Sports Camps
P.O. Box 463
Richmond, VT 05477
802-434-2199

Wolfeboro
Box 390
Wolfeboro, NH 03894
603-569-3451

Woodberry Forest School
Woodberry Forest, VA 22989
703-672-3900

Wyonegonic Camps
RR 1, Box 186
Denmark, ME 04022
207-452-2051

Chapter 10

Save the Planet

Adventure Careers

Work in environmental activism—conservation—and related areas is hot. The job opportunities are many and growing. By the time today's twenty-something job seekers are middle-aged, competency in the areas of environmentalism and conservation will be highly valued in the job market, and even big companies will be hiring conservationists. Also, we found in our conversations with many college students, recent graduates and older working stiffs, that conservation adventures feature prominently in the career and personal development of more people, whether they specialize in conservation or not.

Like travel, conservation experience seems to be a fertile source of adventure and learning that can be applied in a great variety of future jobs and careers. What this means is that the experiences and information described in this chapter are for everyone—for career planeteers and also for those whose main interests lie elsewhere—they can and do benefit from experience in the area of conservation.

This chapter is about the many urgent activities that organizations and people are undertaking to slow the human assault on the environment—and how you can participate and, in so doing, expand your experience or your career options. To many, conservation is the most important issue on the global agenda at present.

If we could better understand and manage the planet of which we are now stewards, we might be able to avoid global warming, feed our growing populations, lower the rate of extinctions and improve our own immediate environments.

To many, the environment seems like the starting point for a broad range of issues and concerns. We suspect that, before long, environmental problems will be seen as so troubling that almost everyone will become environmental activists, to one degree or another!

Action adventures

Action on the conservation front can take many forms. For Jack Smiley, it meant videotaping a developer's efforts to fill a Detroit-area wetland. Smiley is executive director of the Detroit Audubon Society, and when he heard about plans to turn a cattail marsh into a car wash, he informed the appropriate city council that a permit was needed from the Michigan Department of Natural Resources.

But the city (Westland, Mich.) went ahead and approved the developer's plans without the permit. This should have been the end of the story, and the marsh. But Smiley borrowed a video camera and headed for the marsh, arriving in time to document the bulldozing and filling. When he showed the tape to authorities at the Department of Natural Resources, they ordered a stop to the development and prevented similar development projects on nearby wetlands. Smiley even made the news with his video, which was shown on local television and helped develop community support for the efforts of the Detroit Audubon Society.

In a moment we will review some other examples of grassroots action, these suggested by The EarthWorks Group, which published the best-selling *50 Simple Things You Can Do to Save the Earth* in 1989. This book focused on personal actions, and now EarthWorks is collecting and disseminating methods that go the next step, from personal to grassroots community action. Here is how John Javna of The EarthWorks Group describes it:

> *Judging from our mail, people now feel they really can make a difference. They've switched to canvas shopping*

bags, bought low-phosphate detergents, started recycling aluminum cans and planted trees. But we're concerned about what happens next. Snipping six-pack rings may be a start, but it's not the solution. It's important to harness that enthusiasm and new-found sense of personal power to take The Next Step. It's time to reach out to the community. (From *The Next Step: 50 More Things You Can Do to Save the Earth*, Andrews and McMeel, The EarthWorks Press, 1991.)

Here are some of the ways people have been reaching out to their communities.

Recycling Guide Map. The East Bay Conservation Corps prepared a map of the recycling facilities in its area (the Eastern side of San Francisco Bay) and has distributed more than 10,000 copies to residents. Why? Because a survey found that 43 percent of people who do not recycle would do so if they knew where facilities were located. Give them a map, and many will start recycling. (Did you know that we recycle about 10 percent of our trash in the U.S., compared with 50 percent to 60 percent in many European countries?)

Lobby for Local Ordinances. Is your town a nuclear-free zone? It may seem silly at first to address global problems with local legislation. But individual towns and cities can have at least a symbolic impact on global issues, and in many cases a practical one as well. For example, Soldier's Grove, Wis., recently adopted an ordinance that requires businesses in the town to obtain 50 percent of their heat from the sun. This may seem impractical at first, but in fact it is well within current technology (for more information, contact National Appropriate Technology Assistance Service, Conservation and Renewable Energy Inquiry and Referral Service, Solar Energy Research Institute, or Passive Industries Council from the directory in this chapter).

Environmental activism is an appealing career because of the importance of the work, but for many activists it is remarkably unremunerative. Grassroots activism in your local community is a rich source of experience and adventure, but rarely a rich source of compensation. However, many people go on to larger-scale efforts and larger organizations that are capable of paying a living wage. And those who work up to high-level staff positions in larger organizations are able to achieve both financial and environmental success!

Personal Account

Julie: One good tern deserves another

Julie Zickefoose graduated from Harvard with a major in biology, and worked in tern and plover conservation from 1983 to 1986. She currently is a full-time freelance artist, specializing in birds and mammals. Her work has appeared in the New Yorker, Bird Watcher's Digest, American Birds, Bird Observer, *and numerous U.S.* Fish and Wildlife Service *publications. She recently illustrated the book,* Six Backyard Birds *(Harper Collins, 1993).*

The vistas of limitless sand and ocean, once common on Cape Cod and all along the East Coast of the United States, are now peopled with houses, malls, marinas and summer crowds. The "mackerel gulls," an old-fashioned name for the graceful terns that dive for fish, have felt the impact. People, their RVs, dogs and parties, have a powerful impact on the birds that make their nests on the sand.

Of the terns, a delicate species called the Least Tern is most vulnerable because it favors mainland beaches over the remote island outposts other species have retreated to. On the same beaches, the small Piping Plover has also felt the effects of human intrusion. Both species are near extinction in Massachusetts, Connecticut and other coastal states.

I worked with the Nature Conservancy, which acquires and manages land in order to preserve important habitats around the country. Initially I generated a list of what we called the "best and last" in the state of Connecticut. This formed an agenda for the organization's acquisition and preservation efforts. Through this

236

work I became aware of the plight of Least Terns and Piping Plovers. I developed a program to protect the nesting sites of both species because it was absolutely essential for the survival of the birds. We initiated the idea of protecting individual Piping Plover nests. Now the state fences about 30 nests individually every year. That bird would have been extinct in 15 years if we hadn't done something.

When we started, dogs were running through the colonies. Four-wheel drive vehicles were crushing them. In three years I had built up a group of 30 volunteers to guard nests. For example, on the Fourth of July, when the nests are usually destroyed in great numbers, we would unofficially "close" sensitive beaches to keep parties off the colonies. We had no authority to close the beaches, but we'd set up sawhorses and ropes around nests, and we'd wear khaki clothes with little tin sheriff's badges and carry flashlights. That usually worked, and we scared away a lot of partiers!

I was cannon fodder for the conservation movement for six years. They knew I cared so much that they had me hooked. They paid me less every year. But to be fair, I actively avoided promotion. I could have taken a desk job, but I didn't want to because I wanted to be out in the field, working directly to save endangered species. This kind of work may never pay well because there are so many people who care and the funding is always in short supply, but I would recommend it anyway. Everyone should do a stint in conservation, even though many may not go on to make a permanent career of it.

I'll always be a conservationist as a result. I think you get sensitized as to how much there is to do out there. It colors your viewpoint. You realize that nothing in life is free, that the good things in life have to be cared for, and in a sense paid for. Now I see that it starts at home. I've gradually turned my own backyard into an oasis for wildlife. And in my work as an artist I work on conservation in an oblique way. For example, people or groups who are trying to do something good in the world get an incredible break on my prices.

Save the Planet Directory

Many groups in this directory have full-time staff who are paid decent salaries and receive benefits. Most of these organizations do not recruit on college campuses. Further, there are many internships or entry-level work opportunities.

The lists in Chapter 9 and Chapter 4 may also be of interest.

Local and State Audubon Societies
For information on the many local organizations, contact:
Chapter Services
National Audubon Society
666 Pennsylvania Ave. SE
Washington, DC 20003
202-547-9009

The National Audubon Society, is perhaps best known for its efforts in education and public awareness. But for many environmental activists, the front-line workers, the *local* Audubon chapters are where the action is. Local chapters focus on local and regional issues. The annual Earth Defender Awards go to chapters for exceptional local conservation actions. Some winners of the 1991 Earth Defender Award include:

- **Columbia Gorge** Audubon Society in Hood River, Ore., which won an award for its lobbying and education designed to protect white oak stands in Washington and Oregon.

- **Pine Woods** Audubon Society in Hattiesburg, Miss., which blocked exchange of important wildlife habitat from the U.S. Forest Service to the military for training grounds.

Join the national organization for $20 at time of writing. Even better, send an additional $15 to: *Audubon Activist*, 950 Third Avenue, New York, NY 10022. The monthly newsletter *Audubon Activist*, reports on the activities of state councils and local chapters. (Note that *Audubon Activist* itself often has an opening for an intern.) The local and state Audubon Societies are excellent sources of jobs and internships in conservation.

Greenpeace USA
1436 U St. NW
Washington, DC 20009
202-462-1177

Howard Cannon, from the Seattle Greenpeace office, climbed down a tall cliff on a Quebec river to unfurl a huge banner saying "SAUVONS LES BELUGAS" (let us save the beluga whales). This was a dangerous undertaking since the cliff face was loose and the wind strong, but it attracted considerable media attention with an important conservation message. That is the *modus operandi* of Greenpeace, which often enters dangerous situations in the name of conservation action.

But Greenpeace is more than its media image suggests. It has a strong lobbying program at the local, national and international levels. It commissions and conducts scientific research. It works with international organizations like the UN, International Whaling Commission and the European Economic Commission. It even has a scientific base in Antarctica.

In addition to membership-drive assistance, Greenpeace offices around the world have other openings. Whether you want to manage an office or drive a rubber raft under the bow of a Japanese whaling ship, Greenpeace may be able to put you in harness.

Greenpeace generally takes in about 15 paid interns in its Washington, D.C., office for three- to nine-month stints.

Additional listings

Aspen Center for Environmental Studies
Education Coordinator
Summer Naturalist Intern Program
P.O. Box 8777
Aspen, CO 81612
303-925-5756

This is a paid summer internship with free housing provided. Interns help with all kinds of things—landscaping, giving talks on the Birds of Prey program, rehabilitating injured animals and birds, teaching natural history classes to children and adults, and leading nature walks.

Bernie Environmental Education Center
Director of Outdoor Education
RD 2, Turkey Top Rd.
Port Murray, NJ 07865
908-832-5315; Fax: 908-832-9078

Internships (with stipend) of flexible duration in a year-round resident outdoor or environmental education center. Possibility of full-time employment, placement assistance provided, free housing and meals. Should have college or professional preparation in outdoor or natural science or environmental education or related field and knowledge of or interest in pond, stream, forest or field ecologies, group initiative and problem solving, mapping/orienteering, bird study or astronomy.

Brookfield Zoo
Intern Program Office Coordinator
3300 South Golf Rd.
Brookfield, IL 60513
708-485-0263

Considered an excellent internship by those in the field of zookeeping because you work like a regular employee—directly with the animals. A terrific starting point if you're interested in this line of work.

Center for Marine Conservation
1725 DeSales St. NW, Suite 500
Washington, DC 20036
202-429-5609

Unpaid internships, three months.

CSERGE
School of Environmental Science
University of East Anglia
Norwich, NR4 7TJ
United Kingdom
44-0-603-593176; Fax: 44-0-603-250588

The United Kingdom Centre for Social and Economic Research on the Global Environment is the UK's premier interdisciplinary research center and specializes in the study of the social change aspects of global environmental change. Its goal is to conduct policy-relevant research aimed at informing policymakers about the causes, consequences and implications of global environmental problems.

Environmental Action
1525 New Hampshire Ave. NW
Washington, DC 20036
202-745-4870

Unpaid internships; credit.

The Environmental Careers Organization
286 Congress St.
Boston, MA 02210-1009
617-426-4375

Environmental Protection Agency
NNEMS National Program Manager
US EPA (1707)
401 M St. SW
Washington, DC 20460
202-260-4965

Global Tomorrow Coalition
1325 G St. NW, #915
Washington, DC 20005
202-628-4016

Paid internships in lobbying, legislative research, publications or administration. College juniors and beyond.

Government Relations Office
National Audubon Society
666 Pennsylvania Ave. SE, #301
Washington, DC 20003
202-547-9009

Unpaid internships involving research and lobbying. These are popular.

National Wildlife Federation
Resources Conservation Internship Program
1400 Sixteenth St. NW
Washington, DC 20036-2266
202-797-6800

Surfrider Foundation
Internship Program
122 South El Camino Real, #67
San Clemente, CA 92672
800-743-SURF

Major conservation organizations worldwide

ACTION
1100 Vermont Ave. NW
Washington, DC 20525

Alliance to Save Energy
1725 K St. NW, Suite 509
Washington, DC 20006-1401
202-857-0666

American Forest Council
1111 19th St. NW, #700
Washington, DC 20036
202-463-2455

American Fisheries Society
5410 Grosvenor Lane, Suite 110
Bethesda, MD 20814-2199
301-897-8616

American Conservation Association
30 Rockefeller Plaza, Room 5600
New York, NY 10112
212-649-5600

American Council for an Energy Efficient Economy
1001 Connecticut Ave. NW, Ste. 801
Washington, DC 20036
202-429-8873

American Institute of Biomedical Climatology
1023 Welsh Rd.
Philadelphia, PA 19115
215-673-8368

American Resources Group
Signet Bank Building
374 Maple Ave. East, Suite 210
Vienna, VA 22180
703-255-2700

Committee on Agriculture
Longworth House Office Building
Room 1301
Washington, DC 20515
202-225-2171

The Conservation Foundation
1250 24th St. NW
Washington, DC 20037
202-293-4800

Ecological Society of America
University of Wyoming
Laramie, WY 82071
307-766-3291

Energy Conservation Coalition
1525 New Hampshire Ave. NW
Washington, DC 20036
202-745-4874

Environmental Defense Fund
257 Park Ave. South
New York, NY 10010
212-505-2100

Funds for Animals
200 W. 57th St.
New York, NY 10019
212-246-2096

Environmental Technology Council
915 15th St. NW
Washington, DC 20005
202-783-0870

International Rain Forest Workshop
International Expeditions, Inc.
1776 Independence Court
Birmingham, AL 35216
800-633-4734

Adventure Careers

International Union for Conservation of Nature and Natural Resources
Avenue de Mont-Blanc
CH-1196 Gland, Switzerland
022-64 91 14

National Geographic Society
1145 17th St.
Washington, DC 20036
202-857-7000

National Wildlife Federation
1400 Sixteenth St. NW
Washington, DC 20036-2266
202-797-6800

The Nature Conservancy
1815 North Lynn St.
Arlington, VA 22209
703-841-5300

Radioactive Waste Campaign
625 Broadway, 2nd Fl.
New York, NY 10012-2611
212-437-7390

The Sierra Club Foundation
730 Polk St.
San Francisco, CA 94109
415-776-2211

Smithsonian Institution
Office of Fellowships and Grants
L'Enfant Plaza SW, Room 7300
Washington, DC 20560
202-287-3271

Society of American Foresters
5400 Grosvenor Lane
Bethesda, MD 20814

Society for Environmental Geochemistry and Health
Center for Environmental Sciences
Box 136, University of Colorado
Denver, CO 80204
303-556-3460

United Nations Environment Programme
1889 F St. NW
Washington, DC 20006
202-289-8456

U.S. Department of the Interior
1849 C St. NW
Washington, DC 20240
202-208-5048

Bureau of Land Management
C St. btwn. 18th & 19th Streets
Washington, DC 20240
202-343-9435

Fish and Wildlife Service
C St. btwn. 18th & 19th Streets
Washington, DC 20240
202-343-5634

National Park Service
C St. btwn. 18th & 19th Streets
Washington, DC 20240
202-208-6843

Union of Concerned Scientists
Public Information Officer, UCS
26 Church St.
Cambridge, MA 02238
617-547-5552

UCS is a nonprofit, public policy organization that conducts independent technical studies and public education programs; publishes books, reports and a quarterly magazine, Nucleus; and seeks to influence government policy at the local, state, federal and international levels.

U.S. Environmental Protection Agency (EPA)
401 M St. SW
Washington, DC 20460
202-797-6829

Wilderness Society
1400 I St. NW, Suite 550
Washington, DC 20005
202-842-3400

**Women's Occupational Health
Resource Center**
117 St. John's Place
Brooklyn, NY 11217
718-230-8822

World Health Organization
Avenue Appia CH-1211
Geneva 27, Switzerland

World Women in the Environment
1250 24th St. NW, Suite 500
Washington, DC 20037
202-331-9863

Reading and references

Breakfast of Biodiversity. John Vandermeer and Ivette Perfecto. (Food First, San Francisco, CA.)
A book about social change and conservation. Orders: 800-274-7826.

The New Complete Guide to Environmental Careers. The Environmental Careers Organization. (Island Press, Washington, DC, 1993.)

Citizens, Political Communication, and Interest Groups: Environmental Organizations in Canada and the United States. John C. Pierce, Mary Ann E. Steger, Brent S. Steel and Nicholas P. Lovrich. (Praeger Publishers, Westport, CT, 1992.)

Environmental Career Directory. Edited by Bradley J. Morgan and Joseph M. Palmisano. (Visible Ink Press, Detroit, MI, 1993.)

Environment. (Heldref Publications, 1319 Eighteenth St. NW, Washington, DC 20077-6117.)

The Ecologist. (MIT Press Journals, 55 Hayward St., Cambridge, MA 02142-1399.)

The Journal of Environmental Education. (Heldref Publications, 1319 Eighteenth St. NW, Washington, DC 20036-1802.)

Chapter 11

Spiritual Work: Careers and Self-Exploration

People say that what we're all seeking is a meaning for life. I don't think that's what we're really seeking. I think that what we're seeking is an experience of being alive, so that our life experiences on the purely physical plane will have resonance within our own innermost being and reality, so that we actually feel the rapture of being alive.
—Joseph Campbell, writer and philosopher

The Earth can no longer be healed on a physical level. Only a spiritual healing can change the course of the probable futures of mankind.
—Tom Brown, Jr., from *The Quest*

The pursuit of spiritual development stems from the belief that we, as humans, are not only physical beings, but also spiritual beings. Thus our work, in addition to maintaining our physical well-being and promoting worldly prosperity, should include care and development of our spiritual aspects.

Spiritual exploration can be undertaken in many ways, whether you build a career that has spiritual or healing origins, or you pursue your spiritual development through personal discipline and study. This work, while the most personal and intimate you may undertake in your life, is not personally limited. It has important application in the real world of career and community.

Even if your spiritual work is that of personal study and practice, you will find that this inward work has great influence on your outward work and may have profound impact on your career development. It is through inward exploration that many people discover their true selves, their true aspirations and their true "calling," or vocation. Also, it is through spiritual development that you can cultivate an inner reservoir of strength and insight that will empower you and contribute to your effectiveness in your career in the world.

In the words of the Dalai Lama, "The Essence is to live one's life within the noble principles of the *dharma* [transformative process] and give direction and a purpose to one's life. If one can adopt such an outlook, the *dharma* will not only be beneficial to oneself as an individual but will also contribute to the betterment of the community in which one lives." (*Path of Bliss: A Practical Guide to States of Meditation,* by H.H. the Dalai Lama, Tenzin Gyatso Snow Lion Publications, Ithaca, New York). The process of self-development offers a framing for your entire life and a structure for the building of a career.

Whether your career or your study, work in the world of spirit is not an escape or a prescription to ease the stress of everyday life. On the contrary, this is a process that is often difficult, for it can cause a dramatic shift in the way you view yourself and your work. But it is this shift, this transformation, that can provide the opportunity for profound growth and development, both personally and professionally.

The discovery of the spiritual work that is compelling for you is an important step unto itself, whether you work as a healer, church worker, yoga student or volunteer at a meditation center. Spiritual development, in many ways, is self-sustaining. When you begin to ask yourself, "What spiritual work should I be doing?" the answers may come easily and naturally. You may be struck by a book you notice at the bookstore, a sermon or a Sabbath prayer.

Or you may pass a yoga school that you have walked by 100 times, and today you decide to stop and pick up a class/lecture schedule. Or you may be struck by a discussion your friends are having about meditation and know that something in this teaching seems right for you.

Work and adventure during great change

Spiritual work, whether your career, your practice or discipline, will add a character and a flavor to your life. In the outside world of community, work in the spiritual domain will bring you into contact with a growing group of people who share a spiritual focus. Within your inner world of personal growth and well-being, spiritual practice can provide an inner anchor for you as you pursue your work and develop your career. We are not suggesting you move to an Ashram for the rest of your life. On the contrary, we promote that you lead a dynamic and powerful life in the world. For the prosperous and peaceful design of our future, in many ways, depends on your participation and your contribution.

We live in a time of great change, many say a time of transformation. Old prescriptions for work, career, contribution and community may no longer seem relevant or important. Many scholars, scientists and spiritual teachers believe this to be a time of unprecedented change, that will have far reaching implications: change in social and political systems; change in the manner we relate; even a dramatic change in human consciousness.

As we have said throughout this book, it is for you to discover what work and career is important for you and how, in this changing world, you will add your own personal contribution. In this chapter and the directory that follows we hope to have offered some—however small—support to you as you work to develop a life and a career in which your experiences on the purely physical plane will have resonances within your innermost being and reality.

Personal Accounts

We include two personal accounts that offer insight and two methods of spiritual development: meditation and yoga. We are not suggesting that the few methods we mention in the text or the organizations that we list in the directory that follows are necessarily the ones for you. There are countless traditions, practices and rapidly growing career opportunities for you to pursue. Many of you may have been working for years in the world of the spirit, by observing religious practice or through your customary walks alone in the woods. Always keep in mind that this is your personal journey, your own developmental process, your own spiritual work and adventure.

Jay: Meditation and self-discovery

Jay Siemore is a Ph.D. candidate in zoology. He has discovered that meditation has been a powerful tool in his career development as well as personal discovery.

We all know moments of groundedness and of feeling powerfully "alive." Walking through a field on a summer morning, looking into a child's smiling face in the park, seconds after making love, or in early morning. No matter how lightly this sense of being whole touches our lives, we all know these moments.

Through my work as a student of zoology, specifically the study of birds and their learning patterns, I have brought this sense of spirit into my life on a consistent basis. The study of pure science

249

is like the study of the mystery and the power of nature for me—the study of the world of spirit. Whether I am observing nesting patterns of robins in the forest of northern Wisconsin or conducting laboratory experiments to track how chickadees learn, my academic/professional work in intertwined with my spiritual work.

When I complete my study and my dissertation, in the next two years, I will go on to teach at a university or to conduct research for the government. I have already begun to teach college-level courses as part of my doctoral work, finding it rewarding and challenging. This whole process has been a combination of rewards and difficult challenges. I use the practice of daily meditation to avoid being upset by difficult or unpleasant situations. I use meditation to ground me and to sustain me while I continue in my development, my work and my study.

Discussion of Vipassana meditation

Steps along the path of personal growth are taken when one works to see things "as they really are." Vipassana meditation is an ancient meditation technique used by the Buddha, that allows for the seeing of things as they are, in the pure sense. Through the continued practice of Vipassana meditation, a person can begin to live in the world of *action* instead of reaction.

According to the teachings of the Buddha, the inability to see things as they really are is the root of much human suffering and of wrong work and wrong action. When people live life through their perceptions, certain things as good and certain things as bad, instead of living through the pure consciousness that sees things simply "as they are," a miserable cycle of craving and aversion is set in motion. People crave things they perceive to be pleasurable and run from things they perceive to be unpleasant. This practice of meditation allows for the breaking of the cycle of craving and aversion.

The Vipassana practice focuses on the process of observing body sensations without reacting, whether the sensations be pleasant or unpleasant. The process combines self-observation with gentle and persistent calming of a roaming mind. With the Vipassana training, you simultaneously heighten your ability to observe sensations (develop awareness of what is happening) while removing the old habits of reaction. Students of Vipassana meditation begin to "see" that all sensations, isolated from perception and interpretation, are in essence the same—forever changing.

It is within this constantly changing world that aware people must discover their true "function," or career in the world. Many people live their entire lives doing things that they have been conditioned to do because they "look good" instead of because they are the right work for that individual. Meditation is a powerful tool for this process of discovery and a great support as you carry out your work.

Maggie: Athletic interests lead to career in massage therapy

Maggie Mead was always tuned into her love of athletics and physical activity. But not until after she earned a business degree, did she realize that only a career in bodywork would fulfill her true interests.

I have always been athletic. I grew up with three brothers, and in high school I was considered a "jock." I went to college to study business and discovered that the college tennis team, summer wind surfing and camping were much more interesting than formulas and cash-flow charts. My attention was never on the books, but always on the body. I was fascinated by how beautiful people were when they were moving, how powerful, yet graceful, but at the same time how tender and in need of touch and care.

I didn't realize until a year after I, by the grace of God, graduated from college, that the body was beautiful and powerful because it served as the physical home of the spirit and the soul. It was this union of body and spirit, of flesh and energy and light, that made people wonderful. And it was at this time that I realized that my work should be as a healer, a bodyworker, a coach for the training and conditioning of the spirit while in the body.

At this time I decided to return to school, but this time to study the healing art of massage. I worked through a two-year program at a school in Western Massachusetts. I studied massage techniques, physiology, pathology, but I also studied the techniques for healing body and spirit. And I began to learn to do this healing for myself, and to strengthen my spiritual self. It was through this personal healing and strengthening process that I have developed into a healer of others.

Choosing bodywork as a profession also introduced me to a unique and wonderful community of other healers and practitioners. In some parts of the country, these communities are very visible. In other parts of the country they are not as noticeable. But I know that in some way or another, spiritual communities are developing everywhere. And what is so remarkable about a spiritual community is how quickly it seems to grow and develop, and how these people work in so many aspects of the community. Spiritual people are not limited to the healing fields. They are teachers, often psychologists, artists, environmentalists—the list is limitless. What unites these people is the way that they give of themselves with caring and commitment, and how they share a vision of the future that is filled with peace and love.

The work of supporting and healing people in the broader context of building a spiritual community is not always easy in this world. You are often confronted by resistance to a peaceful world—fear, anger, hate and pain. I feel it every day when I work on my massage clients. For me, because I am so physical, daily yoga practice is my technique for supporting myself in my work and to maintain my personal well-being. Also, I garner strength and hope by watching the development of spirit and strength in the world around me.

Discussion of yoga

Yoga, training that combines exercise of the body and the mind, is another technique that can be employed to move into a clear state. "It is indeed a fact that the mind is always telling us to go here, go there, do this, do that—it is always telling us which way to turn," says Swami Prabhupada, the founder of the International Society for Krishna Consciousness. "Thus the sum and substance of the yoga system is to control the agitated mind," he explains. (*The Perfection of Yoga by His Divine Grace A.C. Bhaktivedanta Swami Prabhupada,* The Bhaktivedanta Book Trust). In many forms and techniques, yoga is the practice of body posturing, movements and breathing that strengthens while relaxing both the physical and mental bodies.

The manual for beginners of Hatha Yoga put out by the Integral Yoga Institute explains the basic mind/body connection made through the yoga practice: "By learning proper relaxation the body comes to its own natural state of health and ease. These practices also have a profound effect on the mind, making it more relaxed, poised and centered." (*Step by Step Instruction for Beginners: Integral Yoga Hatha,* Integral Yoga Institute, Integral Yoga Publications: Buckingham, Virginia.) Many people practice yoga daily, from basic to advanced techniques, to develop centering and balance that provides effectiveness and strength in other daily endeavors.

Spiritual Work Directory

Spiritual centers and retreats

The National Center for the Laity
In Support of the Christian Vocation in and to the Modern World
205 West Monroe St., #300
Chicago, IL 60606
312-849-2772

The National Center publishes a newspaper called *Initiatives* six times a year. It's a digest of news and views regarding the initiatives ordinary Christians are taking to improve work, family and neighborhood life. They also host a Good Work Retreat twice a year. Call 708-719-1620 for information. In addition, there is a support and action group called Business Executives for Economic Justice. One can obtain pamphlets concerning spirituality relating to specific occupations: nursing, law, education, unemployment, business and homemaking, with one on the military due out in 1995.

JPUSA
925 West Wilson Ave.
Chicago, IL 60640
312-561-2450

JPUSA stands for Jesus People USA. JPUSA is a Christian community in inner-city Chicago. More than 500 people share a 10-floor hotel building just three blocks from Lake Michigan. Started in the early '70s by a bunch of Jesus Freaks whose bus broke down in Chicago, JPUSA is now a teeming hub of activity with a roofing company, a carpentry crew, an annual music festival for 15,000 people, a magazine called Cornerstone, a shelter for homeless women and their children and much more. People can come to visit or come to live from one month to a lifetime. If you want to see diversity in action, there's no place like JPUSA. The members of the community range from ex-addicts and ex-prostitutes to hippies, punks and plain old "ordinary" folk. People come from all over the world to visit and live. One family group might contain three Germans, two Swiss-Germans, a missionary from Peru, an Australian bank executive, an East Coast college student, a couple from Guam or natives of Chicago.

JPUSA uses a "common purse," meaning that every community member works (though "working" could mean a graphic art internship or spending nights in the homeless shelter), and room and board is covered by the community.

Call to get brochures or other information.

L'Abri Fellowship
49 Lynbrook Road
Southborough, MA 01772

L'Abri is French for "shelter." In 1955, Francis and Edith Schaeffer began a Christian study center in their home in Switzerland. The center in the U.S. is in Southborough, but there are L'Abri's all over the world. L'Abri is a place where honest questions on life and its meaning can be pursued from a Biblical perspective. People come from every state, many other countries and a great diversity of backgrounds. Students range in age from their late teens to their late eighties. Some have seen themselves as Christians, others have not. Anyone who is interested in learning, questioning and growing is welcome. Students come for varying lengths of time, from one or two days to three months. There is a minimal charge per night; that cost is available upon request.

As part of their study program, L'Abri brings in speakers Friday night during each three-month session. Topics range from Feminism and Christianity to a history of Christian apologetics. Following the lecture, there is an open question and answer session that goes on as long as there are people to ask questions (and the speaker has energy). This is a great place to pursue an intellectual as well as an emotional understanding of Christian belief and practice.

Landmark Education

Central Office:
450 Mission St., Ste. 403
San Francisco, CA 94105
415-882-6300

New York City:
425 Fifth Ave.
New York, NY 10016
212-447-2100

Landmark is an employee-owned company that conducts workshops and seminars that support people in leading lives of "possibility." The Forum workshop is the introduction course and prerequisite for other Landmark classes. The Forum, a weekend workshop conducted at locations throughout the country, introduces participants to the "technology" that supports people in shaping their own lives—in areas of effectiveness, creativity, vitality and self-expression.

There are more than 30 permanent Landmark centers in the U.S. as well as centers in Australia, Brazil, Canada, England, Germany, India, Israel, Mexico, New Zealand, Sweden and Switzerland.

Adventure Careers

Kripalu Center for Yoga and Health
Box 793
Lenox, MA 01240
413-637-3280

Kripalu is a well-known center that offers programs in yoga, self-discovery, spiritual attunement, health and fitness, bodywork, and rest and renewal. Guests can come to the Center for self-determined lengths of stay. Yoga classes, meditations and spiritual trainings are scheduled throughout the days. Fees vary depending on chosen accommodations and additional bodywork. Also, workshops such as Yoga Weekends are offered.

The Spiritual Lifestyle Training Program lasts for two to four months, during which the volunteer lives free of charge and participates in study groups and workshops in exchange for 40 hours of work per week. Tasks usually involve kitchen assignment or household maintenance. There is a $25 application fee and $25 for notebooks and other materials needed during the training. Ages range greatly, and the major requirements are that an individual be able to maintain the 40-hour work week and have an interest in the Center.

The Omega Institute
Lake Drive, RD 2, Box 377
Rhinebeck, NY 12572
914-338-6030 (Before the end of May)
914-266-4301 (Late May until late September)

Omega is a summertime institute known for its workshops that teach and support spiritual and creative development, and well-being. The Center, located in the New York Hudson River Valley, puts on week-long and weekend workshops ranging from yoga training to traditional Chinese medicine to writing and dance. Fees for workshops range between $200 and $300. Omega also organizes "Adventures," travel workshops in locations such as Italy and the Swiss Alps.

For those who want to spend the whole summer at the Institute, there is a work exchange program. For 40 hours of work per week (housekeeping, child care, kitchen or garden work), workers receive free room, board, attendance to one workshop and $50 per week. Also, the Holistic Studies Program is organized specifically for workers, and offers courses throughout the summer. Summer work exchanges run from the end of May until Labor Day or until September 27. There are about 180 workers throughout the summer.

Insight Meditation Society
Pleasant St.
Barre, MA 01005
508-355-4378

Another center that teaches the Vipassana meditation technique. Courses run from two-day weekends to 12 days. The fee, which includes room and board, is $26 a day for a nine-day course, but doesn't include payment to teachers which is a voluntary donation. A two-day retreat for $90 is also offered. Resident work/study programs are available.

Esalen Institute
Big Sur, CA 93920
408-667-3000

Opened in the 1960s, this is one of the early centers working in the "human potential movement." Now this is a spiritual/healing center offering gestalt therapy, psychosynthesis, Ericksonian hypnosis, shamanic healing and rolfing.

Institute of Core Energetics
115 E. 23rd St., 12th floor
New York, NY 10010
212-505-6767.

The work conducted at the Institute of Core Energetics combines different dimensions of human existence (body, feeling, mind and spirit) into the teaching of therapy and healing.

The Vipassana Meditation Center
Dhamma Dhara
P.O. Box 24
Shelburne Falls, MA 01370
413-625-2160

The 10-day introductory course is open to anyone over 18 (younger people have taken courses with special permission from the center). Completion of the course, or *sit*, is a prerequisite for self-courses that can be of a self-determined length or longer sits often extending up to 20 days. Many courses are offered throughout the year.

The 10-day course, held in total silence, sticks to a rigorous timetable of meditation periods, interrupted by two daily meals, rest periods, evening tea, and a nighttime discourse that provides instruction for the next day of work. The meditation practice and a code of discipline are taught.

There is no set fee for the courses, but donations, or "metta," are requested in the sum that each person feels he or she can offer. All of the money received is put back into the Center to support courses for other students. There are four permanent centers in the U.S. with others in India, Nepal, Australia, New Zealand, Japan, Thailand, France and England. The Shelburne Falls Center can be contacted for more information on centers, their locations and schedules of courses to he held at temporary locations.

Adventure Careers

The Waldorf Institute
260 Hungry Hollow Rd.
Spring Valley, NY 10977
914-425-0055

Rudolf Steiner, the brilliant writer, lecturer and teacher who lived during the early part of this century, developed new practices in the areas of medicine, education, the arts, architecture, farming and gardening, and social life. The Orientation Year at the Waldorf Institute provides a foundation in Steiner's organic view of the world through intensive courses in spirituality, the arts and humanity. Teacher trainees in this program become qualified for teaching in a Waldorf school. The Institute is part of the Threefold Community, which includes the Green Meadow Waldorf School, the School of Eurythmy and Weleda—the makers of Anthroposophical remedies.

Dai Bosatsu Zendo
HCR 1, Box 171
Livingston Manor, NY 12758
914-439-4566
Fax: 914-439-3119

Zen studies society introduces Zen Buddhism to the West. Center accommodates 75 men and women with a charge of $50 per night.

Living Dharma Center
Box 304
Amherst, MA 01004
413-259-1611

Contact: Richard Clark
505 Pratt Corner Rd.
Amherst, MA 01002

Center for Zen training offers workshops, weekly *zazen* meditations, *dokusan* (private interviews on practice) and *sesshin* (prolonged meditation retreats), at both its Massachusetts and Connecticut locations. The practice taught is that of self-empowerment in a context of psychospiritual evolution.

Sunray Meditation Society
Office of Spiritual Director
Ven. Dhyani Ywahoo
P.O. Box 269
Bristol, VT 05443
413-256-1721

Sunray Meditation Society is an international spiritual society dedicated to planetary peace. Using sacred techniques of the Etowah Cherokee nation, Sunray is also a Dharma center of schools of Tibetan Buddhism. Regional offices are located worldwide; contact your local representative through the central office.

Providence Zen Center, Dept. 380
99 Pound Rd.
Cumberland, RI 02864
401-658-1464

This is a center for meditation practice, retreats and residencies. Programs include meditation and daily practice, public talks and tours, introductory workshops, retreats from one to 90 days, conferences and an annual Summer Training Period. Zen is the technique of learning "how to live your life in a simple, non-clinging way, enriching you and allowing you to touch others with compassion."

Other spiritual centers

Sivananda Ashram Yoga Ranch
P.O. Box 195
Woodbourne, NY 12788
914-434-9242

The Expanding Light
14618 Tyler Foote Rd.
Nevada City, CA 95959
916-292-3494

Has a work program.

Camp Lenox
Route 8
Lee, MA 01238
413-243-2223

Feather Pipe Ranch
P.O. Box 1682
Helena, MT 59624
406-442-8196

Naropa Institute
2130 Arapahoe Ave.
Boulder, CO 80302
303-444-0202

Ojai Foundation
P.O. Box 1620
Ojai, CA 93024
805-646-8343

Hollyhock Farm
P.O. Box 127
Manson's Landing
Cortes Island, OBC
Canada, VOP IKO
604-935-6465

Centers and schools for healing and bodywork

Stillpoint Center
P.O. Box 15
Hatfield, MA 01038
413-247-9322

Since 1981 the Stillpoint Center has combined vocational training in massage therapy with courses and other opportunities for personal and spiritual growth. Stillpoint is a training institute for people who want bodywork to be their career. The core of the Center's training includes various massage techniques,

259

anatomy and physiology, pathology and business practices. The course program approved by the American Massage Therapy Association takes 10 months to complete. The Center also offers evening, day and weekend courses, such as Basic Massage, Business Practices for the Bodyworker, and Subtle Anatomy and Bodywork.

Midwest Center for the Study of Oriental Medicine
6226 Banker Rd., Suites 5 & 6   4334 N. Hazel, Suite 206
Racine, WI 53403   Chicago, IL 60613
414-554-2010   312-975-1295

This is a 36-month training program in acupuncture and traditional Oriental medicine, and a one-year course in Oriental massage. Students receive a solid foundation in clinical science, Chinese medical therapy, diagnostics and needle technique for acupuncture.

Bancroft School of Massage Therapy
50 Franklin St.
Worcester, MA 01608
508-757-7923

The Bancroft School has been training professional massage therapists since 1950. Its program includes completion of the following courses: massage techniques, reflexology, positional release, facial anatomy & physiology, Zen Shiatsu, touch and health, pathology, hydrotherapy, sports massage, CPR, first aid, business, psychology and nutrition. A certification program is also offered in Shiatsu Massage Therapy.

Florida School of Massage
64221 SW 13th St.
Gainesville, FL 32608
904-378-7891

The school offers a 1,000-hour course in basic massage, which prepares students for entry into the health care field as massage therapists, eligible for AMTA certification and licensing by the state. Advanced courses are offered in structural bodywork and awareness, sports massage and polarity therapy.

The Alexander Foundation
605 W. Philellena St.
Philadelphia, PA 19119
215-844-0670 (phone and fax)

A community of students and teachers of the (F. Matthias) Alexander Technique, a theory of healing and bodywork. Students enter into an apprenticeship program, which means "giving oneself the time to study and improve the quality of one's attention, coordination and responsiveness." The Foundation also provides a listing of teachers trained there in the Technique and listings of introductory workshops and residential courses taught annually in the U.S. and abroad.

Other schools and institutes

Myotherapy College of Utah
3350 South 2300 East
Salt Lake City, UT 84109
800-HEAL YOU

Two-week (100 hours) intensive training in therapeutic massage and bodywork.

Flynn's School of Herbology
77 E. 4th St.
New York, NY 10003

A five-session course in herbal medicine. Total cost, including tuition and books and notes is just under $200.

Ohio College of Massotherapy
1018 Kenmore Blvd.
Akron, OH 44314
216-745-6170

Blazing Star Herbal School
Gail Ulrich
P.O. Box 6MH
Shelburne Falls, MA 01370
413-625-6875

Short apprenticeships.

The New England Institute for Neuro-Linguistic Programming
RFD3, Pratt Corner Road
Amherst, MA 01002-9805
413-259-1248

Workshops on Neuro-Linguistic Programming (NLP), a mode of understanding the human mind, and influencing behavior. Certification training, and Ericksonian Hypnosis. Licensed by the state department of education.

The Muscular Therapy Institute
122 Rindge Ave.
Cambridge, MA 02140
617-576-1300

Courses in muscular therapy technique, anatomy, physiology, alignment, tension analysis, injury evaluation, prevention and treatment, energy studies, communications skills.

Rolf Institute of Structural Integration
205 Canyon Blvd.
Boulder, CO 80302
303-449-5903

Training programs in rolfing, the systematic reorganization of human structure into an integrated whole.

Bodywork of the Childbearing Year
Advanced Certificate Training
8950 Villa La Jolla Dr., Ste. 2162
La Jolla, CA 92037
619-436-0418

The School of Healing Arts
975 Hornblend, Ste. E-MM
San Diego, CA 92109
619-581-9429

Acupressure Institute
1533 Shattuck
Berkeley, CA 94709
510-845-1059

Adventure Careers

San Francisco School of Massage
2209 Van Ness Ave.
San Francisco, CA 94109
415-474-4600

**Pacific School of Massage and
Healing Arts**
44800 Fish Rock Rd.
Gualala, CA 95445
707-884-3138

**Harbin Hot Springs School of
Shiatsu and Massage**
Box 570-MM
Middletown, CA 95461
707-987-3801

**Diamond Light: The Marin School
of Massage**
Box 5443
Mill Valley, CA 94942
415-454-6651

**Shiatsu Massage School & Tao
Healing Arts Center**
2309 Main St.
Santa Monica, CA 90405
213-396-1877

Pacific School of Tai Chi
Box 962
Solana Beach, CA 92075
619-259-1396

**Hawaiian Island School of Body
Therapies**
Box 390188
Kailua-Kona, HI 96739
808-322-0048

Honolulu School of Massage, Inc.
1123 11th Ave., #301
Honolulu, HI 96816
808-733-0000

**Blue Cliff School of Therapeutic
Massage**
136 S. Acadian Thruway
Baton Rouge, LA 70806
504-387-0885

Health Enrichment Center, Inc.
Schools of Therapeutic Massage,
Shiatsu, Subtle Energy Therapy &
Clinical Approaches
408 Davis Lake Rd.
Lapeer, MI 48446
810-667-9453

**Minneapolis School of Massage
and Bodywork, Inc.**
220 Lowry Ave. NE
Minneapolis, MN 55418
612-788-8907

**New Jersey School of Shiatsu &
Oriental Therapy, Well Being
Center**
100 Valley Rd.
Montclair, NJ 07042
201-744-5667

**The New Mexico Academy of
Massage Healing Arts**
Box 932
Santa Fe, NM 87504
505-988-2621

Somatic Therapy Institute
546 Harkle Rd., Ste. B
Santa Fe, NM 87501
505-983-9695

**The New Center for Holistic
Health Education & Research**
6801 Jericho Turnpike
Syosset, NY 11791-4413
800-9-CAREER

The International Academy of Massage Science
Box 277-M
Glen Riddle, PA 19037
610-558-3140

International Shiatsu Center
Box 187-M
Buckingham, PA 18912
215-340-9918

Richmond Academy of Massage
2004 Bremo Rd., Suite 102
Richmond, VA 23226
804-282-5003

International centers

China Academy of Traditional Chinese Medicine
Guang An Men Hospital
Beijing, PRC

U.S. Foreign Office:
8839 Knox
Skokie, IL 60076
708-676-9891

Intensive professional training in acupuncture, Tuina/Anmo, or Qi Gong (energy balancing) at hospital in China.

Shiatsu School of Canada, Inc.
547 College St.
Toronto, ON, Canada, M6G 1A9
416-323-1818

Professional Shiatsu therapy training.

Rolf Institute of Structural Integration
Europe:
Herzogster, 40
8000 Munich 40, Germany
Australia:
Box 140
Moreland, 3056
Melbourne, Victoria
Australia
Brazil:
Associacao Brasileira de Rolfistas
Caixa Postal 20.978
01498-San Paulo-SP, Brazil

Training in rolfing, the systematic reorganization of human structure into an integrated whole.

Reading and references

The Associated Bodywork & Massage Professionals
P.O. Box 1869
Evergreen, CO 80439
800-458-ABMP

An international professional membership organization devoted to promoting ethical practices, fostering unification and acceptance of the profession, and protecting the rights of massage and bodywork practitioners.

Adventure Careers

National Accreditation Commission for Schools and Colleges of Acupuncture and Oriental Medicine
1424-16th St. NW, Suite 501
Washington, DC 20036
202-265-3370

Jin Shin Do Foundation for Bodymind Acupressure
366 California Ave., #16
Palo Alto, CA 94306
415-328-1811

New Frontier: Magazine of Transformation
(National magazine of the Consciousness Movement)
46 Front St.
Philadelphia, PA 19106

Chapter 12

Making It Happen! The Logistics of Funding & Travel

Adventure Careers

Now listen to what I have to say, and do not forget it. First you will come to the sirens, who bewitch everyone who comes near them. If any man draws near in his innocence, and listens to their voice, he never sees home again...If you wish to hear them yourself, plug your men's ears with wax, and have your men tie you tightly to the mast. When you have got clear of them, there is a choice of two courses, and which you take is up to you. One course will bring you to a pair of precipitous rocks, the Moving Rocks. Not a bird can pass between them without being caught between them. The other course leads between two cliffs. Inside of one the Scylla dwells, and yelps in her dreadful way. She has twelve feet and six enormously long necks, and she grabs a poor wretch with each of her heads from any ship that sails below. Underneath the other cliff Charybdis swallows down black water. Don't be there when she swallows!

—The goddess Circe's advice to Odysseus (or Ulysses), from the ancient Greek epic poem, *The Odyssey*

Fortunately, modern adventurers do not face quite the same degree of peril as that confronting King Odysseus. But, like Odysseus, modern adventurers will do well to seek practical advice and collect as much information as possible before setting to sea—whether metaphorically or literally. Finding the right sources of information is, of course, critical (it's a good thing Odysseus had a goddess handy for advice), and it is important to *use* all the available information to plan the details of a trip, or of any experience, for that matter.

We have endeavored to include practical advice wherever it occurred to us, and you will find ideas on how to implement your own adventures and odysseys—and avoid monsters, clashing rocks and whirlpools—throughout the other chapters of this book. But there is a great deal more to be said on the topic. The logistics of actually implementing your own adventures can be complex, and it is over the details of logistics that most adventures succeed or fail.

For that matter, the success of your planning can determine whether you are able to undertake an adventure in the first place. Planning has a most beneficial effect on cost, for instance. A well-planned school year abroad may cost you very little—discounted airfares and lodging, a grant to pick up your tuition, or a part-time job can all contribute to a financially successful trip. Without some planning in these areas, you may be unable to afford a trip, or, more likely, you will not be able to afford as much of a trip. The clever planner is able to do more and go farther—for example, by adding a summer of low-cost rail travel or an interesting workcamp experience onto a spring semester of study in Europe.

This is especially true when your adventures require long-distance travel, since travel is inherently costly, and more preparation is needed the farther you go from home. But it is also true of adventures in nonspacial dimensions. An adventurous experiment in a new career will go better if you do not go broke in the first month. Careful financial planning and prioritizing can make many adventures and rewarding experiences possible. For example, once you decide you want to take a low-paying internship for the next summer, you can develop a detailed financial plan to make the experience possible.

Personal financial planning

The first and most essential step in financial planning, for an individual as much as for any business, is accurate financial information. Where does your money go now? Look at your monthly expenses.

Your checkbook ledger, or better yet, the canceled checks from your last statement, will tell you what you spent your money on. Your statement will also tell you how much cash you took out from ATMs and from checks written to "cash." If you don't think the month is representative, combine it with another monthly statement or adjust it by eye. And don't forget to make a list of those occasional big payments, such as taxes, quarterly insurance payments, tuition, or occasional health care and car repair bills, and convert them to a per-month basis for the sake of your analysis. When you are done itemizing specific expense categories and the typical monthly expenditures in them, prioritize by size and make a list of the top 10. The rest will not amount to enough to make much difference in your financial planning. (Yet ironically it is on the little items that most people concentrate when they try to save money. Going out to fewer movies will not solve any major financial shortfalls!)

With your top 10 monthly expenses listed in front of you, it is a relatively easy task to think about how you might alter them. Let's say you want to quit a boring sales job and take on an interesting internship to learn wooden boat-building, but this would cut your income by a few hundred every month. Look at your list of expenses and come up with a way to cut them by the same amount or more.

You can do it. Really. For example, sell the car and move to a cheaper apartment within walking distance of the new internship, and you will probably cut your monthly expenses by at least half. (No gas, repairs or auto insurance—think about it!) You can always move into a larger apartment later, and you can always buy or lease another car, but you cannot replicate the impact of today's career experience and personal development later in your life.

Funding for study abroad

Are there public funding sources available? Yes, although most of the funding for which you will qualify is likely to be in considerable demand. It takes care and foresight to target the right funding sources and prepare yourself to be an ideal candidate.

There are hundreds of sources of funding. That's the good news. The bad news is that the majority provide scholarships or research stipends for graduate students—often for their doctorate or postdoctorate research projects. This is fine, if you are a Ph.D.

student, but the majority of readers are not. (Further, if you are a Ph.D. student, your school and professors should be able to orient you to the major sources of funding in your field.)

If you are not a Ph.D. student, or not even a student at all, do not give up all hope. There are still many options. Undergraduate college students, high-school students, and people with high-school or college degrees but little or no current academic work, can also qualify for a range of grants and subsidized programs.

There are a number of good annual directories of sources of grants and other types of funding. The best place to start is at the local library (or the nearest big city or university library). Here are two excellent sources that will help you determine whether you are eligible for any of the hundreds of awards listed:

Annual Register of Grant Support. National Register Publications Co., Macmillan Directory Division. Wilmette, IL.

Directory of Grants in the Humanities. Oryx Press. Phoenix, AZ.

More publications are included in the directory in this chapter—be sure to review them and order any that are relevant to your interests and plans.

The listings in Directory 1 include grant-giving organizations, selected primarily for their accessibility to a wide range of applicants. Most of these give awards to undergraduates and even nonstudents in addition to graduate students. And many support alternative educational experiences, such as travel or research abroad.

You will find that every college and university has its own scholarships and stipends, both at the graduate and undergraduate levels, for traditional students. In some cases a scholarship or stipend for at-home study can also be used for a period of study abroad.

Fund-raising strategies

How do you use the directory, or the hefty volumes listed in this chapter? Think of the granting organizations as customers looking to purchase certain types of people or projects. You are not a chameleon on plaid. You cannot repackage yourself for every possible grant or award. But neither are you completely inflexible. The idea is to fund an *adventure*, after all, so you must be open to the unexpected. Define some general areas of interest and expertise. Then cull out the grants that apply to those areas of interest. Contact the sponsoring organizations for details. And then, once you have a handful of well-defined funding alternatives, start defining the details of what you want to do.

In many cases, as will be obvious when you read the listings in the directories, you need specific qualifications to obtain the funding. This may mean speaking a foreign language (as in most grants for study in Turkey or France, for example). If you really want to pursue such a grant, but do not have the requisite language skills, enroll in a language course—this ought to convince the grantors of your sincerity! Requirements can be far more specific—for example, there are grants (not listed in the directory) for Ph.D. students of Irish descent who are studying Irish history, as well as a growing number of grants for minorities (a few of which we have included in our directory).

In some cases, the grants are given more on the strength of a project than the person proposing it. If you want to work on an economic development project in the Caribbean, or a peace development project anywhere in the world, there are groups that might like to fund your work. For these types of grants, it should be obvious that you need a well-developed project proposal. It is prudent to run your proposal by as many experts as you can find before submitting it for funding consideration.

Many granting organizations work on strange calendars. They may only consider applications once or twice a year when their directors convene to read the applications. This confounds short-term plans and it is generally wise to work on *next year's* adventure rather than this year's as a result.

Smart travel buying

Why pay less when you can pay more? This is the implicit motto of most travelers. Let's review some of the tactics that can help you reverse it.

1. Airplane tickets: Airlines offer cheap promotional fares. Use them. Read the newspapers for advertised promotional fares from major airlines—this is especially useful if you can be flexible in timing. However, if you must leave and return on a strict schedule, all is not lost. Consolidators usually offer the cheapest tickets to Asia, the cheapest unrestricted fares to Europe and, occasionally, the cheapest fares within North America. Because of fare wars, special *restricted* promotional fares to Europe are often cheaper, but be careful of those restrictions. If it is important for you to be able to change your flight plans, an unrestricted coach fare from a consolidator is preferable to a cheaper restricted promotional fare.

Consolidators buy tickets in bulk from airlines—generally tickets the airlines do not think they can sell at their regular fares. Most consolidators sell their tickets to travel agents, but many are also happy to sell them directly to individual travelers. Discounts may be 25 percent to 35 percent.

Be forewarned that most consolidator tickets are "non-endorsable," meaning you cannot use them on another airline if the one that issued them flakes out on you—and that, if the ticket cannot be used, you will probably have to pursue a refund from the consolidator, not the airline—so make sure you have confidence in the solvency of airline and consolidator before purchasing! (Note that many consolidators also offer discounts on hotels, so check all options available.) Directory 2 features major consolidators. We are basing this list on a Consumer Reports survey of the industry. They do business by telephone, and where 800 numbers exist we have listed them.

A further note of warning for smart travelers: Do not travel on tickets, script or vouchers with *someone else's name* on them! Many an unwary traveler has purchased a ticket issued to someone else, only to be bumped from the flight at the gate or hassled in customs upon arrival. It's *not* worth the extra discount to run these risks.

In general, make sure you are dealing with a legitimate company (listed telephone numbers, real office or storefront with full-time employees, clear and helpful customer service, a business track record in a single location), and that your tickets are normal-looking and issued in your name. If you are in doubt, take the ticket to a travel agent for a second opinion. Don't be talked into spending any money under suspicious circumstances—discount-hunters are easy prey for scam artists, and they often use time-pressure to keep buyers from researching the offer and discovering the scam.

2. Discounted travel: Also consider last-minute travel clubs. Clubs sell airline tickets, cruises and other travel packages at very low prices, providing you are able to jump on a listing, drop everything, and go at the last minute. This can be integrated into a long-term plan. For example, if you arrange a flexible internship or job in Europe over the summer, you might join a travel club in the spring and wait for the right fare before going to Europe. Joining a club gives you access to listings, either via a phone hotline or a regular newsletter. Annual membership is usually less than $50. Directory 3 lists a number of clubs. We hear that local clubs work best for travel out of their areas, and that the big national clubs (Sears, R&R, DTI) are better otherwise—also these large clubs handle hotels and car rentals as well as air travel.

3. Bartered travel: Travel companies sometimes pay suppliers with travel *credits* instead of cash, and these credits are often transferable. When the suppliers sell the credits for cash, they can end up in the traveler's hands at discounts of 25 percent, 50 percent or more. But you generally have to work through a specialized broker to find bartered airplane tickets, hotel rooms and the like (they often issue their own credit cards, usable at specific airlines, hotels, restaurants, and so forth). Try the services listed in Directory 4.

4. Rail passes: Every passenger railroad offers one or more discounted rail passes, and many offer special discounts to students or seniors as well. The Eurailpass, which can be used for travel throughout Western Europe, with the single exception of Great Britain, is probably the most well-known. In general, the Eurailpasses (there are a variety depending upon your age, student status and the length of time you wish to travel) are good deals if you plan to travel, on average, more than a couple hundred miles a day. Some of the longer-term passes, such as the 21-day pass, are a good deal if you travel only 100 miles a day on average. But if you do not expect to travel at least this much, you are better off buying single-ride tickets as needed.

There are similar rail passes for many individual countries both within and beyond the boundaries of the Eurailpass, including England, Ireland, Greece, Poland, Japan and Portugal. Such rail passes can only be obtained from travel agents in the U.S., but if your agent is not knowledgeable, you can also go through the organizations listed in Directory 5.

Contact Amtrak at 800-872-7245 for information on U.S. rail passes and your travel agent, tourist information office or embassy of the country for information on passes in countries not included.

5. Cheap/free housing on the road: Travel agents can and will book you into major hotels anywhere in the world, and if you join a discount club, buy a discount card or go to other special efforts, you can often obtain significant discounts at such hotels. Holiday Inns have a discount program that gives people from the U.S. discounts on their hotels in Europe, for example.

If you want to spend your money with a local business (see Eco-Travel), then you should stay away from all the major hotel chains. There are bed & breakfast listings in the yellow pages (or equivalent) of most cities in the world. Chambers of commerce also can provide references to local bed & breakfasts, youth hostels and small, locally owned inns.

One helpful strategy is to book your first night in a new city at a big hotel, since reservations can be made so easily at them and there is usually free transportation from the airport. Then plan to spend the next day finding an inexpensive bed & breakfast. The search will take you all over the new city, making you an authority on its geography, neighborhoods and sights, and you will be able to select a bed & breakfast in person rather than from afar.

Another strategy is to select a program that includes room, or room and board. Many of the directories in this book list overseas study programs, wilderness trips, internships, jobs and other experiences *that include room and board*. This generally makes them pretty economical. At first, a several-thousand-dollar summer program may seem expensive, but if you do not have to spend any other money on food and lodging, it may actually allow you to live less expensively than if you stayed home!

Believe it or not, you may be able to find *free lodging* when you travel, whether within or outside of the U.S. Well, not exactly free, but available at no cost other than the willingness to provide lodging to others when they need it. There are two approaches: Hospitality exchanges allow you to be a guest at someone's home for shorter trips. And housing exchanges permit you to use others' homes when they are away. In both cases, you are expected to reciprocate. You do not have to own a mansion to reciprocate. Nor should you expect to be put up in splendor—many members of such exchanges have beautiful homes, and many others live in small apartments. But all are willing to offer hospitality to fellow travelers.

Directory 6 lists hospitality clubs and housing exchanges. Contact sources for brochures and membership information as far in advance as possible. (Or try *Worldwide Home and Hospitality Clubs and Services*, available for $6 plus 90 cents postage from TAAS Guides, Box 344, Amherst, MA 01004, or *Vacation Home Exchanging and Hospitality Guide*, for $14.95 plus $2 shipping, from Kimco Communications, 4242 West Dayton, Fresno, CA 93722.)

Organizations such as these are really nothing more than international networks of people who have two things in common: They like to travel, and they are willing to let other travelers use their homes. With this thought in mind, you should consider whether you belong to any other networks that could lead you to free or inexpensive housing while traveling. For example, if you are in academics, you can obtain an ID on one of the international computer networks used (generally for free) by academics. (Check with the computer sciences department of your school, college or university for options and instructions.) You will find there are electronic bulletin boards through which you can send out requests to others on the network. And if you belong to any clubs or professional associations, you may be able to network though their newsletters or foreign offices.

We also recommend these two newsletters featuring considerable information on bed & breakfasts, housing exchanges, and more:

The Newsletter of International Living
Expatworld
Box 1341
Raffles City, Singapore
(Send $5 U.S. for an airmailed copy and information.)

Traveler's Information Exchange
The Traveler
356 Boylston St.
Boston, MA 02116
(Send stamped, self-addressed envelope for a copy.)

6. Half-price hotels: Another way to defray the cost of lodging is to take advantage of the deep discounts on hotel rooms available through a number of half-price hotel clubs. If you expect to spend a week or more in hotel rooms during the course of a year, it is probably well worth the annual membership fees—generally less than $100—to join one of these clubs. Directory 7 includes several clubs that offer a wide selection of U.S. hotel accommodations at half price.

7. Travel ID cards: You should obtain an International Student Identity Card (ISIC), a GO25 International Youth Travel Card or the International Teacher Identity Card. These three ID cards are your passport to saving money.

An ID card is one of the cheapest ways to obtain discounts and insurance. The youth cards cost $16, while the teacher card is $17. The student ID card is accepted around the world as proof of student status and allows you to receive the discounts appropriate on tickets, museums, movies, plays, etc. The cards also provide access to reduced airfares on major international airlines. When you purchase a student card you receive a 32-page *International Student Identity Card Handbook;* the other two cards also have their respective handbooks.

When you buy the ISIC or the GO25 card, you receive basic sickness and accident insurance while you travel outside the U.S. The coverage includes $100/day for in-hospital expenses, up to $3,000 for accident-related medical costs and up to $10,000 for emergency evacuation to a medical treatment center (either there or in the U.S.). The Summary of Coverage is available upon request from CIEE, INS Dept., 205 East 42nd St., New York, NY 10017-5706.

An additional bonus when you buy a card is a 24-hour help line. When you dial, you are put in touch with a multilingual staff member. This person is equipped to direct you to the appropriate medical facilities, advise you on required immunizations, make arrangements for emergency evacuations, locate an English-speaking attorney, secure bail bonds, help replace stolen passports or traveler's checks and arrange travel should an emergency arise at home.

You can buy a card at one of 450 college/university issuing offices. Call 212-661-1414, ext. 1109, or send a computer online message to ISICOFFICES@CIEE.ORG and mention the state in which you live.

8. CIEE: Working your way around the world can be another great travel buy. One way to do this is through the Council of International Educational Exchange (CIEE). Council Travel, an extension of CIEE, has information on CIEE's work, volunteer and study programs around the world. Council Travel is a great resource for cheap airfare, Eurailpasses, adventure tours, youth hostel memberships, low cost car rentals, insurance, gear, guidebooks and international ID cards. They also provide great info on adventure tours. For example, they can set you up with the cheapest fare for an around-the-world trek.

Listed below are regional offices for Council Travel. Check out the On the Road Chapter or the directory in Chapter 3 for additional information on CIEE.

Council Travel

San Francisco, CA
530 Bush St., Ground Fl.
San Francisco, CA 94108
415-421-3473

Boulder, CO
1138 13th St.
Boulder, CO 80302
303-447-8101

Miami, FL
One Datran Center, Suite 320
9100 S. Dadeland Blvd.
Miami, FL 33156
305-670-9261

Chicago, IL
1153 N. Dearborn St., 2nd Fl.
Chicago, IL 60610
312-951-0585

Boston, MA
729 Boylston St., Suite 201
Boston, MA 02116
617-266-1926

New York, NY
205 E. 42nd St.
New York, NY 10017-5706
212-661-1450

Austin, TX
2000 Guadalupe St.
Austin, TX 78705
512-472-4931

Seattle, WA
1314 NE 43rd St., Suite 210
Seattle, WA 98105
206-632-2448

Safety issues

The most common problem travelers to foreign countries experience is illness. Be prepared to deal with a major illness by traveling with health insurance that will cover you where you will be, and by knowing where the nearest decent health care facilities are and how to get to them in an emergency.

In countries like Egypt, Turkey, and many Latin American and Asian countries, dysentery is common because contaminated water and food are likely to be encountered. This risk can be minimized by taking certain precautions—in rural parts of many undeveloped countries, for example, it is advisable to treat any water by boiling or chlorinating it before drinking it or using it in cooking. Similarly, it may be advisable to avoid raw fruit and vegetables in some countries.

A doctor or university health service ought to be able to provide detailed information about health hazards and how to avoid them, and can give you various vaccinations appropriate to your destination.

Robbery and violent crimes are, of course, possible in any place where people live, and you need to do some research on the area you plan to visit to determine the level of risk and how to minimize it. Politically turbulent areas pose additional risks for American travelers, and in some cases should be avoided entirely. The U.S. State Department tracks such hazards around the globe, issuing travel advisories when appropriate. A warning advisory means you should stay away. A caution means you should probably stay away. A notice indicates there's something you ought to know about before going. Travel agents generally receive and file all such travel advisories or can access them via their online computer system.

You can avoid being robbed of large sums of cash by not carrying large sums of cash. Some travelers now leave their cash at home in the bank, and use their ATM card to access it in foreign countries (check with your bank concerning availability of ATM machines in the country you will be visiting). Of course travelers checks are an excellent protection against theft, provided you keep a record of the checks and the slip giving their serial numbers in a place where it cannot be stolen along with the checks. Credit cards also avoid the cash problem, provided you can qualify for one.

Trip insurance can be obtained through American Express (if you have a card) and through a number of other companies listed in Directory 8. It covers expensive emergency costs like being flown back to America with a medical escort, or being returned deceased (try to avoid this, please). Contact these companies for information about their services and costs.

A general piece of advice for travelers and adventurers, regardless of destination: Avoid any illegal activities, plan travel and lodging in advance, and come prepared for local conditions.

Some pointers for college students

A good adviser is an invaluable resource throughout your college sojourn—especially if you plan to study abroad. If you're not assigned one your freshman year, ask a faculty member you admire to be your adviser.

Be prepared to take the bureaucracy by the tail and handle your own program planning and travel logistics. If you've picked an off-campus program, take care of transferring credits and such details *before* you depart.

Campus travel centers can be helpful in charting a trip once you know what you want to do and where you want to go. While many college programs that lead you off campus provide travel plans, some do not. You may also want to supplement the scholastic program with additional travel before you return. Campus travel centers are great for up-to-date information and low-priced travel tickets, as well as details on discounted rates on travel in foreign countries.

Answering questions: using research skills

Not only should you ask questions—you should answer them. While this book provides considerable information about alternative programs, you will need to put your research skills to work as well. Follow up on the entries to see if anything has changed, or strike out on your own and discover other options. Budget plenty of time for research and planning, and be sure to use all the available primary sources (program directors, faculty members, other students, members of campus clubs and travel groups, your parents and friends), as well as consulting this book and the many other references listed in these pages and in the card catalog of your library.

It takes work to design an alternative educational or work experience and, in fact, the act of planning one is a valuable learning experience in itself—it helps you develop skills that you can use to plan adventures throughout your career. Remember, this is your adventure (and life) and it is up to you to make it great!

Making It Happen! Directory

1. Funding sources for alternative education and travel experience

Institute of Current World Affairs
4 West Wheelock St.
Hanover, NH 03755
603-643-5548

Its purpose is "to identify areas or issues of the world outside the U.S. in need of in-depth understanding, and then to select young persons of outstanding promise and character to study and write about those areas or issues." They provide funding for nondegree work, and the grants are available to people of diverse backgrounds. Application is made by letter with a brief proposal and resume enclosed. But send for the brochure first to get a better idea of what the Institute is interested in. In general, it funds two-year programs overseas.

Institute of International Education
U.S. Student Programs
809 United Nations Plaza
New York, NY 10017
212-984-5330

This organization is the source of a diversity of grants for school years abroad, including Italian language and culture scholarships, Swiss Universities Grants, Polish Government Grants, Romanian and Israeli grants, and the Fulbright U.S. Student Program.

African Studies Association
Credit Union Bldg., Emory University
Atlanta, GA 30322
404-329-6410

Supports a wide range of research in the field of African studies.

Adventure Careers

American Academy in Rome
7 East 60th St.
New York, NY 10022
212-517-7200

Fellowships to college students.

American Council of Learned Societies
228 East 45th St.
New York, NY 10017
212-697-1505, ext. 136 or 138

Postdoctorate grants only, but a wide range available.

American Research Institute in Turkey
University Museum
33rd and Spruce Streets
Philadelphia, PA 19104
215-898-3474

Bosphorus University summer program for intensive advanced Turkish language study.

The American-Scandinavian Foundation
725 Park Ave.
New York, NY 10021
212-879-9779

For college graduates only.

Austrian Cultural Institute
11 E. 52nd St.
New York, NY 10022
212-759-5165

Grants for 20-35 year-olds only.

Austro-American Association of Boston
48 Davis Ave.
West Newton, MA 02165
617-969-9324

British Universities Summer Schools Joint Committee
Dept. for Continuing Education
1 Wellington Square
Oxford, 0x1, 2JA, England
(0865) 270378

Canadian Institute for Internal Peace and Security
360 Albert St., Suite 900
Ottawa, ON, Canada, K1R 7X7
613-990-1593

Projects contributing to peace.

Centre European
Universitaire Carnot
15, Place Carnot
54042 Nancy Cedex, France
83.36.52.84

Limited to exchange students with college degrees; French language is important.

The East-West Center
1777 East-West Rd.
Honolulu, HI 96848
808-944-7111

A variety of options for Asia-bound students.

Herbert Scoville, Jr., Peace Development Program
110 Maryland Ave. NE, Rm. 211
Washington, DC 20002
202-546-0795

Inter-American Foundation
901 N. Stewart St.
Arlington, VA 22203
703-841-3864

Japan Information Center
Consulate General of Japan
299 Park Ave., 18th Fl.
New York, NY 10171
212-371-8222

The Mongolia Society
321-322 Goodbody Hall
Indiana University
Bloomington, IN 47504
812-855-4078

United States-Japan Foundation
145 E. 32nd St.
New York, NY 10016
212-481-8753

Winston Churchill Foundation of the U.S.
P.O. Box 1240, Gracie Station
New York, NY 10028
212-879-3480

Scholarships to Cambridge.

---

2. Airline tickets

Access International
800-333-7280, 212-465-0707
Europe

British European
800-747-1476, 408-984-7576
Everywhere

Char-Tours
800-323-4444, 415-495-8881
U.S., Europe and more

C&H
800-833-8888, 213-387-2288
Asia and the South Pacific, Europe

Canatours
213-223-1111
Asia and Canada

Compare
312-853-1144
Everywhere

Venton Tours:
Euro Asia Express
800-782-9625, 415-692-9996
Europe, Asia including China

European-American
800-848-6789, 202-782-2255
Europe and Latin America

Jetway
800-421-8771, 213-382-2477
China and the Far East

Magical Holidays
800-433-7773, 415-325-9944
Africa, Latin America, the Middle East

Sunline Express
800-786-5463, 415-541-7800
Latin America, U.S. and elsewhere

Travel Ave.
800-333-3335, 312-876-1116
Everywhere

U.S. International
800-759-7373, 219-255-7272
Europe and Eastern Europe; in conjunction with other airlines: India, Oman, Damascus, Far East, Africa.

3. Discount travel clubs

Moment's Notice Discount Travel
425 Madison Ave., Suite 702
New York, NY 10017
212-486-0500

The One Travel Place
200 North Martingale Rd.
Schaumberg, IL 60173
800-621-5505

Sears Discount Travel Club
3033 South Parker Rd.
Aurora, CO 80114
800-331-0257

Travelers Advantage
Box 1015
Trumbull, CT 06611
800-548-1116

Up 'N Go Travel
44 Front St.
Worcester, MA 01608
800-888-8190

Vacations To Go
2411 Fountain View
Houston, TX 77057
800-338-4962

4. Bartered travel services

Travel World Leisure Club
225 W. 34th St., Suite 909
New York, NY 10122
800-444-8952, 212-239-4855

5. Rail passes

You must purchase your rail passes before you leave the U.S. They are available at Council Travel offices, as well as through the offices listed here. The Eurailpass is good for Austria, Belgium, Denmark, Finland, France, Germany, Greece, Holland, Hungary, Ireland, Italy, Luxembourg, Norway, Portugal, Spain, Sweden and Switzerland.

Rail Europe
226-230 Westchester Ave.
White Plains, NY 10604
914-682-5172
2100 Central Ave., 200
Boulder, CO 80301
800-438-7245, 303-443-5100
Fax: 800-432-1329
    Passes for European countries.

Netherlands Board of Tourism
225 North Michigan Ave.
Suite 326
Chicago, IL 60601
312-819-0300

6. Hospitality clubs and housing exchanges

Globetrotters
BCM/Roving
London, England WC1N 3XX

Hospitality Exchange
Wayne and Kathie Phillips
704 Birch
Helena, MT 95601
406-449-2103

Members offer lodging and hospitality for one or two nights free of charge. Annual membership fee: $15.

INNterlodging Co-op
P.O. Box 7044
Tacoma, WA 98407
206-756-0343

International Home Exchange
Intervac USA
P.O. Box 190070
San Francisco, CA 94119
415-435-3497; Fax: 415-435-7440

Invented City
41 Sutter St., Suite 1090T
San Francisco, CA 94104
415-673-0347

This organization arranges for housing exchanges between travelers from the United States and Europe.

Teacher Swap
P.O. Box 4130
Rocky Point, NY 11778
516-272-2039

Worldwide Home Exchange Club
45 Hans Place
London SW1X OJZ
England

7. Half-price hotel clubs

America at 50 Percent Discount
Taste Publications
1031 Cromwell-Bridge Rd.
Baltimore, MD 21286
410-882-9726

Entertainment Publications
2125 Butterfield Rd.
Troy, MI 48084
800-477-3234

Publishes coupon booklets ranging in price from $28 to $53. The Half-Price Europe coupon book, $53, provides good coverage of Europe, including all Sheraton hotels. Also publishes booklets for individual European countries in their local language; these booklets are more likely to include smaller and less expensive hotels. They offer a discount edition price of $28 after the purchase of one full-priced booklet.

Solid Gold
101-1715 Book St.
Vancouver, Canada, B5Y3J6
604-874-0821

Deep discounts on hotels.

Quest International
402 E. Yakima Ave., Suite 1200
Yakima, WA 98901
509-248-7512

Mostly U.S. listings, but check to see if they cover your foreign destination as well.

International Travel Card
6001 North Clark St.
Chicago, IL 60660
800-342-0558, 312-465-8891

Costs $36 per calendar year, and provides discounts at more than 2,000 hotels around the world.

Holland Welcome Vouchers
Netherlands Service Center for Tourism
225 North Michigan Ave.
Suite 326
Chicago, IL 60601
312-819-0300

Scandinavian BonusPass
From travel agencies, including:
Borton Overseas, 800-843-0602
Holiday Tours of America,
800-677-6454
Nordic American Travel,
612-827-3853

8. Sources of trip insurance

Access America, Inc.
6600 W. Broad St.
Richmond, VA 23286
800-424-3391

American Express Travel Protection Plan
6440 Lusk Blvd., Suite D-205
San Diego, CA 92121
800-234-0375

Travel Assistance International
1133 15th St. NW, Suite 400
Washington, DC 20005
800-821-2828, 201-331-1609

Travel Insured International
The Travelers Companies
P.O. Box 280568
East Hartford, CT 06128-0568
800-243-3174; Fax: 203-528-8005

Reading and references

Here are some references of relevance to planning and logistics, including finding foreign jobs and funding for overseas travel, and paying appropriate U.S. taxes on what you earn abroad (you do need to file a tax return—sorry!).

Books

Study Abroad. The Unesco Press, Paris. Order from Unipub, Inc., 4611-F Assembly Dr., Lanham, MD 20706. This annual directory contains listings of organizations with scholarships and fellowships for students worldwide.

Student Travel Catalog. CIEE Publications Dept., 205 E. 42nd St., New York, NY 10017. Annual, $1. Helpful guide to low-cost transportation and also information on obtaining student identity cards, jobs in foreign countries and other practical matters.

Survival Kit for Overseas Living. L. Kohls. Intercultural Press, P.O. Box 700, Yarmouth, ME 04096.

Work, Study, Travel Abroad: The Whole World Handbook. Del Franz, Editor. CIEE Publications, 205 East 42nd St., New York, NY 10017.

Consumer Reports Travel Buying Guide. Consumer Reports Books, 9180 LeSaint Drive, Fairfield, OH 45014. Annual; this source provided much of the detailed information concerning where and how to find discounts of travel and lodgings for this chapter.

Publications and pamphlets

Tax Guide for U.S. Citizens Abroad (Publication 54). Forms Distribution Center, P.O. Box 25866, Richmond, VA 23260. Free; also kept in stock by larger tax accounting firms.

Scholarships and Fellowships (Publication 520). Forms Distribution Center, P.O. Box 25866, Richmond, VA 23260. Free.

Visa Requirements of Foreign Governments (Publication M-264). Office of Passport Services, Room 386, 1425 K St. NW, Washington, DC 20524.

Other resources

Financial resources for international study
IIE and Peterson's Guides. Annual description of awards available for college, graduate, post-graduate students and professionals to study abroad. Peterson's Guides, P.O. Box 2123, Princeton, NJ 08543.

Fulbright and other grants for graduate study abroad
A free annual pamphlet listing IIE-administered financial assistance programs for U.S. graduate students to study abroad. Also includes an application form. If you are enrolled in a college or university, request this publication from the campus Fulbright Program adviser (talk to Financial Aid or Job Placement Offices if you need help locating this person or, as a last resort, contact IIE for the name of the adviser on your campus). If you are *not* an enrolled student, you can still apply: Request the booklet from IIE/Student Programs, 809 U.N. Plaza, New York, NY 10017.